PRAISE FOR
Uncommon Waters

"The range of contributors is impressive. . . . The quality of the writing is uniformly high. . . . A book of vision, beauty and depth."
—*Fly Fisherman*

"A powerful and revealing anthology."
—*Chicago Tribune*

"This splendid anthology should be read by all male angler-authors who will learn—if they didn't know it already—that women have a marvelously personal way of looking at fish and fishing: perceptive, evocative, intense and sometimes charmingly wary, downright humorous and disarmingly ingenuous."
—Nelson Bryant, *The New York Times*

"If you're a man and love to fish, you'll want to buy two copies: One for yourself, so you can open some mental doors, and one for your niece, daughter, granddaughter, wife or significant other, so your future fishing partner can start with a tradition, with a voice, with a touchstone. *Uncommon Waters* could be the best investment you make in a long time."
—Tom Rosenbauer, *Orvis News*

"Bravo! *Uncommon Waters* is a unique and extremely important book."
—Nick Lyons

"For women who fish, these pieces may serve as a deeply encouraging affirmation. For those who don't, the book may serve as an invitation. . . . Or it may evoke reflections on the way activities we glibly classify as sports and recreation may restore us to a larger awareness and lightness of being. . . . It honors the venerable business of fishing in terms of its practical pleasures and its rich metaphorical possibility. . . . *Uncommon Waters* is a book to be savored equally for its whimsicality and its sudden moments of vision."
—*The Women's Review of Books*

"This collection should inspire more women to record their outdoor experiences and in so doing create a new vision of feminine independence."
—*Publishers Weekly*

"A marvelous anthology of essays, poems and stories by women anglers. . . . All anglers will find this book full of insight, charm, humor, and honesty."
—*The International Angler*

"*Uncommon Waters* is a wonderfully literary volume about fishing, as told by women. . . . A delightful, amazing and entertaining book offering the unbeatable combination of good reading about good fishing. Armchair Rating: ☆☆☆☆☆   —*Marlin: The International Sportsfishing Magazine*

UNCOMMON
WATERS

WOMEN WRITE ABOUT FISHING

EDITED BY HOLLY MORRIS

PREFACE BY MARGOT PAGE

ILLUSTRATIONS BY SANDY SCOTT

The Seal Press

Cover art by Kris Wiltse.
Interior art by Sandy Scott.
Design by Clare Conrad.

Library of Congress Cataloging-in-Publication Data
Uncommon waters : women write about fishing / edited by Holly Morris.
   p.   cm.
   ISBN 1-878067-10-9
   1. Fishing--Literary collections. 2. Women fishers--United States--Literary collections. 3. American literature--Women authors. 4. Fishing stories. American.   I. Morris, Holly, 1965-
PS509.F5U53   1991
810.8'0355-dc20

91-21455
CIP

Printed in the United States of America
First printing, October 1991
10 9 8 7 6 5 4 3 2

Foreign Distribution:
In Canada: Raincoast Book Distribution, Vancouver, B.C.
In the U.K. and Europe: Airlift Book Company, London

Grateful acknowledgement is made for the use of the following previously published material: "Fishing for Eel Totems" by Margaret Atwood. Originally appeared in *Procedures for Underground*. Copyright © 1970 by Oxford University Press Canada; reprinted by permission of Oxford University Press Canada. "Fish" by Judith Barrington. Originally appeared in *History and Geography* (Portland, Oregon: The Eighth Mountain Press, 1989). Copyright © 1989 Judith Barrington; reprinted by permission of the author and publisher. "The Treatise of Fishing with an Angle" by Dame Juliana Berners, and corresponding footnotes, from John McDonald's *Origins of Angling*. Copyright © 1957, 1963 by Time Inc.; reprinted by permission of Time Inc./Doubleday. "The Emerger" by Mallory Burton. Originally appeared in *Fly Fishing News, Views & Reviews*; reprinted by permission of the author. "Woman's Hour has Struck" appeared as "A New Hand at the Rod" in *Fishing in North America 1876–1910*. Copyright © 1986 by Castle Books; reprinted by permission of Castle Books. "A Little Short of the Record" by Elizabeth Enright. Copyright © 1951 by Elizabeth Enright, renewed in 1979 by Elizabeth Enright. Reprinted by permission of Russell and Volkening as agents for the author. "The Bassing Gal" by Sugar Ferris. Originally appeared in somewhat different form in *Bass'n Gal* magazine; reprinted by permission of the author. "Boat Ride" by Tess Gallagher. Originally appeared in *Amplitude: New and Selected Poems*. Copyright © 1987 by Tess Gallagher; reprinted by permission of Graywolf Press. "The Young Woman and the Sea" by Lorian Hemingway. Originally appeared in *The New York Times*; reprinted by permission of the author. "Fishing" by Linda Hogan. Originally appeared in *Savings*. Copyright © 1988 by Linda Hogan; reprinted by permission of Coffee House Press. "King Bait" by Keri Hulme. Originally appeared in *Te Kaihau: The Windeater*. Copyright © 1986 by Keri Hulme and Mary Bodger; reprinted by permission of George Braziller, Inc. "A Day in the Life" by Mari Lochhaas. Originally appeared as "Fisher" in *Hard Hatted Women: Stories of Struggle and Success in the Trades*. Copyright © 1988 by Molly Martin; reprinted by permission of Seal Press. "Fishing the White Water" is reprinted from *Our Dead Behind Us*, Poems by Audre Lorde; by permission of W.W. Norton & Company, Inc. Copyright © 1986 by Audre Lorde. "Ahn-ka-tee" originally appeared in somewhat different form as "Marya Moses" in *Winds of Change: Women in Northwest Commercial Fishing* by Charlene J. Allison, Sue-Ellen Jacobs and Mary A. Porter. Copyright © 1989 by The University of Washington Press; reprinted by permission of the University of Washington Press. "Cut and Paste" by Jean Rysstad. Originally appeared in *Travelling In*. Copyright © 1990 by Jean Rysstad; reprinted by permission of Oolichan Books. "The Long Light" by Le Anne Schreiber. Originally appeared in *The Independent* (Columbia County, New York); reprinted by permission of the author. "A Buncha Guys, a Coupla Fish and ME: The Opening of Trout Season, Roscoe, New York" by Viva. Originally appeared in *New York Woman*; reprinted by permission of the author. "Without a Backward Cast: Notes of an Angler" by Katharine Weber. Originally appeared in somewhat different form in *The Boston Monthly*; reprinted by permission of the author. "Where I Want to Be" by Joan Wulff. Originally appeared in *Trout*; reprinted by permission of the author.

Editor's Acknowledgements

I am grateful to the many people who gave knowledge and inspiration to this project, especially Dan Boorman, Laura Funk Boorman, Jeannie Morris and my mentors, Botts and John Hatteberg. A very special thanks to Jamie Nichols, whose support, both emotional and technical, was invaluable.

The women of Seal Press have been a part of this endeavor from the start and I am greatly indebted to them; especially to Faith Conlon, who provided a much appreciated wealth of wisdom and editorial expertise, and Clare Conrad for her many hours and fine job of book design. Thanks also to Cathy Johnson for her feedback and careful copyediting.

Lastly, my warm appreciation goes out to all the contributors to this anthology who were a pleasure to work with and whose enthusiasm and talent made this book possible.

Contents

Preface

It is astonishing to me that the book you hold in your hands is a first. In all the centuries of fishing literature, this volume represents the first collection of women's writing on the subject of angling: a vivid compendium of women's experience in a sport that has, with rare exceptions, been written about primarily by men and whose traditions and legacy to date have been exclusively male.

Here is the drama of a woman's fifteen-year quest for a great swordfish; the voice of a Native American woman who supports her family off the ocean with a $150 boat; a girl who hooked a branch that rolled over to become a dead man; the tragicomedy of the ladylike nineteenth-century C. R. C. who dares to borrow a camp rod, wets her best shoes, rents her dress, hooks a tree and finally summons up the nerve to venture out onto a log to catch her first trout. Here is the bone-chilling story of a lone woman in a men's fishing camp; an account of Viva's fly-fishing baptism at the Antrim Lodge in the Catskills; the life and death poetry of Tess Gallagher. Deep and rich, edged with heat or tenderness or both, these narratives compose an anthology of distinction and resonance.

Because of the outdoor recreation boom over the past two decades, women have been fishing in growing numbers and have begun to define their own terms for enjoying the sport. We have scrounged for babysitters and planned family meals in advance; settled for ill-fitting waders (marketed, for the most part, in men's sizes only); read patronizing or offensive books, cartoons, magazine articles and advertisements; waded not only pushy rivers but also into crowds of good old boys and withstood their staring and their braggadocio—all so that we could get to the water, that diamond-studded, liquid metaphor that blinds one's eyes while allowing one to see ever more clearly; that makes us forget woes big and little; that offers us watery gurgles and the flash of a living wild thing from another world.

And the literature of the sport is beginning to reflect the change. As more women go down to the water, more is written about their experience. It is particularly gratifying to me to read the accounts of women because as the editor of a quarterly museum journal devoted to the history of angling, I am used to seeing the relatively one-dimensional writing—either scholarly or technical—of the male professional writer. Coming across these multilayered works has been like living abroad for many years and discovering that just around the block live people who grew up in my hometown. I have fallen upon each story eagerly, with hands outstretched, a smile on my face. Hello, welcome!

Of course, women have always fished, ever since the first net, trap and hook helped us put food on the table (or ground, as it were). But the numbers of men involved in the professional, commercial, and recreational aspects of fishing have been greater than those of women, and, perhaps more importantly, men have had more access to the primary means of recording history—published writing. Written experience begets history begets tradition begets legacy. It follows that history and the weight and authority of tradition have built upon each other, so that customs, clubs, and social groups have often excluded women.

A noted writer friend of mine remarks that he rarely encounters women fishing alone on the stream, and the reason for this, he says, is that most women are afraid of the woods, fearful of the dark forests. I don't agree: If women are reluctant to fish by themselves, it may be because, in part, they are stepping into a masculine arena which can make one feel alone and intimidated. And however rewarding or, in the case of fly fishing, graceful, angling is, the truth is that it is a large, and potentially dangerous, outdoor experience. It requires a basic knowledge of entomology and an ability to read the water. It necessitates a significant amount of free time (a couple of hours is "significant" when you're the primary child-caregiver). And it all takes place on the raw, unpredictable stage of nature. Angling requires confidence: a strength born of experience and knowledge, a strength fostered by opportunity, which many of us haven't been afforded. We haven't received the training that would help us feel comfortable in this setting. Fishing with Mom down at "the Hole" wasn't the rite of passage for girls that it was for many boys with Dad.

For instance, my grandfather, the writer Sparse Grey Hackle, only took male teen-aged grandchildren on initiation trips to the Catskills to introduce them to fly fishing. It wasn't until I was motivated to learn to fly fish in my early thirties that I got a chance to fish with my grandmother—Louise Brewster Miller, as passionate a fisher as my grandfather—then eighty-six years old, allowing me rare insight into this woman's private and fiercely held fifty-year-old treasure. It is poignant that in her five decades of fishing she fished with only a few—maybe four—other women, myself included. With her proud nature, she struggled—in this respect—in the shadow of her more famous husband. Some say she was the better fisher. "Think of me when you fish," she once told me wistfully.

My own fishing is both a family affair and a solitary adventure. I started to fly fish out of curiosity—what did my grandparents see in this eccentric recreation that involved slimy fish and funny pants?—and also so that I would understand my husband-to-be's hunger, for I had an idea what our life could be like if I sat on the sidelines. The surge of excitement when I caught my first wild Vermont brookies surprised me, for I fancied myself somewhat of a New York Sophisticate and I was bemused that I had fallen in love with an outdoor man. But it wasn't long before I could cast well enough among the cow flops that lined the Vermont streams to inspire pride. From then on it was a matter of moving to the country and hoping that our marriage—and then parenthood—could adapt to two independent-minded people who both desired the experience of fly fishing, but who couldn't always afford a babysitter.

Over the years, fishing as a woman among men has meant that at times I have been lonely in a buddy-buddy, macho world. I have been reluctant to call up fishing friends to arrange an outing because they are almost all men and I didn't want to appear brazen. If I trudge more than a half mile in my boot-foot waders I get blisters because they're sized for men and don't fit. I have heard more times than I care to count a whispered "Was that a WOMAN?" after I pass on the stream.

The intelligent, reflective and various voices in this book have been there too, and they know it all goes deeper than a crude remark or ill-fitting gear—that's why we have persevered. We fish to ease the pain of a divorce or the death of a beloved; to earn a living; to remember or to forget who we may have been and who we may have loved; or just to get the hell out of some jagged, hectic place and into some other place—slower, prettier. Some of the writers here compare the often indescribable urge to find a silvery ribbon of water that hides wild creatures within to the process of writing itself—casting a line onto a surface and waiting, waiting, for something from the depths to make its appearance—or they link fishing to the landscape of dreams in which fish are said to represent intuition. These women speak of our desire for temporary freedom from sobering human foibles, weighty professional and domestic responsibilities; they describe our struggle to find our way; and they are testimony to our wish for communion with the majestic natural world, of which we are, after all, just another species.

This book answers the questions I and others have asked: Where are the other women who like to fish, and who are they? These voices, that of the polished writer, the professional guide, the commercial fisher, the remembered child and the sorrowing mother, will enrich and deepen the existing body of fishing literature. Because of this book, and the women in it, girls like my daughter Brooke will have role models. Here they are. There they were. *That's* how you do it.

These writings will add to all of our perspectives as we—male and female alike—try to make sense of the hours we share on this splendid planet, admiring in a clear pool of water, or a limitless ocean horizon, the mystery, the system and the grace of it all.

Margot Page
East Arlington, Vermont
May 1991

Introduction

The summer I turned seven, having mastered the two-wheeler and having just finished first grade, I embarked on my first real fishing trip. I had been hook-and-bobbering the lakes and ponds of suburban Chicago and now felt ready to take on the Pacific Northwest—a region that seemed an eternity away and teeming with fish. I happily left my parents and three siblings behind to join my grandparents for what was to be the first of many timeless fishing trips. I know now that my excitement did not come solely from childlike anticipation. Perched beside those ponds and lakes near my home, having set out alone on a misty morning, I'd already sensed that fishing offered something deeper: a certainty of self, a feeling of rightness in nature's order, an independence that young girls rarely get to explore.

I have vivid memories from those summer trips—like my grandmother's floppy white cotton hat with turquoise trim. Finishing an article in whatever magazine she had her nose in that day, she would dip the hat in the water, wring it a bit and then put it back on her head to stay cool. Aside from an occasional outburst about the villainy of Richard Nixon, or some such political editorial, she was quiet.

I remember my grandfather intently tinkering with the small outboard motor which seemed to be attached to our rickety rowboat as an afterthought. If he became satisfied with the motor, he'd take an interest in the contents of the musty tackle box—lures, split shot, warm worms.

I remember the hours drifting by and the freedom I felt in spite of the oversized life jacket which bound my body and propped up my chin. I was never bored watching the tip of my rod because, at any given moment. . . *boom, a strike!*—and the world would collapse into itself like a black hole and every bit of self a seven-year-old could muster would be balanced at the end of that pole, completely focused, adrenaline pumping.

When a fish was on, chaos ensued. Magazines flew, tackle was scattered, advice was bellowed—all of fishing's etiquette went overboard. But somehow the three of us, partners in angling, managed to land our fish.

This scene transpired several times a day—never losing its thrill in repetition. Each evening, sunburned and satisfied, I motored our boat back to the dock and proceeded to gut and clean all of our fish—two chores I insisted on doing. These were my tasks; each of my grandparents had theirs. Between the three of us, we composed a day of splendor in which the only surprises came on the end of a line.

During those long days of summer, the thrill of the take highlighted other lessons: the comfort of ritual, the rewards of a quiet afternoon, the magic of my grandfather's campfire stories, his youthful adventures, intimately told, somehow extending through the years to give a little girl her place in the world. Even together with my companions, fishing was a solitary venture, my own. I felt free, selfsufficient, competent, and those powerful feelings of self-discovery bred a lifelong passion for the sport. Fall and spring—even winter— my love of fishing was sustained by suburban bluegill and an occasional bass, but each summer I boarded an airplane alone and flew west where angling, eating and sleeping became the stuff of life.

There is little doubt in my mind that the special joys and fundamental values of those early fishing experiences were part of what drew me back to the Northwest nearly twenty years later. The rhythms of fishing are the same, but other things have changed. The size and number of fish I catch are of much less consequence. Scores don't count, it's all in the process. As you will read in these pages, fishing both as sport and vocation has many variations. But the beauty of it lies precisely in the fact that it touches each of its impassioned adherents in a place deep inside the self and connects us, at that level, to the natural world. Fishing seems to be the most evocative of sports, which perhaps explains why throughout literature it has become a powerful and often used metaphor for life.

This evocative nature of angling has, over the years, sent me to its vast and rich body of writing. I read a story about a sea captain who had a love-hate relationship with a whale. I read another about an old man who battled and killed a great marlin that killed him. I read about a young man whose father taught him to fly cast by metronome. I read about fish and men, fishermen.

I easily related to the themes and passions in fishing literature, but there was a whole range of experience missing: the female experience. I did find one woman depicted, the fishing widow, but she was not someone with whom I could identify. I knew I wasn't the lone woman in the male domain of fishing, but there stood the fact: In fishing, as in many areas of life and literature, women's voices had yet to be clearly heard. And with this realization the need for a women's anthology of writing about fishing became very apparent. Women anglers needed a forum to fill a void, create a community and validate and celebrate our outdoor experiences.

So when I began this project I went back to the fishing canon and scoured it—this time looking for women—with sparse, yet valuable results. I waded through stacks of short stories and found that women *had* been writing about fishing and their stories were scattered throughout literature. But the most exciting part of the project was soliciting new and unpublished writing. Some women had to be convinced that what they had to write about themselves and their fishing was important and interesting, others eagerly brought forth pieces that had been gathering dust for years and many others were thrilled at the opportunity to write about angling for the first time.

Throughout the selection process I looked specifically for writing that told what it meant to be a *woman* fishing, that reflected the diversity of our experience and that testified to the scope of our participation. You find the results in this anthology: fiction and nonfiction that represent several countries and more than one century—all about women who fish.

Although this is the first anthology of its kind to feature women's voices, women have fished since antiquity and have at times written about their experiences. The best known and most important female figure in angling history is Dame Juliana Berners. The first essay on the subject of sport fishing, "The Treatise of Fishing with an Angle," written circa 1421, is widely attributed to her. There is debate among scholars over Berner's authorship, but the romantic legend that places her as nun, noblewoman and angler lives on. And the treatise's most important legacy, the twelve fly-tying patterns called "The Berners Flies," endures to this day and remains deeply embedded in angling history.

Since Dame Juliana, there have been other women who have made their mark on fishing. Some of the most well-documented are in the arena of fly fishing. Mary Orvis Marbury ran Orvis's commercial fly-tying business, and in 1892 she published her landmark book *Favorite Flies and Their Histories.* Cornelia "Fly Rod" Crosby (1854–1946), a Maine guide and one of the first women outdoor journalists, wrote of angling news in her newspaper column "Fly Rod's Notebook." Contemporary greats include Joan Wulff, renowned teacher, author and fly-casting champion, and fly-tying masters Helen Shaw and Carrie Stevens. In 1977, bass angling pioneer Sugar Ferris started Bass'n Gal—a 26,000-member women's fishing organization—and then went on to form a women's bass tournament circuit. This handful of recognizable women represents millions of unknown women, whether fishing for sport or sustenance, who make up our collective fishing history and our contemporary fishing community.

According to the National Sporting Goods Association (NSGA), approximately eighteen million women sport fish in this country alone—a full one-third of the fishing population. We spend over 150 million dollars annually on fishing equipment and buy thirty percent of all rods and reels sold. The Orvis Company of Manchester, Vermont, currently boasts a thirty percent, and climbing, women's enrollment in its fly-fishing classes. That's twelve thousand more women who will don waders and take their places midstream this year.

In the light of these figures, it's not surprising that recent years have seen an increase in women's numbers in fishing organizations that have traditionally had a predominantly male membership. But women have also formed their own national organizations like the Texas-based Bass'n Gal, the Louisiana-based Lady Bass, the International Women's Fishing Association (IWFA) and many community and regional groups where women are networking, socially and politically, with other women who share a love of fishing.

As the number of women anglers increases, fishing traditions will evolve. Many of these stories chart the evolution of the fishing experience—one typically thought, as much of the literature suggests, to take place in the company of men, men and boys, men alone. But this image is changing, and will continue to change, in part because of writings like these that tell of another experience—that of girls and women. Many of the women in this book had male fishing mentors— fathers and grandfathers who have left them with varied legacies. But these women have gone on to become the teachers, mentors and guides themselves, and are in turn drawing more girls and women into angling and enriching the experiences of boys and men. Some of the women tell stories of fishing with their husbands and partners and explore how that affects their experience. Others share this outdoor experience with mothers and sisters, adding a new dimension to basic relationships. Still others fish alone, in pursuit of the thrills and awareness of self and the natural environment that fishing offers.

The literature that angling so powerfully inspires will also evolve, if only slowly, to reflect the reality and diversity of women's presence. This collection is a start. I have tried to bring together the finest writing that celebrates and captures the depth and enjoyment of our midstream and high seas adventure. With luck, this writing will not only entertain, but will also inspire and open doors for the women who have been denied a rod, been shunned at the docks or been simply unaware of the pleasures of fishing. I hope it will pave a way for a growing genre of women's fishing literature—for we certainly have more stories to tell.

Holly Morris
Seattle, Washington
June 1991

UNCOMMON WATERS

THE LONG LIGHT

LE ANNE SCHREIBER

I WAS BORN CRAVING SUMMER, not for its warmth or colors or breezes. From the womb, I wanted light, as much of it as my freshly opened eyes could withstand. Since I was born in early August, I was born satisfied, or at least I would like to think so. But that first dark November, and every one since then, came as a blow.

It's not that summer light is more beautiful than any other season's; it's just that there's more of it, and, make no mistake, when it comes to light, more is better; ask any Scandinavian; ask any sufferer of seasonally adjusted depression; ask me.

Being outdoors on a sunlit day is the only self-justifying state of existence I know; it follows that being indoors on sunlit days requires a lot of explaining, and what explanations I have been able to provide never suffice. I was born knowing this, as I say, but it took me forty Novembers to arrange my life around the knowledge. Lacking independent wealth or the skills of a forest ranger (they spend too much time in the shade anyway), it took some doing.

The ten years I spent working in high-pay, low-light jobs helped, especially the thirty months I toiled in the windowless precincts of a newspaper sports department. After long fluorescent days, I was too depressed, too without desire, to spend the money I earned. So I toiled in darkness, saving for a sunny day.

On the brink of forty, single and self-propelled, I left offices behind. I climbed my way out from under the rock of Manhattan and moved to Ancram, New York. There I quickly discovered that getting in the vicinity of light isn't enough. You still have to figure out how to let it fall on you, which is not as easy as it sounds.

There is simple basking, which has a lot to be said for it, but most of us lack the sublime temperament for prolonged, purposeless delight. It's the price we pay for not being lizards. There's sun bathing, which is just a hazardous form of napping, or one can simply do outdoors the things one routinely does indoors, like reading and dining. The trouble is, doing outdoors what one might better do indoors just leads to an indoor frame of mind. Who needs those page-flapping breezes anyway?

Which brings me to fishing. I was resistant at first. I remembered summer vacations as a child, fishing with my father in a tippy aluminum rowboat on a lake in Wisconsin, snagging weeds and getting sunburned. We were after plump, tasty bass, but the usual reward for long periods of strictly enforced silence, broken only by an occasional racket of squeaky oarlocks, was the sight of a lean, mean, ugly, oily, snaggle-toothed fish called northern pike.

So when my tackle-bearing father visited me for Thanksgiving that first country fall, I politely thanked him for the hand-me-down rods and spared him my memories. Since legal fishing season was months away, there was no immediate need to confess my utter lack of interest. I looked attentive as he demonstrated his fly-casting skills in my snow-crusted backyard and kept up pretenses by showing him my favorite spot on the stream whose steep bank formed the back border of my property.

In my early searches for idyllic basking sites, I had discovered a fallen sycamore whose double trunk spanned the stream from bank to bank, offering itself first as a cradle for my early, failed attempts at basking, later as seat and footrest for my contemplation of that failure.

One light-filled afternoon, while pondering the difference between humans and lizards, I noticed a flash of silver in the water, which marked the beginning of my life as a fish watcher. Nearly every day since then I had spent an hour or two sitting on my perch staring into the water, watching dark shadows dart across the streambed at my approach and then slowly slink back as the creatures that cast them realized it was just the lady without a pole.

By Thanksgiving, we had reached the point in our relationship where I could intentionally cast a shadow over their backs and they wouldn't bother to stir. Hooks were out of the question, I thought, as my father and I sidestepped together across the frosty log to the center of the stream. "Trout," he said, gazing into the swirling water with a wide smile of anticipation.

I had planned to keep my vigil on the sycamore all through the winter, not suspecting, of course, that within two weeks, the stream would be frozen solid from bank to bank. By Christmas, an opaque veil of ice stood between me and my fish, and nothing but spring could draw the veil back.

I waited. Those rods, stashed and forgotten in the rear of an up-stairs closet, waited. Slowly, the afternoons began to lengthen. The ice thinned, turned transparent and finally succumbed to the swollen urgency of the stream rushing beneath it.

April came, and I resumed my perch on the sycamore log. May came, and I wanted to get into the water I was watching. What's the harm, I thought, in just pretending I'm fishing, strolling rod in hand through the sun-flicked stream, catching reflections. I could walk a stretch of the stream sufficiently distant from the sycamore that the fish gathered there would never have to see that suspicious long ex-tension of my arm's shadow.

Some days I started downstream from the sycamore, at a shallow, fast-flowing stretch of the stream that suddenly stilled and deepened as it went round a bend and under a bridge. Other days I headed way upstream to a series of small falls and pools, always stopping well short of the sycamore.

Taking tips from neighborhood boys, I fished first with live bait—minnows and worms. I was rewarded with nibbles, which seemed enough. I wasn't really fishing, after all, just playing a game of hide and seek with the trout, and I counted each quick tug as a tag. I was getting to know the stream, certain stretches of it inch by inch. My sneakered feet searched the rocky streambed for secure footings while my eyes scanned the surface for signals. I took my cues from light and its interruptions, from shadows cast by overhanging trees or passing clouds or birds flying overhead, the darkening of the water over a sub-merged boulder or a deep hole in the streambed. Standing in light, I cast into darknesses where a trout might rest—cool, still, hidden—waiting for a morsel to tempt him into movement.

Then I caught my first fish, not on live bait, but on a twirling three-hooked lure that embedded itself, irretrievably, two hooks up and one down, deep in the throat of a very young, inexperienced, pink-finned brook trout. I watched it gasp and flap in my hand, watched its shimmering vibrancy turn dull and listless, then still and blacken.

I had fallen in love with my light-filled game without ever believing it might come to this end. Nothing in my father's smile on the sycamore log that day contained a warning, nothing in my memory of our days on those Wisconsin lakes prepared me for this mangling. Catching, cleaning, eating, yes, but not this purposeless kill.

I called my father, and without blaming him outright for my sins, I let him know I wished he had never left those rods behind. He understood my distress but drew a different conclusion. The fault was not in fishing but in how one fished. For a different end, I needed a different means. I needed a fly rod, and if I would look in that closet again, I would see he left me two—"both real honeys," a fiberglass and an "old split bamboo."

He would tie me some flies on hooks too small to hurt the most newly spawned fish. I could remove them from a fish lip with a flick of the wrist and release a trout, no sadder but wiser, to the stream. Should the hook be embedded more deeply, he had just the thing—a scissor-handled surgical clamp, the kind doctors use to remove stitches from humans.

Within three days I was back in the stream, unencumbered by minnow bucket or worm can or tackle box full of lures. I traveled light now, just a few bits of string and feather wrapped around tiny hooks, stuck in sponge and stuffed in my vest pocket. And a whippy, near-weightless rod.

Since my goal now was to imitate what hovers just above the water, I raised my sights a notch, taking in the air and light as well as the water they stir and dapple. My focus lengthened, as did the summer afternoons, which now extended well into evening before I even considered leaving the stream.

To my father's and my amazement, I began to catch respectable-sized trout almost immediately. With his help I mastered the art of quick release; the trick is patience, taking the time to play the fish out before reeling him in, so he arrives quietly in your hand, too tired to resist the flip of the wrist that will free him.

We were in league with the trout, allies in their progress from season to season, training them to fend off the harsher assaults of worm-danglers and hardware flingers. At the end of long days in the stream, I called my father with news of the catch: a ten-inch brookie, a twelve-inch brown, the sight of a great blue heron lifting off at my approach, an eight-point buck crossing the stream at the riffles, a sleek-headed muskrat diving for the cover of his underwater door in the bank.

I described whatever flitted above the stream, and he tied its likeness for me. Our phones seemed connected not by fiber optics but by the most delicately tapered of leaders, so sensitive that he felt the float of each fly, felt each slow swish of tail as the just-released trout steadied itself in the water before racing out of my loosely cupped hand.

He made my learning easy, but one thing I learned the hard way. "That's too bad," is all my father said when I told him I had broken the tip of my rod on a careless back cast into a tree branch. The next day, when I took the "old split bamboo" to the tackle shop for repair, I was unprepared for the whistles of appreciation and dismay that greeted the sight of my broken rod. In my ignorance, I had chosen it over the fiberglass as the best rod for a beginner to bumble with.

"Do you know what you've got here?" the shop owner asked, and I pretended that I had always known what I was just beginning to understand. He told me he knew a guy over in Massachusetts who used to repair split bamboo just for the love of it, but he might be out of business now, because hardly anybody who has a split bamboo rod actually fishes with it anymore. They just hold on to them as investments.

When I told my father the guy in Massachusetts thought the rod could be repaired but it would never be whippy again, he said, "Well, I've caught a lot of good fish on fiberglass." For the next three trout seasons, so did I.

The phone and mail flowed between us like the stream, rising to its highest level in late spring and tapering off to a trickle in the fall.

He sent me flies, and I sent him photographs of my favorite stretch of the stream; one time I even included a diagram showing the exact spots where I had seen the buck crossing, the heron lifting off, the big one that always gets away. Each year he planned a visit so we could enter the stream together, but each summer he was detained, first by my mother's illness, then by his own.

On my last visit to him, I saw that he kept those pictures at his bedside. Thumbworn at the corners, they still glistened at the center. One August morning, he asked if we could talk about a few things, "just in case." He said he would like a portion of his ashes to enter the stream, and I said I knew just where. No, not where the sycamore spanned the stream; the winter after my mother died, the sycamore had been pried loose from its mooring on the bank by the force of high water released during a rare January thaw. Without the fallen sycamore to slow and deepen the stream, there was nothing special to keep the fish there and they had departed.

There was a better spot now, I told him, and picking up a photograph, I pointed to the riffles where I had seen the buck highstep, head erect, across the stream and disappear into the woods. Anything that entered the stream there would flow downstream past all the spots marked on the diagram to the stretches I would explore next summer and the summer after that. He smiled at the idea, and that's all it was, an idea, "just in case."

Then he asked me to go down to the basement, to the workshop where he tied flies and fixed whatever was broken, because there were some things down there he wanted me to have some day.

His work table was in order, cleared of projects for the first time in my memory. Sitting on the table was the wicker creel I had seen in pictures of him fishing as a young man. I looked closely this time, saw the well-oiled leather of the creel's shoulder strap and harness, its polished silver clasps. Next to the creel was a long oak case that I had never seen before. I opened it and found five pristine sections of split bamboo rod, with three different end sections of varying weights and whippiness.

It is spring now. The afternoons are beginning to linger. Rod and creel and ashes wait with me for summer, for the long light, when they will enter the stream at the riffles. Sometimes I wonder if the creel is his permission for me to keep what I catch. Right now, it seems more important that he taught me how to release.

This summer I will carry the creel, empty, and bear the wicker weight of his absence. They say death comes as an invitation to light. I hope so. I would like to think of life as a progress from light to light.

THE EMERGER

MALLORY BURTON

SEVERAL YEARS AGO, at the beginning of fishing season, I bought my eight-year-old son a light-action spinning rod and reel. Anthony was already a veteran fisherman by this time, having netted sizable bass and northerns at his grandparents' place back East. My father ran a guiding service in northern Ontario, and anyone who ventured out in a boat with him was guaranteed to have a successful trip. Members of the immediate family were not only guaranteed but obligated to catch fish.

"Mum," said Anthony as we drove away from the tackle shop. "Is this really my very own fishing rod?"

"Of course it's your rod," I said, slightly irritated that he would ask. I had become a confirmed fly fisher and hadn't touched a spinning rod since before he was born.

I hoped, of course, that my son would eventually develop an interest in fly fishing, but I wasn't going to push him. Fly fishing isn't like that. Either it calls you or it doesn't.

We fished many of the lakes and rivers between Prince Rupert and Terrace, British Columbia, that season, from the tiny Lost Lake with its doubtful rowboats to the fast-flowing Copper River. Anthony fished with worms and briny-smelling gobs of salmon roe, while I persisted in trying to raise trout to a floating fly.

Anthony enviously admired the stringers of cutthroat and Dolly Varden taken by the bait fishermen we encountered on rivers and lake shores. He had almost given up trying to persuade me to keep the fish I caught, watching incredulously as I removed the barbless hooks and slipped the fish back into the water.

"But that's a keeper," he'd protest. "Why do you have to put him back?"

Because he took the fly so deliberately. Because he was a wild trout, not a hatchery fish. Because the exhausted fish came to my feet so quietly, with none of the panicked, thrashing resistance that might have sparked some killing instinct in me. They were not the kinds of reasons that would have made sense to an eight-year-old.

Occasionally I took pictures of the fish I released, especially the dark-spotted cutts, with their scarlet slash below the gill cover, or the sleek, bright steelhead trout. Anthony kept all of his regulation-size fish. We had an agreement that I would fish for picture fish while he fished for food fish.

Fortunately, the wild stocks were in no danger from my fish-killing son, who wasn't patient enough to be very deadly. His tolerance was limited to one netted fish, one lost lure or one hopelessly tangled line, whichever came first. After that, he was content to build luxurious toad habitats or holding ponds, where he watched his captured sculpins swim until they found a hole between the rocks and darted away.

"They don't mind," he said of the imprisoned fish. "It's like a puzzle for them. It makes them smarter." At his age I'd constructed similar mazes, subjecting insects to treacherous obstacle courses and congratulating myself on their intelligent escapes.

He shared my childhood enthusiasm for collecting dragonfly nymphs and caddis-fly larvae, which he put into plastic bug boxes and scrutinized with a cracked magnifying glass. Occasionally he would extract a caddis worm from its cylinder and dissect the tube of gravel bits and bark, marveling at the strength of the silk that held the bits together.

Once he waded into the Lakelse River during a mayfly hatch to observe the wormlike nymphs floating up from the bottom of the river and emerging as winged adults. Together we watched the newly hatched adults drift across the surface to dry their wings for a few seconds before coming off the water. Later he sat beside me for hours as I tied nymph, emerger and adult insect imitations on small hooks, advising me on their correct size and color for the waters we were fishing.

"I'd like to try that," he announced one evening. He was disappointed when I suggested he start with a much larger hook and an easier pattern.

Eventually Anthony fished with a fly I had tied. After the Kloiya River closed for the season, I lost interest in fishing, but Anthony was still keen on visiting the lakes. Near the end of August, he decided to try his luck at a pair of tiny lakes outside Prince Rupert that were really better suited for picnicking than angling. There might have been some larger fish in their depths, but I secretly doubted that any really decent fish would live in lakes named Tweedledum and Tweedledee. Anthony fished while I picked berries nearby.

I could tell it was going to be a short expedition. Arriving on the marshy shore, Anthony promptly stepped into the bog, filling his gum boots with reeking slime. And he was rapidly using his supply of worms, winging them right off the hook with vigorous casts or losing them to the minnows that boiled around his bobber like a school of miniature piranhas.

"Are you ready to call it a day?" I asked him when the worms ran out.

"No," he called. "Look there." Several larger rings on the water's surface suggested better fish. I set down my berry pail and quickly knotted a trailing leader of six inches to a thumbnail spinner. I tied on a fly called a Muddler Minnow and handed it to him. He looked dubiously at the fly setup but recognized it as a sculpin imitation and clipped it on the swivel in place of the bobber.

His ferocious cast plunked the spinner well on the other side of the rising fish. Reeling in rapidly, he tried to jerk the tackle clear of a clump of reeds as it came within four feet of the bank, but the spinner caught in the rushes. As Anthony tugged on the snagged spinner, the trailing fly flopped wildly on the surface. Suddenly a fourteen-inch trout sailed through the air, nailing the Muddler with an angry splash. The force of its impact freed the snagged spinner, and the fish was airborne a second time. In moments, Anthony horsed it out of the water onto the shore. The cutthroat was legal size and therefore a goner. I thought.

To my surprise Anthony picked up the fish, carefully removed the hook and gently eased the trout back into the water. He watched it swim away and turned with an odd expression on his face.

"What an incredible fish! Did you see the way he hit that fly?" I nodded. "Do they always hit a floating fly like that?"

"They don't often sail through the air, but you usually see the take."

My son's hands trembled slightly as he picked up his rod and slowly reeled in the line. He took a deep breath and shook his head.

"Awesome," he said. I knew the feeling.

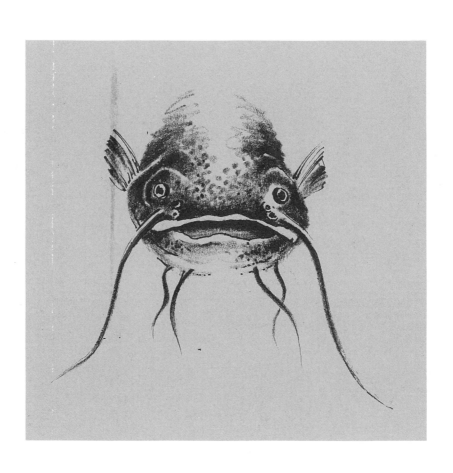

ABE LINCOLN FISHED HERE

LIN SUTHERLAND

M Y MOTHER WAS A fishing fanatic despite her Charleston, South Carolina, blue-blood upbringing. When she was twenty she graduated magna cum laude from the College of Charleston and left that city of history and suffocating social rules forever. With the twenty-dollar gold piece she got for the Math Prize, she bought a railroad ticket for as far west as it would get her. Austin, Texas, was $19.02 away.

There she met my father, a poet and horseman, and proceeded to have seven children—all girls. She also took up fishing, and by the time I was born, she had enough tackle, lawn chairs and fishing hats to fill a steamer trunk. To my father's horror, her favorite lure was blood bait. Bass and catfish were her prey.

Every summer it was my mother's custom to pack the seven of us girls into the DeSoto and drive from Austin to Charleston to visit our grandparents. We camped and fished the whole way.

Mama's preparations for the fifteen-hundred-mile trip consisted of packing the car with seven army cots, a basket of Stonewall peaches and sixteen gallons of live bait, with her tackle box and assorted rods and reels thrown in. Her idea of successful traveling was to get us all in the car without one of us sitting on the blood bait or being left at a gas station. Once she'd done a head count and ascertained the security of the bait, she'd drive like A. J. Foyt until it was too dark to go any farther. This meant we were usually tired, hungry and lost on some back road in the middle of Louisiana or Mississippi when we stopped to camp.

"Stopping to camp" in our case meant suddenly swerving off the road when my mother spied a river or lake that stirred her sporting blood. She never once planned our stops like normal people do, timing themselves to arrive at a campsite or park around dusk. But this was the 1950s, when people still slept with the screen door unlocked and left the keys in the car. We felt perfectly safe at any roadside area, and we were.

The trip that brought us face to face with history was the one we took in the summer of 1958 when I was ten. It started normally enough. We had driven all day from Austin, into the dark and the Deep South. From the back seat, groggy and weary from the hours of travel, my sisters and I felt our mother wheel the car onto the shoulder and turn off the motor.

In the dim glow of our flashlights, we pulled out the army cots, set them up and sucked on leftover peach pits. We wanted to drop into a dead sleep, but as far as Mama was concerned, this was a perfect time to go fishing.

The problem was, Mama never seemed to notice that she was the only one who ever caught anything bigger than a deck of cards. She also failed to recognize that she had borne seven girls, not seven Captain Ahabs. She lived under the illusion that everyone had the same enthusiasm as she did for sitting on rocks at waterside and waiting hours for something to steal the bait. Which of course never happened to her.

While we slouched around the camp making unintelligible grumbling noises, she unloaded the gallons of blood bait and her tackle box and got to work.

"Look at that big dark pool just under those cypress knees, honey," she said. "You just *know* there's a ten-pound bass waiting for me in there! I hope it's a stupid one." She whistled a snatch of "High Noon" as she explored her stock of lures, jigs and spoons.

Mama was very Zen about her fishing, giving it her complete concentration and ritualized observation. She examined each item in the tackle box with pleasure, murmuring to herself. She emerged from this reverie only when she decided on the right lure to use.

This night she announced, "I think I'll use my Good Luck Lure

Number 242 on this baby." She glanced in my direction to see if I was watching and abruptly emitted a theatrical, diabolical laugh.

"He'll never escape my Magic Lucky Lure!" she went on. "We have ways of making fish welcome here at our little fish camp... no, Herr Lucky Lure?" Then, adjusting her fishing hat, she addressed the water in a tough-guy voice: "Prepare to meet your Maker, Lord Bass-ship."

And she cast perfectly into the heart of the cypress-root pool.

For her children, the enthusiasm and high drama my mother created around fishing was more intriguing than the activity itself. She was ceaselessly energetic and entertaining, and when she went up against a largemouth bass with a brain the size and density of a dust mote, it was no contest.

Fifteen minutes later she was addressing the bass in person as she cleaned it.

"I regret to inform you, Lord Bass-ship, that the inscrutable order of the universe has destined you to serve in the dual role of Main Guest and Dish at this evening's festivities. You have my deepest sympathy. On the other hand, the jig's up for everybody at one time or another, Bud. Fire up the logs, girls. Dinner just arrived."

Our second day on the road we passed trees dripping with Spanish moss, stately old homes and vast fields of cotton and snap beans. We sang and talked and Mama told fish stories. And finally, in the pitch black somewhere deep into Mississippi, she stopped the car.

"I hear running water," she announced.

We bailed out of the DeSoto and traipsed down from the road until we found a place where the ground got gravelly. We figured we were far enough from the road so we wouldn't be run over in the middle of the night, and we set up our cots in the usual manner: jammed against each other in line, so that if, during the night, one of us flopped an arm or leg out, the warm body of a sister would be felt. Sitting cross-legged on the cots, we munched Vienna sausage and Wonderbread sandwiches and watched Mama fish in the fast-running creek next to us. Then we fell asleep, exhausted.

As the dawn light began to come up, something like a gentle lapping at my side awoke me. I slowly let a foot slide over the edge of my cot. It fell into two feet of cold water. I bolted upright and saw that seven sisters and their mother were about to float away.

My mother had camped us in a creekbed. The water had risen during the night from rains upstream and had us surrounded. We practically had to swim to the car, pulling our cots behind us.

The third night found us somewhere in the mountains of Kentucky. I was never quite sure where we were at any given point on these trips, since I knew only one landmark—the tree-lined road to my grandparents' house—the finish line. But again, we had driven for hours into the night futilely looking for water. When we finally pulled off the road, the hills around us were black as midnight under a skillet. Then a slice of a quarter moon slid out from behind a cloud and delicately illuminated a rock gate in front of us.

"Oh, look!" Mama cried, "a national park."

There was an audible sigh of relief from the back seat. "Let's camp here, Mama!" we clamored urgently.

Since she had been slapping her cheeks for the last hour to stay awake, she agreed.

We cruised down a black dirt road into the parking area. Nestled nearby was the outline of a log cabin. Beyond that, the glint of water.

"See that!" Mama said excitedly. "A sleeping cabin. By some kind of lake. This is paradise."

We parked and unloaded the car, dragging our stuff into the log cabin.

It was open and empty. We could see it was very old and rudimentary, but it had a bathroom with running water. For us it was luxury quarters. We bathed and ate our dinner of kipper snacks and soda crackers, with Moon Pies for dessert. Then we snuggled into the cots that we'd fixed up in the one bare room.

Mama set off with long strides toward the water, gear in hand. The faint murmur of her voice as she conversed with her tackle box drifted through the open windows. With that and a cozy roof overhead, my sisters curled up and fell to sleep like a litter of puppies.

I picked up my rod and reel and, still in my pajamas, slipped quietly out the door. Across the damp grass I could see my mother's silhouette making casting motions. For a moment I felt the thrill of anticipation inherent in fishing: there was a fat catfish with my name on it waiting out there, I just knew it.

I joined my mother and we fished together. Just us, the water and the quarter moon. It was one of those moments that form a permanent part in the book of parent-child memories, though it was destined to be brief. Mama could practically conjure fish up to her, and sure enough, within half an hour she got a strike and brought in a fourteen-pound cat. Probably *my* Fat-Cat, I thought irritably.

"Look," she said, bending around me, her hands grasping mine as I held my rod. "Let me show you . . . " She made a deft flicking motion and suddenly my line shot across the water. The light of the moon made it look like the trail of a shooting star. It fell silently on the dark water and disappeared. "Right *there*," she said lowly. "Hold tight to it."

She turned away and began cleaning her fish. I gripped the rod until my knuckles were white. I had a feeling for what was coming. Suddenly, the line lurched tight and my arms shot forward. I almost flew into the black water of the lake.

"It's a big one, Mama!" I yelled. "I don't think I can hold it." My feet were slipping down the bank, and the mud had oozed up to my ankles. "Mama, quick!"

She grasped me around the waist and yanked me back up the bank. The pull on the line lessened. "Now! Bring it in now!" she shouted. I reeled in as hard as I could. Suddenly the fish was right there below me, lying in shallow water. It was a big one, all right. Almost as big as Mama's.

"Good work," she said, leaning over and carefully pulling the catfish onto the bank. It slapped the wet grass angrily. I was exhausted. We took our fish back to the cabin and fell into a deep sleep.

It seemed only minutes later that sleep was penetrated by voices. Lots of voices. Suddenly, the door of the cabin burst open and sunlight and a large group of people led by a woman in a uniform flowed into the room. The uniformed person was in the middle of a speech. "And here we have the boyhood home of President Abraham Lincoln—Aagghhhh!!"

We all screamed at once. My mother, protective in her own quixotic way, leapt off the cot, her chenille bathrobe flapping, and shouted at the intruders, "Who do you think you are, bursting in on a sleeping family like this?"

The guide was struck speechless. She gathered herself with visible effort. "Ma'am, I don't know who *you* are, but this is Abraham Lincoln's Birthplace National Historic Park," she reported tersely. Her eyes quickly shifted sideways to take in two huge catfish lying on the floor. Though she tried to conceal it, her lips pursed with disgust. I knew right off she wasn't a fisherman.

"And his log cabin," she continued, "is *not* an overnight stopover for fishing expeditions. This is a restricted area with guided tours beginning at 7 a.m. and . . ."

"Oh my God, we overslept!" Mama shouted. "Pack the car, girls. We've got to get on the road!"

We lurched into a flurry of experienced cot-folding and were out the door in seconds.

"But, ma'am," the guide called at my mother's disappearing back, "You weren't supposed to sleep in here. This is Lincoln's Log Cabin. *It's a National Treasure!*"

"We treasure our night here," my mother shouted back, as she gunned the car around. "Abe wouldn't have minded."

With that we roared off in the direction of South Carolina. I saw a sign as we left: "Leaving Hodgenville, Kentucky, Abraham Lincoln's Birthplace. Ya'll Come Back."

"Not likely," my mother laughed. "A good fishing spot, but I hate to do anything twice, don't you?"

And that's how it happened that, during the summer I was ten, the course of history was changed. Unofficially, to be sure, but if there'd been a historical marker by that lake, it would now have to read ABE LINCOLN FISHED HERE . . . AND SO DID I.

BOAT RIDE

TESS GALLAGHER

for Galway

Since my girlhood, in that small boat
we had gone together for salmon
with the town still sleeping and the wake
a white groove in the black water, black
as it is when the gulls are just stirring and
the ships in the harbor are sparked with lights
like the casinos of Lucerne.
That morning my friend had driven an hour
in darkness to go with us, my father
and me. There'd been an all-night party.
My friend's face so tired I thought, *Eskimo-eyes.*
He sighed, as if stretched out
on a couch at the back of his mind.

Getting the bait and tackle. What
about breakfast? No breakfast.
Bad luck to eat breakfast before fishing, but
good luck to take smoked salmon to eat
on the water in full sun. Was my friend's coat
warm enough? The wind can come up.
Loaning him my brother's plaid jacket.

Being early on the water, like getting first
to heaven and looking back through memory
and longing at the town. Talking little, and
with the low, tender part
of our voices; not sentences but
friendlier, as in nodding to one who already
knows what you mean.

Father in his rain-slicker—seaweed green over
his coat, over blue work shirt, over cream-

colored thermal underwear that makes a white V
at his neck. His mouth open so the breath
doesn't know if it's coming or going—like any
other wave without a shore. His mind
in the no-thought of guiding the boat.
I stare into the water folding
along the bow, *gentian*—the blue with darkness
engraved into its name, so the sound
petals open with mystery.

Motor-sound, a low burbling with a chuckle
revolving in the *smack smack* of the bow
spanking water. *You hear me, but you don't
hear me*, the motor says
to the fish. A few stars
over the mountains above the town.
I think *pigtails*, and that the water under us
is at least as high as those mountains, deep
as the word *cello* whispered under water—
cello, cello until it frees a greeting.

We pass the Coast Guard station, its tower
flashing cranky white lights beside
the barracks where the seamen sleep in
long rows. Past the buoy, its sullen red bell
tilting above water. All this time
without fishing—important to get out of
the harbor before letting the lines
down, not time wasted but time
preparing, which includes invitation and
forgetting, so the self is occupied freely
in idleness.

"Just a boat ride," my father says, squinting
where sun has edged the sky toward Dungeness
a hazy mix of violet and pink. "Boat ride?"

I say. "But we want salmon."
"I'll take cod, halibut, old shoes, anything
that's going," says my friend. "And you'll get
dogfish," my father says. "There's enough
dogfish down there to feed all Japan."
He's baiting up, pushing the double hooks
through the herring. He watches us
let the lines out. "That's plenty," he says,
like it's plain this won't come
to much.

Sitting then, nothing to say for a while,
poles nodding slightly. My friend, slipping
a little toward sleep, closes his eyes.
Car lights easing along Ediz Hook, some
movement in the town, Port of the Angels,
the angels turning on kitchen lights,
wood smoke stumbling among scattered hemlock,
burning up questions, the angels telling
their children to get up, planning the future
that is one day long.

"Hand me that coffee bottle, Sis," my father
says. "Cup of coffee always makes the fish
bite." Sure enough, as he lifts the cup,
my pole hesitates, then dips. I brace
and reel. "Damned dogfish!" my father says,
throwing his cigarette into the water. "How
does he know?" my friend asks. "No fight,"
I say. "They swallow the hook down
their gullets. You have to cut
the leader."

No sun-flash on silver scales when it
breaks water, but thin-bellied brown, shark-
like, and the yellow-eyed insignia

that says: *there will be more of us.*
Dogfish. Swallower of hooks, waster of hopes
and tackle. My father grabs the line, yanks
the fish toward the knife, slashes twice,
gashing the throat and underbelly so
the blood spills over his hand.
"There's one that won't come back," he says.

My friend witnesses without comment or
judgment the death and mutilation
of the dogfish. The sun is up. My friend
is wide awake now. We are all wide
awake. The dogfish floats away, and a tenderness
for my father wells up in me, my father
whom I want my friend to love and who intends,
if he must, as he will, to humor us, to keep
fishing, to be recorded in the annals
of dogfish as a scourge on the nation of
dogfish which has fouled his line, which is
unworthy and which he will single-handedly
wipe out.

When the next fish hits my friend's line
and the reel won't sing, I take out my
Instamatic camera: "That's a beautiful
dogfish!" I say. "I'll tell them in New York
it's a marlin," my friend says. I snap
his picture, the fish held like
a trophy. My father leans out of
the frame, then cuts the line.

In a lull I get him to tell stories,
the one where he's a coal miner in Ottumwa,
Iowa, during the Depression and the boss
tries to send the men into a mine where
a shaft collapsed the day before. "You'll

go down there or I'll run you out of
this town," the boss says. "You don't
have to run me. I'm not just leaving
your town, I'm leaving your whole goddamned
state!" my father says, and he turns
and heads on foot out of the town, some
of the miners with him, hitching from there
to the next work in the next state.

My father knows he was free
back there in 1935 in Ottumwa, Iowa, and he
means you to know you don't have to risk
your life for pay if you can tell the boss to
go to hell and turn your heel. What
he doesn't tell is thirty years on the docks,
not a day missed—working, raising
a family.

I unwrap smoked salmon sandwiches and we bite
into them. It is the last fishing trip
I will have with my father. He
is ready to tell the one about the time
he nearly robbed the Seminole Bank in
Seminole, Oklahoma, but got drunk
instead and fell asleep.
He is going to kill five more dogfish
without remorse; and I am going to
carry a chair outside for him
onto the lawn of the Evergreen Radiation
Center where he will sit and smoke
and neither of us feels like talking, just
his—"The sun feels good."
After treatments, after going back
to my sister's where he plays with her baby—
"There's my gal! Is the Kiss Bank
open?"—in the night, rising up in the dream

of his going to say, "Get my billfold," as if
even his belongings might be pulled into
the vortex of what would come.

We won't catch a single salmon that day.
No strikes even. My friend and I
will share a beer and reminisce in advance
about the wonderful dogfishing we had.
My father wipes blood from his knife
across his knee and doesn't
look up. He believes nothing
will survive of his spirit or body. His god
takes everything and will not be
satisfied, will not be assuaged by the hopes, by
the pitiful half-measures of the living.
If he is remembered, that too
will pass.

It is good then,
to eat salmon on the water, to bait the hook
again, even for dogfish, to stare back at
the shore as one who withholds nothing, who,
in the last of himself, cannot put together
that meaning, and need not, but yields in thought
so peacefully to the stubborn brightness of
light and water: we are awake with him

as if we lay asleep. Good memory,
if you are such a boat, tell me
we did not falter in the vastness
when we walked ashore.

KING BAIT

KERI HULME

I THINK THIS SEASON'LL BE the last, you know. Well, I mean, Coasters have their channels for spreading news, mainly ex-Coasters. From such people, news filters through to friends of ex-Coasters, not to mention relations, and eventually travels the length and breadth of the country. So maybe everybody knows why, and maybe everybody doesn't, yet.

Here I am, wound round in a welter of words, with a mystery on my hands, and very uncertain what to say about it. But this is the core of the matter, the heart of the nut: King Bait.

One thing everybody does know about the Coast is bait. Whitebait. That succulent little fish, quick and lucent, likened in an old haiku to the "spirit of the waters"—

> The whitebait:
> as though the spirit of the waters
> were moving.

And every beginning spring, Coasters in their hundreds flock to the rivers and streams to swoop and scoop and blind-drag as many as possible out of sanctuary. When it's a good season, tons are lovingly packed into freezers against the lean, non-bait portion of the year; tons more are railed and flown over the hill, weekly. The Coast becomes a joyous place, the Coaster a contented being.

Of course, quite a few hundred-weight get converted meantime into patties and omelettes and—well, whatevers. How did your mother cook them when she got them from the shop? I'm from Christchurch, we eke out the bait with flour and other foreign bodies. But here! Prodigality . . .

Take half a pound of bait per person, add an egg (two eggs, if you really like them), stir vigorously until fish and egg is a viscous froth full of strange little eyes. Add half a teaspoon of baking powder, a little salt, a smidgen of pepper and fry the mix quickly, but with care. There you have a Coast feed, two right-sized whitebait patties, a subtly flavoured delight for anyone with a tongue in their head.

Last year, I missed the whitebait season. I was newly arrived from Christchurch and, unaware of Coast ways, bought my bait from a local fish-shop, and was well content to get it forty cents cheaper the pound than the family over the Hill. Last year, I couldn't have told you the difference between a net for the Tere, and one used in the Grey. Nor what the advantages of supplejack over duraluminum. Set nets were strangers, and the joys of very early morning tea in a tin shack on a riverside also unknown. The haiku was just a pleasant poetic fancy, blind-dragging was peculiar terminology and the great runs—well, myths of the past, a nice concept to beguile the tourists.

This year, I'm all enthusiasm. Buy myself the regulation round Grey net, and a bloody great pole to go with it. Equip myself with gumboots, get out old fishing clothes and head down to the river at odd hours, waiting on changing tides. Drag that net, eyes strained, shoulders filled with a dead ache, hopeful of a nice little pudding in the bottom of the nylon bag. Or a very large one, for the season's started out a boomer. Tons of bait about. Happy faces all around, reflecting my smug grin. Full stomachs abounding, appetite satisfied, bankbook replete and yet expecting much, much, more.

Things are just beginning. All over the Coast the hiss of hot fat and the crunching of little eyes . . .

And you know what? I thinks it's the end.

A very strange thing happened yesterday, twenty to nine under Cobden bridge; a strange, a horrible, a holy thing.

Friday night was a good night. I'd been to the local juicery, talked a lot, sung a bit, drank to capacity, happy among happy people.

Came home with the white moon high over the sea. A windless peace-filled night, the only sound that liquid continuous chirruping of treefrogs. I cooked a couple of patties, ate them with a last cold beer from the fridge and went to bed. Relaxed, full, content, perfectly at ease . . . ah, sweet.

And then, the morning. I woke suddenly, dropped abruptly out of sleep. For a moment I couldn't place the awakening factor, and then, there it was. A most peculiar hysterical liveness, filling the quiet street, streaking up my quiet hill, a shrill cacophony of voices.

"Berloody kids," I think, and go to turn over, back to sleep.

It penetrates then:

"Whitebait running WHITEBAIT RUNNING WHITE-BAIT . . ."

The words and the strangeness were enough. I shot out of bed, into my denims and t-shirt faster than it's said, grabbed my boots and the net and screamed out of the door and down the hill far more quickly than I've ever done. In fact, I'd reached the bottom before I realized that I've left the pole back in the house. Or asked myself why somebody should tell everybody about a good thing.

But the street is alive as never before. The old lady recluse, who's probably never seen the light of day outside for years, is standing there, mouth open, staring-eyed, looking shrunken and untidy on the footpath. The new family at the corner is running in a graduated straggle round the corner, all eleven of them. As they vanish, the bloke next door and his wife with the new kid rush out. He's got the net and pole, and she has one arm full of kerosene tins and plastic bags, and one arm full of baby, and I swear it's not the former she's going to drop. I don't wait round looking anymore. Bugger the pole, I hive off through a shortcut down into Bright Street. And believe me, all ambulant Cobden seems to be there; I'm a heavy sleeper, late waker, and the street is now crowded with everyone before me, running, walking, staggering, hell for leather for the river.

Well, it's normally a ten-minute walk from my place to the bridge, but even with the crowd I make it in a three-minute run. After getting through lame oldies and slow small fry, it's much easier of course. There was the risk of being skewered by poles or having the breath thumped from one by a carelessly swung kero tin. Christchurch Friday-night-in-the-Square experience came to the fore here, though, and I'm in the van of the rush as we reach the river, that stretch just before the north end of the bridge.

Down the bank, trampling bush, slipping, kicking someone, grazing my hand on a tree I use to break my headlong eagerness a moment. All pulsing wild excitement to get a spot.

And stop aghast. Because, before God, the Grey is solid white-bait, bank to bank.

A fabulous mass of life, so thick in the river that water isn't seen. Just a seething froth of bait, frantic yet purposeful, a live river flowing in from the sea. And the hiss of disturbed water from their passing is louder than rain, louder than rapids, as spirited and loud as great falls.

I scoop, holding the rim of the net. It's FULL, absolutely chokka, and I drag it, elated, to the shore. The nylon is strained to its limits. Damn, nowhere to put the catch! But the bait, contrary to the nor-mal lively whipping efforts to get out of the net and into the river, lie there like a sacrifice and peacefully begin to die.

Strange. All my feverish desire to catch whitebait is gone. I lay the net with gentleness on the riversand at my feet, and all along the bank, as the people come slithering excitedly down, and then stop, stunned, they are now doing the same. Over on the Greymouth side, the weird thing happens, as the crowds gather and swell and burst to the riverside. Horrified reverence for this impossible dream-run.

Except one man.

I don't know who he is, a thigh-booted dungareed individual, made distant and inhuman by his action. For he is swinging his net like an automaton, scooping the bait, flinging it silver and anywhere onto the shore. There is saliva hanging in a shining string from the corner of his mouth, and I am not so far away that I can't see the money-glaze on his eyes. It's inevitable, a feeling of disaster growing. Stop it you bastard, from voices in the crowd, leave them alone. But he continues shoveling up the unresisting harvest.

. . . an eddy in the river of bait, or an eddy of the crowd, pushing harder out? I don't know, but he is suddenly off his feet, falling with grotesque flailing slowness into the froth of eyes. The bait-river moves on, and how to swim when the water is gone, how to swim in the viscous moving jelly? His dark head is above the river once, shining all over with lucid bodies, mouth gaping open, nostrils flaring wide, but full of writhing fish...

If ever a man died in dream turned nightmare, that was him. And yet, not a movement or sound is heard from any of us. Just a shared feeling of wonderment, of rightness and inevitability, as the whitebait we caught die on the shore. Things move to a conclusion.

And then there is an unforgettable sound, a vast wind of indrawn breath coming from the seaward end of the river. People astonished, bereft of all movement except the gasp of awe. Slowly it swells, welling along the banks of the river, both sides of the river, while we who have no knowledge, wait and there, midstream, lambent, borne on the living tide, the spirit of the waters, moving.

We disagreed how big today. Ten or maybe twelve feet of lighted perfection. Clear as the most clear water, except for the fine line of black speckling on his sides, and the slender dark-drawn rays of his four fins and tail... and the goldened brain in the top of his head... and the eyes, the great silver eyes, intensely circled black centers, burnished globes on the inward side of his head. They reflect neither intelligence nor love, nor malignity, but show forth pure being. Summation. A complete benign magnificence.

For as the multitude of whitebait had gathered to protect this one by sheer pacific numbers, so was there nothing to fear from him. Watch with calm incredulity as he passes.

King Bait.

And as much bait flowed behind in that protective solid wall, now unharried by fish or bird or man, as came to be preyed on before. I thought of the millions upon millions of ridiculous harmless little fish, who had been sacrificed to provide a safe passage for that majesty, and did not wonder much therefore at feeling echoes of their massed consuming joy.

There is nothing in the river, except the white slimefroth of their passing, and the water. And somebody says, loud in the quiet that follows after,

"Hell, I hope they make it to wherever that is going. I hope they get there."

And somebody near me, voicing all the other thought of the people,

"God love us all, but are they ever coming back?"

THE YOUNG WOMAN
AND THE SEA

LORIAN HEMINGWAY

THE NAME IS A JOKE to those too smug to believe in the enduring power of a heritage. Others see it as an accident, a casual gift that allows Hemingway family members to walk the world with their heads high, never quite knowing why they do. And I have heard some say that the name is a curse, something made volatile by the memory of the despairs and exhilarations of a fine writer too long dead.

It has been all things to me: self-doubt, strength, justice and abomination. It has been a wish to drink hard and relentlessly, to paper myself with the guilt that is the other legacy Papa's name bestows. But for all the fine and the sinister gifts my grandfather's name has given to three generations of his family, there is one we all embrace without question. The belief in luck that Papa lived by makes the name worthwhile; a legacy of luck for the proud, confused children on whom Ernest was such an influence.

I'm glad we do not have to try to kill the stars. Imagine if a man each day must try to kill the moon. The moon runs away. But imagine if a man each day should have to try to kill the sun. We are born lucky. Yes, we are born lucky.

—The Old Man and the Sea

There was a cocktail party the night before. It was the second night of the third annual Hemingway Billfishing Tournament, and many participants had been working on a decent, stabilizing drunk for several days. I had had my share of beer. Enough to float one of the sunken sailboats in Bimini's harbor.

Had I been sober, I would have looked less kindly upon the scene before me. The rich yachting types who courted Papa, and whom Papa swore he never liked, were all around. They were perfect-looking men and women, dressed in perfect sports clothes, and were standing around the pool at the Blue Water Marina, talking of marlin fishing and Ernest Hemingway and their suntans. I had a good suntan, but my clothes weren't perfect and there was a Band-Aid over my right eye (a testimonial to the rough and clumsy night before). But I made many friends and was jealous of them because they would be fishing the next day for something my grandfather had loved —something I had wanted for years, and had actually fished for several times, but had never caught.

"You want to catch a marlin, don't you?" asked Dr. Howard Engle, an old friend of Papa's and a new friend of mine. "I can tell by your eyes," he said.

Dr. Engle was right. I had wanted to fight a marlin for three years, ever since I had come upon that wondrous yearly event my great-uncle Leicester, Ernest's brother, had decided to call the Hemingway Billfishing Tournament. There are four kinds of marlin — blue, black, white and striped. Of these, the blue is most prized on Bimini because it is the largest and fights hardest.

But I wasn't entered in the tournament. I didn't own a boat, and if I had wished to charter one, I would have been milked for $650 for a day's fishing.

"The very rich are different from you and me," F. Scott Fitzgerald said.

"Yes," Ernest told the world. "They have more money."

It's a good thing they do, because if Dr. Engle hadn't befriended Capt. Marion Merritt, a fugitive from the Mau Mau rebellion in Kenya some thirty years ago, then I would have been left behind, sipping beer on the dock for the remaining three days of the tournament.

I had met Captain Marion the year before and had a healthy

respect for his Georgia accent and his stories about the ruthlessness of the Mau Mau. He had bought a boat and named it Kembé in honor of the Watusi tribal chief who had helped him escape from Africa.

"Young lady," Captain Marion told me, after Dr. Engle had spent two hours at the party helping to convince him of my desperate need to fish, "you are gonna catch a marlin your granddaddy would be proud of. But you're gonna do every damn bit of work yourself."

Melodrama, perhaps. But those were the words I had wanted to hear.

"You be down here at 9 a.m. We'll catch us a fish. Where'd you get all those gray hairs?"

"Too much beer, I guess," I said.

"On you it looks good," he told me. "You need another beer, doncha?"

I told him that I didn't really.

"Yes you do, by God. You wait here while I get you one."

Captain Marion brought me a Budweiser, and, as Papa would say, "it tasted good."

I tried saying, "It tastes good," under my breath just to see if I could make it sound right. I wanted to walk up to everyone at the party, hold out my bottle of beer and say, "It tastes good." Or even "real well." But I wasn't quite ready to start talking like Jake Barnes in *The Sun Also Rises.*

I was, however, ready to fish my heart out as soon as Bimini's dead-heat sun broke the horizon the next morning. It was a good day for fishing. I could tell by the way I felt as I hurried to make it down to the boat. I didn't feel the usual beery stupor too much, but I drank one while I was getting dressed just to make sure the night before wouldn't catch up with me.

"Nothing like a cold beer in the morning," Dr. Engle shouted as he left Les Hemingway's houseboat, on which he was staying. He was heading down to the Kembé to chat with Captain Marion and make everything as right as he could. He had been acting as patriarch of the clan since Leicester had been hospitalized for a blood clot five days before. He had fixed fine meals for my husband, Douglas, and me and for Les's daughter Hilary (my cousin), and he had made our stay in Bimini a good one.

Dr. Engle, with his salt-and-pepper beard and suntanned face, is often mistaken for a Hemingway. We don't all have beards, but there's something about the jaw structure that suggests a need for one. Dr. Engle wears his well. And happily. He was our alarm clock the entire time we were in Bimini, so eager was he to be up and to scout the island for a new adventure. This day he had fixed it so that I could chase one of Papa's perfect fantasies, one which might become real.

Bimini's summer is a great furnace. It must be avoided and re-sisted. And as I walked to Captain Marion's boat that morning, the heat was nearly suffocating. "Eight-thirty in the morning and it's hot-ter than hell," someone said. There was a little breeze that would wilt before the day was over.

"Ready to catch a big one?" Captain Marion bellowed from the bobbing stern as we approached. It was a beautiful boat, a forty-seven-foot custom job with impressive woodwork and a flying bridge designed only for those sure-footed enough to walk a plank in thirty-foot seas. Hilary, Douglas and I went on board. I said good morning to Tommy Sewell, a young man who has the reputation on the island as one of the best mates around.

Captain Marion took me into the cabin and pulled a monstrous rod and reel from one of the overhead supports. Dr. Engle was on the sofa, having his fifth cup of coffee. He watched as Captain Marion began to drill me on the fishing equipment.

"You'll be usin' a rod like this. Fifty-pound test line, so it'll be a little easier on your arms. It's harder to catch a big marlin on 50 pounds because you have to be aware of what you're feeling when he pulls. Too much and it'll break." He handed the rod to me.

The weight of the rod was enough to send me off balance. I sup-ported the butt in my right hand and kept my left on the grip.

"How's it feel?" Captain Marion asked.

"Fine," I lied.

"Now you're gonna be the only one that knows what's going on with that fish. I can only *guess*. Tommy can only guess. You gotta tell us so I know what the hell to do with that boat. We never want the fish to get under the boat."

Captain Marion seemed to know everything. With his white beard and perfectly round red cheeks, he looked like Santa Claus.

And there was that certain integrity in his face that children appreciate: an almost sad willingness to give a part of himself that will later prove valuable to the recipient. But his voice was all business. He was being rough so he could prepare me for what might be ahead.

He taught me all about the rod and reel. And how to set the drag, which controls the amount of pressure a hooked fish has to exert to take out line. "Don't set the thing all the way up," he told me. "If you do, you'll break the line. If you got a five-hundred-pound marlin on the end of this thing, it'll snap like a toothpick unless you do everything right. You gotta let him run once you hook in. Just keep enough pressure on the line so you know he's there. You'll know it when you feel it."

I wasn't sure I would. I had read all of Papa's books, had been told how stupid men lose fish through carelessness, had tried to tell myself that if I ever hooked such a grand thing I would be able to handle it. I was thinking about what I knew about marlin. Not much, but more than the average novice. I heard stories about them from Les Hemingway, Dr. Engle and many experienced captains and mates. One man lost an eye to the needle-sharp bill of a marlin brought alongside the boat before the fight was out of it. Another man was gouged in the side as the marlin took a final leap before the gaff reached it.

I had seen marlin dead on the docks and had seen them thrown, uncut and wasted, into the harbor for the barracuda to feed on. I had seen them mounted, one on the north wall of the Compleat Angler Hotel, where Papa used to stay when he was on Bimini. And I had seen films of them jumping majestically, trying to throw their hooks while great ribbons of scarlet streamed from their intestines.

Papa boated over one hundred marlin in his time. And once they were boated, he either released them or kept them for food and an occasional trophy. He never let them rot as they do on Bimini now, nor did he turn his back on them once they were dead. He kept the memory of the fight and wrote of it so someday a scared kid like me would halfway get over her nerves as she listened to these precise instructions from rough and bearded Captain Marion.

"Look outside there," Captain Marion demanded. "There's two flat lines, girl. There's a left rigger and a right rigger hooked up with them clothespin-lookin' things. When I yell, 'Flat line!' you go to that flat line and take the pole. When I yell right or left rigger, you take that pole and knock the line out of the pin if it's not knocked out already. Get in the chair then, and Tommy will strap you down. *You* set the drag. *You* do it, girl. When I say, 'Let him go,' let him go, then you let the drag run. When I say, 'Hit him,' then set the drag. Here, put this belt on, because if you get a hit on a flat line, you'll need it before you can get to the chair."

He handed me a wide rubber belt that hooked in back and had a cuplike gimbaled socket in front to hold the pole. It was too wide and too loose for someone as small as I am. The doctor helped me adjust it.

"You've got to rest it on the pubic bone," he said. "Otherwise you'll have internal injuries." What have I got myself into, I thought. I grabbed a beer from the cooler. We were headed out of the harbor now, and Tommy was setting the baits.

"OK," Captain Marion yelled from the bridge a few minutes later as we were heading at half-speed toward the Gulf Stream. "This is gonna be your drill. The next time you hear it, it'll be for real. Get used to the pull of the bait on the rigger. It pulls hard, girl. But when you get a marlin on, you damn well better know the difference."

"Flat line! Flat line!" Captain Marion yelled.

I ran to the right side of the stern. I grabbed the pole from its grip and tried to work it into the belt strapped around my waist.

"Let him go! Let him go!"

I set the drag down as low as it would go.

"Hit him!" Captain Marion bellowed.

I set the drag up and pulled on the bait, a mullet as large as a good-sized trout.

"See how it feels, girl?" Captain Marion asked. I told him I did. It took a lot of muscle just to pull the bait out of the wake.

We weren't in the Gulf Stream yet, but there was a light chop, and the sun, at 10 a.m., was as high as it ever seems to get in a northern city like Seattle, where I live. The bank of black clouds in the distance, which had threatened rain the night before, was the backdrop for a sight I had never seen. The waves were green and aqua peaks, as if painted by a seaworthy Van Gogh, with all their madness and tranquility taken into account. There were fish swimming along the cor-

ridors of reefs, their heads and tails flashing colors more brilliant than
the light of the water.

"Right rigger. Right rigger!" Captain Marion yelled now. I stumbled toward the right rigger and grabbed the rod.

"Knock it out!" he demanded. I slapped the pole to my left with
all my weight, grinding the butt of the pole against my right ribs, and
managed to knock the line out of the pin. Then I jumped into the
chair, set the drag, moved it to strike and gave a big tug.

I was feeling proud of myself. A few calisthenics in the morning
never hurt.

"The next time," Captain Marion reminded me, "it'll be for
real."

Dr. Engle helped me adjust my belt again, and I headed to the
cooler for another beer. We were at sea now. Bimini's pastel waters
and the shadowy symmetry of the coral reefs were lost to the purple
shadow of the Gulf Stream passing just east of us.

I sat beside Dr. Engle near the fighting chair. He was waiting as
patiently and as nervously as I. "You're going to have to do the whole
damn thing yourself, Lorian," he told me. "Your grandfather's looking down on you."

"Up at you," my husband corrected.

This wasn't the easy time on a boat I had known before. Sure, I
had gotten my sea legs, learned how to climb the ladder to the bridge
during a storm without falling into the Gulf Stream's warm, almost
thick-looking waters. I knew how to tell a bad squall from an inconse-
quential one, and I knew where the flying fish would settle. But I
never knew, nor had ever conceived, the power and the unalterable
beauty that a marlin at its fiercest and most loyal to its element would
offer.

I was standing by the cabin door, smoking a cigarette, when the yell
came. I thought Captain Marion and Dr. Engle might be teasing me.

"RI-ITE REE-GUH! Rrriii-iite ree-guh!"

Go to hell, I thought.

"Right rigger!" Dr. Engle yelled with comparative calm.

I ran to the rod, clawed my way into the chair and was strapped in
by Tommy and Douglas. The boat came to a rocking halt in the wa-

ter. Everyone except Captain Marion, who was piloting the boat, rushed toward the stern.

"Let him go! Let him go!" Captain Marion yelled.

"He's five-hundred pounds, boss," Tommy said.

"Hit him!" I heard Captain Marion scream. I pulled back and felt the monster take hold.

"Jesus Christ," I whispered.

I could feel the pain in my back as soon as I hooked into him. Tommy had taken off my waist belt and was adjusting the straps on the harness. But it did not fit. I was pulling with all my weight just to keep myself in the chair. My muscles were cramping, and I knew that I had to distribute my weight better or else lose a kidney or have my arm yanked off by this unseen great fish.

I started the business of pulling back on the rod to get some slack and then slowly reeling in as I leaned forward.

"You tell us how it feels," I heard Captain Marion say. "You tell us how it damn well feels. Lorian! Where's he goin' now?"

"Take up the slack," Tommy said. Tommy was at my left, ready to shout at me and keep up my spirit as long as the fish stayed with me. I could feel the brutal pull on my left arm as the fish jerked the line out.

"He's taking out, Tommy," I screamed.

"Slow the boat, boss. He's taking too much." Captain Marion inched the boat back, and I felt a bit of slack on the line and began to take some of it in.

Thirty minutes passed. I knew because, after each ten minutes, Dr. Engle would boom out the length of my fight.

A wet towel had been put on my head. Then a bucket of sea water.

"Give him hell, Lorian," came the rough voice from the bridge.

Douglas kept rubbing my cramped back. My head ached. I dearly wanted to see the thing that was sharing so much pain with me.

"Where the hell is he?" I asked.

The blue marlin brought himself out of the water with a muscular leap. His colors were a deep blur of blues, greens and purples. His bright mouth, open to cast off the hook, was like a red gash.

I let out a yell that made no sense. I screamed and pounded my right fist against my leg and heard all the other screams coming into chorus around me. Then I took up the slack on the line.

I fought him for fifty-seven minutes, the doctor told me, before the line broke. I had watched the weak section of line rushing out as the fish sounded. But I hoped to God that it would hold.

Luck, luck, luck, Papa.

I felt the weight of the fish release as quickly as I had felt it take hold.

I cried.

"That's one big baby you just labored over," I heard Dr. Engle say.

"I never cry," I told them all.

I sat and brooded in the cool of the cabin.

"You didn't do a damn thing wrong," the doctor told me. "You handled the rig like a pro. Papa would be proud of you."

And I felt proud. The fight had been enough for me. I couldn't imagine holding onto a fish like that for twelve hours. And I couldn't imagine losing him either. But I began to hope that the whole day was over and that Captain Marion would decide to head back to the dock.

No chance.

"The next one's going to be a tough one," the doctor told me, "so get your strength back and be ready."

I laughed to myself and thought never again would I put myself through such pain. I remembered a man I had met several years before who had fought a marlin for just thirty minutes before his arm cramped into an indefinable shape. My left arm was still shaking, and my mouth was still dry after two more beers. I needed to take a nap, to lose my consciousness to the slow rock of the boat.

But I kept myself awake just to wait for what I might possibly see. I felt my work was over, but I wanted to wait for another unimaginable delight that might tear itself from the ocean, which now looked like a mirror under the high sun.

"You don't need any more beer," my husband told me when I suggested what my lunch would be.

"I sweated it all off out there," I told him.

"It'll make you weak if you drink any more."

"*You* go out and try to fight the fish." I was getting a little testy. "Beer won't hurt me. Pour it over my head. I'll take a sip when it runs into my mouth."

I was feeling rather tough now. The true fisherwoman. Out at sea. Never seasick. I was hard and tough and a lot of fun, just like Papa. Or so I thought. I had to think that way to keep myself ready for what everyone on the boat considered the true test. I hoped it would not come. At 104 pounds, my body was not ready for another beating.

"Ri-ite rigger. Damnit, Tommy. Ri-ite rigger!" Tommy, Douglas and I fought our way out of the cabin. Tommy let out a scream that shocked even him. Hilary crashed down from the tower to take a place near the chair.

I grabbed the rod in a panic, and Tommy and Douglas strapped me in again. I felt the same pull when I hooked in as I had the last time. I listened to Captain Marion's directions and did exactly as he said until I was sure the fish was solid.

"He's hooked in the jaw, girl. He's hooked solid."

Then the work was mine. Bloody, wrenching, brutal work. I commended Papa for his courage. My hands were blistered from the previous fight. I could see the pink skin on my hands bubbling into some gelatinous shape I had seen only in science-fiction movies.

"Get the gloves on her," Tommy yelled.

The rod was set securely in the gimbals, and I was hooked to it. I could feel the unerring strength of the fish as he took out the line, steadily, against my own weight.

"What is it?" I hollered to no one in particular.

"It's a blue, baby," Dr. Engle called back.

Whatever was said after that bit of news I only vaguely remember. There was Tommy's steady talk at my left. A litany: "Reel. Pull. Just take an inch, no more. Save your strength. Half an inch is good. Get the belt under you. Don't give him any slack. She needs water. Doug! Pour some water over her. Keep the tip up! Keep the tip *UP!* Take up the drag."

"There is no drag, Tommy," I would hear myself mumble. "He's pulling me in."

"Back her up, boss. Back her up. He's taking too much. Put that towel on her head. More water! She'll die out here in this calm if she don't have water. Get it in her eyes. Don't matter."

And so on. The talk was constant and beautiful. Everyone was with me. Captain Marion and Dr. Engle called me names to make me mad enough to hold on to the monster that was tearing at my muscles. And I called them names back, just to please them and also because I was overflowing with anger.

"Reel, you dummy," Captain Marion yelled.

"REEL, damn it!" came Dr. Engle's voice.

"I am reeling!"

"Lorian, are you OK?" I heard Hilary, Les's daughter, ask.

Then the violins came up, and I grimaced at the idea of being such a sentimental kid.

You are killing me, fish, the old man thought. But you have a right to. Never have I seen a greater, or more beautiful or a calmer or more noble thing than you, brother. Come on and kill me. I do not care who kills who.

—The Old Man and the Sea

The fish had sounded four times. I had got him in to the leader wire, which connects with the hook, three times, thinking that the unconquerable pain in my arms and back was over. But as soon as I'd get him close enough, he'd take off like a madman, sounding the line until I thought there would be none left. I was using eighty-pound test line this time, which allowed this marlin to pull harder than the first one without the line breaking. Hilary and Douglas held me down in the chair at one point. My back was bowed against the unpredictable leaps and dives the marlin was taking under the water.

All the things Papa wrote about the fight are true. There is not another strength as holy and unrestrained as the strength of that one beautifully mad fish. Once it is hooked, it will seek its freedom a thousand times before it gives up.

Before, I had thought it was all foolishness, this man's business of fighting a fish. But it is not. There is luck involved in the testing of one life against another. And you *do* begin to love the fish because all the pain you are going through just to keep him on the line is equal to the pain he feels in his attempts to lose the thing that has gripped him.

I became nearly delirious after an hour and a half in the chair. The sun was high and there were no clouds or even a faint breeze. The wet towel was still on my head and countless buckets of sea water from the Gulf Stream had been poured over me. The salt had dried on my arms and I could taste the brine running down the parched back of my throat. I had a few sips of beer, a drag off a cigarette and a Fig Newton that Hilary crammed into my mouth. My feet were cramping because I had to strain to reach the footplates on the fighting chair.

I kept trying desperately to find the horizon and some sign of the blue marlin that Tommy said weighed four hundred pounds and that was feeling heavier by the minute. But I wasn't seeing too well. There were silver spots floating before me and my heart was skipping beats.

Heatstroke. Sunstroke, I thought. Maybe just a good, old-fashioned stroke. I'll fall off this chair and never be able to walk again and then they'll be sorry for what they've put me through.

But please know I would have stopped this long ago except that I know that if David catches this fish he'll have something inside him for all his life and it will make everything else easier.

—Islands in the Stream

I was stretched flat-out in the chair. The back was down and I was holding onto the fish with everything I had left. And I was cursing Papa in my head. Just a good-luck curse is all.

Hilary looked worried. She poured another bucket of water over me.

"He's comin'! He's comin', boss. Comin' up!"

"Reel! Damn it, Lorian, REEL!"

"I can't reel."

"YES, YOU CAN!"

If the screams hadn't been so loud, I would have passed into the perfectly peaceful unconsciousness I had already begun to dream about. I took up the slack, sitting forward in that huge chair built for a man or a large woman. I am neither.

And I saw my friend standing on his tail in the water, moving that body that was all muscle and the same amount of fury. His colors could never be duplicated, not even in the memory of Papa. He was shot with purple streaks, and his body threw off sparks of green and spinning marbles of sea water. He was as blue as the finest robe of the finest silk worn by the grandest Emperor of China. He stood in twisting power on the water as if he could walk, and he threw his head furiously. His open mouth was that brilliant red seldom seen anywhere but in the most perfect of tropical flowers.

"Lorian!" Hilary screamed. "Do you see him!"

"I see him Hilary!"

He was going down again, but everyone knew it was almost over. I wasn't betting on it, though, because he was one hell of a fine fish.

The cries grew around me, louder than any amplified rock band. And they were full of so much love and excitement that I could do nothing but respond to them with what was left of my arms. My muscles were torn, but there was enough strength left for the thing I had not finished.

"REEL! PULL! REEL! PULL!"

"You come down and fight him," I screamed. "I AM REELING!"

I watched the line grow fatter on the reel. I had watched it run out five times and had lost my heart each time. Now I was gaining on him, and I could feel that he was tired.

When Hilary asked if I wanted to bring him on board or let him go, I told her I did not care. But when I reeled him in to the leader wire with the last of my strength (it *always* seemed like the last of my strength), I knew what I would do.

Someone helped me out of the chair. I think it was Douglas. I staggered over to the side where Tommy was holding onto the wire. Three feet from his hand, just breaking the surface of the purple water, was the marlin, belly up, silver and huge, His length dissolved into shadows, and I could not see where he began or ended. Unbelievable, perfect of form, definite and true, he had run himself to the pure edge of death, and in that honored state had surrendered. Only two confused fins on his belly twitched in the air to declare he was still alive.

"Will he live?" I asked

"I think he's dead," Hilary said.

Captain Marion and Tommy pulled the body back and forth in the water to resuscitate him, and I watched as he gave a half-turn.

"He's alive," Captain Marion said.

"Let him go," I said. "Let him go."

"That marlin's got your name on him, girl. He's gonna give somebody else hell one of these days," Captain Marion told me. Tommy reached over the side and separated the leader wire from the hook. The hook was left in the marlin's jaw, where it would dissolve in time.

The fish pushed his bill down with what instinct was left to him and paddled slowly away. Dr. Engle presented me with the wire that had held him for two hours.

It wasn't the longest fight on the record. But it was the one I had wanted. Papa would have pounded me on the back and given me a shot of the best whiskey for my effort. Captain Marion pulled the cork on some champagne, and we all cavorted in a mad sequence of hugging. And we all praised the damnable spirit of the fish that had fought its imprisonment so spectacularly.

I see now that what I felt during the marlin fight sounds like the makings of tall and foolish stories. But it is not. Papa had it right all along in *The Old Man and the Sea*: "But who knows. Maybe when luck comes your way you are ready."

Captain Marion flew the "Fish Caught — Released" flag when we headed into Bimini's harbor. He broadcast our day at sea over the radio to anyone who would listen.

"An average of eighteen days' fishing it takes to get a look at a marlin, and you hook two in one day," Dr. Engle applauded. "And then you let it go. Papa was smiling on you today."

Someone threw me in the drink because it was the thing to do. Time-honored on Bimini, I was told. My bruised and swollen hands were grabbed by everyone who passed me.

And as I remembered the slow and perfect agony of the fight, even days later when my right arm swelled to the size of my thigh, I believed that Papa had conned someone into testing me. It could have been Captain Marion. It could have been Dr. Engle. It could have been the fish itself. And wouldn't it be fine to think so?

ADDENDUM

I have always believed a writer grows in response to demands made on her character. New ways of looking at past experiences occur during this growth process, and one day the writer will pick up an old piece of writing—her own—read it, and wonder who the hell the person was who wrote it. It was this way when I reread my marlin story. I know the woman in this story as I know friends from years past, vaguely, their faces lacking definition, their antics legendary.

At the time I wrote "The Young Woman and the Sea," I was very studiously trying to be enamored of my grandfather's legend. It was something that did not come naturally. From the time I was a kid, I resented his unseen influence on my life; the funny way people would act when they knew my last name; the way teachers expected me, by sheer right of this last name, to be brilliant; his suicide, kept from me as if it were a shameful thing, until I read of it in a magazine. I winced when I read the endearment "Papa" throughout my story. I never called him Papa, as the world did, nor did I identify with his writings. Until the age of twenty, I refused to read his work. Yet in this story I have recreated a Hemingway world in which the granddaughter embraces some of her grandfather's most sacred territory. Why? Because I wanted to belong, somehow, to a sense of family. All my life I had been told I had certain characteristics because I was a Hemingway. It was time for proof, for a birthright to be recognized, and I believed this proof existed in trying my damndest to be like the man: fishing, drinking, living on an adventurous edge that grew more precarious as the years passed. For a time I believed it was real, even praying to my grandfather's spirit when something went wrong, as if prayer to a dead man could fix my life.

When I reread the actual marlin fights, I recalled—I hope accurately—the actual pain and exhilaration of the experience. It *was* fun. It *was* a test of strength. And I still believe that on some ultraconscious level I did communicate with the fish. But what it was not was an experience manipulated by the ghost of Ernest Hemingway. If anything it was a generous gift from Dr. Engle and Captain Marion. I see this now, no longer clouded by alcohol as I was both the day I fished *and* wrote the story.

What stands out in this piece now, for me stronger than the determination of the fight, is the drinking. The article is, as one *New York Times* editor put it, "afloat in beer." Even so, it was accepted by my editors and by those who read it as part of the day's adventure. I look back to that day off Bimini and see that the drinking ritual I kept then—all day long, starting in the morning—was one I would perfect over the years until I ended up in a detox ward vomiting blood, a peculiar sort of landsickness common to chronic alcoholics. I was alcoholic then. I am now. But then I drank and called it heritage. Now I do not and call it grace.

What I did not understand back in 1980, when I was nobly trying to keep up the Hemingway drinking image, was that my grandfather was debilitated by drinking and that it was indeed the major contributing factor to his suicide. Hemingway scholars argue with me over this, believing in the superhuman myth and the man. But I understand the pain and degradation my grandfather endured when his drinking began to destroy his talent, his health. It is the one thing we truly had in common, and not one I need pretend to. And this understanding allows me compassion for a man who bore the necessary cross of being human and for the young woman in the story who had not yet recognized the dimensions of her own cross.

There have been changes, too, in my views of big game fishing. All too often it is wholesale slaughter, fish taken for prize money in big game tournaments, and I cannot participate in the slow and certain decimation of these fish populations. As a woman who fishes, I have forsaken this arena of big game fish, partly because having caught and released marlin, tarpon, shark and barracuda, I find it more enjoyable to spend time on a lake or in a trout stream. The physical energy required is not as great, and the conscience rests easier.

And there is also nothing left to prove. Maybe there never was. If I proved anything it was that ghosts and legends can grow beyond their boundaries into powers great enough to consume those who take them on. But I have a freedom now from this business of legends. Caught and released, in a way.

WOMAN'S HOUR HAS STRUCK

C . R . C . (1 8 9 0)

ALL SUMMER LONG I have waited my opportunity. I have seen the male members of the camp, incased in rubber boots and armed with bamboo rods, go striding off down the gulch, while conversational fragments relating to reels, flies and "leaders" were wafted to my envious ears. I have frequently seen them come back wet, torn and triumphant, sometimes loaded with fish, and sometimes not, as luck favored them; but always with stories. I have heard all about the big one that fell back into the water; about the bigger one that got caught in the bushes and jerked off the hook, and about the biggest one of all, "regular Jumbo, by George!" that gave one flop just as he was being dropped into the bag and—vanished!

Why should I not have the privilege of shaping some of these romances?

The camp is deserted.

The brothers and husbands and visiting cousins have all gone to town.

The fish poles lean invitingly against a pine.

"Woman's hour has struck."

I will go fishing.

The selection of a pole becomes the first difficulty and that arises not from the superiority of one pole over another, but from the question as to which man's wrath I can most safely provoke. Lose his knife, break his pipe, mislay his papers, slander his wife, but keep jointed rod holy, is the eleventh commandment of the amateur fisherman. This smaller rod seems the least elaborate; it is also light and easy to hold—besides it belongs to a cousin's friend, who, if anything happens, will have to look pleasant whether he feels so or not. So, Mr. Jones, by your leave, while you are in town getting the mail or ordering provisions, or going to the circus or whatever it is that takes the men off in a body, leaving the camp to the women and children and chipmunks—by your leave, I say, I will borrow your rod. So that matter is settled, only it would be simpler and pleasanter if you had not put two hooks on the line; one at a time is enough to catch in one's hair.

Now for something in which to bring home the fish. The game bag, to be sure, and here it hangs on a branch. Ugh! how it smells! I really cannot hang that thing around my neck. Strange how impervious men's faculties are to disagreeable odors. A basket would answer the purpose, but in this benighted valley of the Arkansas River there is no such thing as a splint basket, the want of which we have discovered to be one of the small housekeeping difficulties of this region. A tin pail would answer the purpose, but it would not be sportsmanlike, look at it in any light you please. The kitchen tent offers nothing else in the way of a receptacle except a deal cracker box with a picture of Pike's Peak on the end; clearly unavailable. Nor will I degrade to such uses my burnt alligator satchel or the case to my camera.

Ah! a handkerchief. Silk, and a large one; I hope it is not Mr. Jones's; but he will forgive me if I bring it home full of trout. A knot in each corner and it will hold a dozen easily. See! And yet they say that women have no adaptability.

What a steep path it is down into this gulch! I say path, but there is not a sign of one except a foothold here and there on a pine root or a bunch of soap weed; elsewhere boulders and long steep stretches of loose gravel. As I dig my heels into the soil, sliding frantically downward, grazing my elbows and peeling the leather in strips from my best shoes, I long unspeakably for an old pair bestowed weeks ago on an ungrateful washerwoman. My scramble comes to an end at the brink of the Cottonwood River, foaming among the rocks at the bottom of the gulch. Steep, chalky cliffs rise on either side and all around the stately pines keeping guard over the solemn fastnesses of a

Rocky Mountain canyon. Ah! this lovely river. How it rushes and swirls and quarrels with the boulders! See that smooth, green slant of water, curving over a granite shelf and breaking into foam below like a Kodak view of Niagara. The color is entrancing: it is not emerald (there is too much ochre in the rocks), but a restful brownish green with an unexpected touch of blue of the Colorado sky. Surely a reflection, for here in the only quiet portion of the troubled surface, I see the inverted outline of Sheep Mountain as it stands blocking the view toward the head of the canyon.

I will paraphrase Wordsworth:

> *Three* voices are these: one is of the sea, Onc is of the mountains, another of a trout stream,

which, if you don't vex yourself unduly about the metre, is a very good version. This pool has a bass voice, a double diapason; the one above, where I can see the pebbles on the bottom, gives out a shallow soprano tinkle as the water ripples lazily along. The silence of this hushed auditorium is further broken only by the wind in the pines and the occasional hoarse call of a magpie or a blue jay. Song birds do not venture above the valleys when the valleys themselves are eight thousand feet above sea level.

However, all this is not fishing, and what will the camp say to an empty game bag at supper time? As soon as I have unhooked the brown fly from my hat and the white fly from my hair I will begin.

Now, let me see; what are the rules of the game? I must stand "upstream" and "cast" down, letting the fly lie as near as possible on the surface, then draw it slowly toward me, so. Then repeat the operation.

This is called "whipping" the stream. One learns a great deal in this world by careful observation, and the camp talk is bearing fruit. Yes, trout fishing is delightful and not at all difficult if only this rock would not tip so. It destroys my equanimity as well as my equilibrium, and one needs both in a trout stream.

It seems as though I ought to have a bite by this time. I have been "repeating the operation" for fully twenty minutes; the sun is hot, and the rapid water makes my head dizzy. I wonder what the men do at this stage? Ah! I remember. According to the professional lingo the fish are not "rising" in this pool, and I must go farther upstream, which I proceed to do as soon as my skirts are tucked up a little more securely. How I regret my incapacity to wear those big rubber boots that fasten around the waist! They would be just the thing for this swampy place.

There! One foot is wet—the other also! Dear me! It would have been wiser to go out on the road and come back to the stream farther on. Still, let me be philosophical. One can no more have trout than fame or riches without some accompanying disadvantages. Emerson says in his essay on compensation—

Is that a fish? Surely—there—to the right, just under the shade of that rock! See him, with his head upstream, his tail lazily waving in rhythm with the water, his pink-spotted sides flashing in the sunlight! Oh, you beauty! How delicious you will taste, served up in bread crumbs with a dash of lemon (or Worcestershire sauce?) and a garnish of watercresses! Do have this nice little brown fly, or the nicer white one at the end. See, I drop them just over your nose and dangle them invitingly. "Will you walk into my parlor?"

Ah! he is gone, and strange to say I did not see him go, though my eyes were on him. That is too bad, but not an uncommon experience if I may judge from our dinner-table talk. Our authoritative angler (alias the Camp Liar) says if you "whip" a pool and the fish sees you there is no use staying in that place any longer.

Now, who would give a trout credit for so much discernment? This one saw my hat and my general get-up, and like a sensible fish, he took himself off directly.

I must now try my luck farther upstream. This trout fishing is a perpetual "movin' on" as arduous as poor Jo's peregrinations, and with as little result.

Oh, for one more safety pin! That last jump loosened my dress skirt, and now there is an appalling rent in the front breadth, the result of the interference of a dead branch. What is to be done? Ah, of course—a hairpin!

There, that will last a little time, and in the meanwhile I will see what is in this pool; it looks trout-full. Or, on second thoughts, I will not. Just on the opposite bank is a cow, and she is looking this way. If it was just an ordinary Ohio cow I would pay no attention to her, but these range cattle have a gaze that would freeze the blood in one's veins.

Shoo! I will move on.

Here at last is the place. A glassy sheet of water surrounded by lichenous purple rocks; a volume of foam pouring in from above and spreading out into ripples below; a dead pine spanning the stream from bank to bank, and cushions of moss meeting the placid water on all sides. Could there be a more ideal spot for fishing or meditation? All around is a grove of quaking asp (first cousin to the poplar). A refined, gentle tree with whispering leaves and ladylike attitudes.

The change is refreshing, for pines, be they ever so poetical, are grim and monotonous, and their blackened trunks covering the side of the mountain speak of fire and storms, snowslides and the roar of beasts in the night. That they should be succeeded in Nature's plan by these clean, white-stemmed trees is a silent allegory. *Post tenebras lux*.

Beneath the trees and among the rocks grow the vivid Colorado wild flowers; not such pale beauties as we find in April in New England and the Middle States, but gorgeous scarlet, yellow and rose pink blossoms, like dabs of pigment on a palette. I really would not dare to carry this bit of scenery home in a water color, except to show to people who have been here. It would seem like an attempt to improve on one's subject.

Now I am going to do something that will show great strength of nerve and will. I am going out on that log. You see it is directly over the pool, and I can throw the fly just where it ought to go. The case is perfectly clear; heretofore I have not been in the proper position. Those men who wear big boots climb right into the water up to their knees, and of course, they catch trout—who couldn't?

Well, here I am, safe and sound, looking down into the very depths of the stream, where I am confident there is a whole panful of trout waiting yearningly for my flies. Not in the least difficult getting out, either, and if one of the gentleman had been here he would have thought it necessary to help me.

What's the matter now? I can't move my pole; the hook is fast in that tree. Dear, dear, how stupid of me to carry it over my shoulder as

Mr. Winkle did his gun! Come off there! I do not wish to be slangy, but really—

No, it won't stir; neither this way not that! Now, I don't wonder that men "say things" when they have such provocation as this. What do they say, anyway, and when they say it how does it work? I would like to make any kind of a remark that I thought would loosen that hook. I have heard Mr. Jones in the remote seclusion of his own tent say, "Gee whang it!" but that is his own particular property, and to borrow a man's jointed rod and his expletive, too, is stretching a privilege in a way my conscience won't allow. Am I to sit here all day? I wonder what a steady pull would do—like *that*. I don't dare to be very forcible, for this log is quite round and—I'll try a series of coaxing jerks with an emphatic yank to finish with.

Ah! there it comes, with the air of saying, "I was not caught at all, only fooling."

Nevertheless the brown fly is left up in the tree, where, it is to be hoped, he will lead a useful and prosperous career. Now, if the trout will only be persuaded that the flavor of this white fly is as fine as that of the brown one, I'll catch a string of fish that will prove me entitled to a rod of my own. No hurry, however. The camp timepiece is Mt. Harvard. When the sun drops behind that wall of granite that towers above us to the west, we know it is a quarter to five. Long before that time chilly shadows fill the gulch and creep up the cliff, and the South Park Range takes on a cold gray, then deepens to purple, while the three snow peaks of Mt. Princeton glow with rosy pink against the evening sky.

According, then, to signs and omens, it must be about half past three o'clock, and as long as the sun continues to warm up this particular nook, I am going to sit and swing my feet over the water. It is comfortable and romantic, and I don't care so much about fish after all. To tell the truth we have had salmon trout for dinner every day for the past two weeks and are thinking of sending to Buena Vista for ham or bacon or some such delicacy for a change. So why should I cast flies?

What are those beautiful lines of Whittier's addressed to Monadnock? They begin with something about a painter and "for her sake." I do not quote readily. I wish I did. Let me see.

First a lake
Tinted with sunset; next the wavy lines
Of far receding hills, and yet more far
Monadnock.

Shades of Izaak Walton, was *that* a bite? That earthquake, that cyclone, that terrific tug that is bending the pole into a letter C and lashing the water into suds. It is never a trout; it is nothing less than a sturgeon, or perhaps a sea serpent, and it is pulling me off the—

  *   *   *   *   *   *   *   *

Something must always be left to the imagination of the reader. When the Russian poet Pushkin is carried beyond the force of language, his emotions explode into a shower of stars. So I find nothing but asterisks will express my situation. Up to my waist in the Cottonwood; the water sweeping my skirts around me; my head dizzy and my hat floating rapidly off toward the Arkansas! But the trout? Ah, yes! Here he is; I seized him with both hands as I took my plunge and he shall *not* get away. He is not so large as I expected. Indeed, quite inside the law, hardly worth cooking for a camp of nine people. Still he is my first trout, and I'll not surrender him to any fish commissioner.

I steal up to camp the back way, and after leaving the rod with its fellows against the tree I seek my own tent.

As the six o'clock horn sounds, I hear Mr. Jones's footsteps going supperward. Will he stop at the pine tree?

He does.

I hear the click of the metal reel and then a growl—

"What in thunder!"

Jesus, Pete, It's a Woman Fly Fishing!

MARY S. KUSS

I SOMETIMES FIND IT HARD to believe that I'm thirty-eight years old and that I've been fishing for thirty-two of those years and fly fishing for twenty-two. It doesn't seem like it's been that long, and I'm amazed at how far I've come. I'm a certified fly-fishing instructor for the Orvis Company of Manchester, Vermont, one of the oldest and most reputable purveyors of fly-fishing tackle in the country, and I've been teaching group classes and private lessons for the Orvis store in Media, Pennsylvania, near my home, for the past ten years.

Sometimes I think that I was born a fly fisher. But are fly fishers born or made? Many are made, certainly, by the circumstances of their birth or the choices they make later in life. When an individual is nurtured by a family that has a tradition of fly fishing, with a parent or grandparent who is an avid fly fisher and wishes the next generation to follow in his or her footsteps, or if there is a family friend who is a fly fisher, someone the youngster likes and respects and wants to emulate, or if one lives in an area with an abundance of high-quality trout streams, a place where an interest in fly fishing has fertile ground in which to grow, it is not surprising that an enthusiasm for the sport may develop. Maybe a spouse is a fly fisher, and the couple wants to enjoy and share the sport together. Any or all of these things may conspire to create a "made" fly fisher. I must have been born a fly fisher, however, because none of these factors applied to me.

I am an only child. My mother prayed for a little girl and wanted

59

nothing more than to make a proper, frilly little lady of me. It was not to be. My strong and apparently permanent "tomboy" streak manifested itself at a very early age.

My father was a nuts-and-bolts bait fisherman and a hunter, but my parents separated when I was six years old and he had little if any influence on my interest in outdoor pursuits. My mother tells me that when I was quite small I thought it was great fun to drag his hip boots from their hiding place under the bed, climb into them and clump around the house.

At age six, after my parents had separated, I took my first steps toward my lifelong love affair with angling. My mother's sister and her husband lived with his parents in a big, old eighteenth-century farmhouse built into the side of a hill overlooking a small lake in the little village of Imlaystown, in west central New Jersey. My uncle's father ran a boat livery on the lake, and I can still remember how he would drag his fleet of heavy, somewhat decrepit wooden rowboats out of storage early each spring to get them ready for the season. He would pound oakum caulk into the seams in the planking and then lay on a coat of paint. Soon the boats would be bobbing along the dock near the huge weeping willow that stood on the bank, overhanging the water, with big, slab-sided bluegills swimming in its shade. He rented his craft to anglers and families for the princely sum of two dollars a day. Each boat came equipped with oars, oarlocks and two coffee cans. One can was for bailing water from the bottom of the boat (a frequent necessity). The other, filled with concrete in which an eye bolt had been embedded and then attached to a length of frayed rope, served as an anchor. Going for rides in Grandpop Malsbury's boats was a ritual part of my childhood, a feature of nearly every trip to Imlaystown, spring through fall.

I don't remember what put the idea into my little head, but during one visit, I decided that I wanted to go fishing and asked my Uncle Marvin to take me. He did his best to ignore me, no doubt hoping that I would shift my focus to something else; fishing was not something for little girls to do. But I gave him no peace, and finally he gave in just to get me out of his hair. I'm sure he thought I would quickly lose interest. How wrong he was!

We went out behind the hen house and cut a fairly long, straight limb from a small tree. Uncle Marvin took a length of black braided nylon line from his baitcast reel and tied it to the tip of the pole. A number ten hook, a small split shot and a round plastic bobber completed my rig. We dug some redworms from the manure pile, put them with some dirt into one of Grandpop Malsbury's tobacco cans and headed for the lake. It was late spring, and the pumpkinseed sunfish were spawning along the banks. Soon we found a sunnie on his nest. He saw us and darted away into the weeds. Uncle Marvin told me not to worry, the fish would soon return. We baited the hook and adjusted the bobber's depth, and I dropped the bait into the nest. Moments later, the sunnie stuck his head out of the weeds for a look; seeing the intruding worm in his nest, he approached warily, picked it up and started to swim away. I watched open-mouthed and mesmerized until I became aware that Uncle Marvin was shouting, "Pull, pull, pull!" When I finally did, it was too late, the sunnie had spit out the baited hook. I think I've spent the rest of my life searching for that fish, catching many others but never the one that got away on that fine spring day.

From then on, I was utterly fascinated with fishing. I fished at every opportunity. On visits to Imlaystown, my mother never had to guess where I was when it was time for a meal or to head for home—I could always be found along the lake. It seemed to me an eternity until the next trip, even though we visited our relatives almost every Saturday. By means of much begging and pleading, I soon persuaded my mother and grandparents to buy me a real fishing rod of my own (no small feat considering the family's perennial financial difficulties) and to take me fishing somewhere near home as often as possible.

Home was Point Pleasant, then a sleepy little resort community on the central New Jersey coast. Although there were plenty of fishing opportunities, there was little trout fishing, and practically no one fly fished. But at that time it didn't matter to me. I participated avidly and eagerly in any kind of fishing that presented itself: bait fishing in the Point Pleasant & Bay Head Canal, the Manasquan River, the Metedeconk River or the numerous small lakes and ponds nearby; crabbing with hand line and net, or dragging a seine for killies, silversides, whatever could be caught, I loved it all.

I devoured fishing in any and all forms. Whenever I could talk my mother into buying me a copy of *Field & Stream*, *Outdoor Life* or *Sports Afield*, I would skip over the hunting articles and carefully scan from cover to cover for anything pertaining to fishing, including all the ads. On Sunday afternoon I would never fail to watch my favorite television program, "Gadabout Gaddis, The Flying Fisherman." My memories of the show are sketchy, but I remember a gentleman—who then seemed elderly, but whom I would now probably consider middle-aged—who was always landing on remote lakes in a float plane and catching lots and lots of big fish. I recall that he did a fair amount of fly fishing, a technique that seemed far too exotic for me to even consider. I felt very lucky that my family had bought me a spinning rod of my very own, and the purchase of a second rod of any kind was clearly out of the question.

My introduction to fly fishing happened almost by accident. Thanks to the charitable efforts of my town's school nurse, I had the opportunity to attend camp each summer during my middle school years and the first two years of high school. The last three of those summers, I went to a camp in Belgrade Lakes, Maine, owned and operated by a group of teachers and administrators from my high school. When I arrived at camp that last summer, I had my spinning rod with me, needless to say. A day or two later when I went down to the lake to wet a line, I saw a young camper struggling with a long, unwieldy fishing rod. I moved in for a closer look, and my suspicions were confirmed. "Wow!" I said, "That's a fly rod!" "Yeah," he said with a notable lack of enthusiasm. "Want to trade for a while?" I asked. "Yeah!" he replied, enviously eyeing my spinning rod. Although those long ago memories are dim, I remember that the rod was split bamboo and carried a braided silk line. Now, with hindsight, I can almost guess how the boy wound up with such a rod. It was probably his grandfather's, and when he asked for fishing gear to take to camp, someone remembered granddad's old "fishing pole" that was stored up in the attic. That rod is probably a valuable collectible today, if it still exists.

Well, the boy was happy with my spinning rod for the duration of his stay at camp, and when the time came to switch back, I did so with more than a little regret. Despite having had no instruction other than watching old Gadabout Gaddis on television and what I'd been able to pick up from the outdoor magazines, I managed to beat the lake to a froth and catch quite a few smallmouth bass in the process. One day one of the other girls from Point Pleasant saw me out along the shoreline with the fly rod. "Do you like to do that?" she asked. "Yes! I really do!" I replied. "Well," she said, "you'll have to come over to my house when we get home and meet my father. He fly fishes all the time."

I made sure to take Barbara up on her offer, and that's how I met Dr. Donald Pyle, the man who would be my principal fly-fishing mentor. Doc gave me my first casting instruction, lent me books, bought me fly-tying tools and materials in exchange for my clumsily tied early flies and fostered my interest in the sport in many other ways.

It took only a single casting lesson with Dr. Pyle to convince me that I just had to get a fly rod of my own. I don't remember if it was by means of S&H Green Stamps or the coupons that my grandfather got with his packs of Raleigh cigarettes, but I soon became the proud owner of a Shakespeare WonderRod and a South Bend Finalist reel, spooled with an eight-weight "Torpedo Tapered" fly line in a garish shade of green. Although crude and heavy by today's standards, I thought my new outfit was just marvelous. I caught sunnies, crappies and small bass on little cork poppers and wet flies.

Soon I was losing flies faster than I could afford to replace them. That was my motivation for taking up fly tying. My earliest attempts were rather primitive, but looking back I think my improvisations with tools and materials were very resourceful. I knew I needed a vise, but a real fly-tying vise was prohibitively expensive. So I bought a cheap, tiny machinist's vise from the Woolworth's Five and Dime. I had hooks—my Eagle Claw bait hooks with the offset bend and the slices in the shank to hold worms in place. I did not know that these hooks were not appropriate for fly tying, but fortunately my intended quarry didn't know it either. Why buy thread, when I could borrow some of my mother's sewing thread? The most effective wet-fly pattern I'd tried to date was a Yellow Sally, so I bought some bright-yellow nylon floss for the body of the fly. I had to buy hackle and wing material, too. There was no way around that. Once again I sacrificed authenticity for economy and bought a packet of long, yellow-dyed saddle hackles to serve both purposes.

At last I was ready to tie. I clamped a hook in the corner of my little vise. With enough fiddling and adjusting, it was reasonably secure. Somehow, with no knowledge of proper technique, I managed to attach thread and floss to the hook and wind a body. I cut and trimmed two little chunks of saddle hackle to shape, lashed them to the sides of the hook to serve as wings, added a wisp of hackle fibers at the throat and tied off the thread. Bless the poor, gullible sunnies for the positive reinforcement they gave me by eagerly accepting these unsophisticated early efforts.

I made enormous strides in both fly fishing and fly tying during the next couple of years with the help and encouragement of Dr. Pyle. Joe Spader and Charlie Anderson, fishing buddies of Doc's, also became friends and mentors to me, the first of many individuals who would aid and influence my development as a fly fisher. I later discovered that this was in keeping with one of the sport's finest traditions—that of veteran fly fishers unselfishly sharing their expertise with novices.

For a couple of summers, Doc sent me and his youngest son, Billy, up to the Beaverkill River in the Catskill Mountains of New York state for a week at a time. He wanted to take Billy fishing, but couldn't get away from his practice and asked if I minded taking him. Doc gave me the keys to his station wagon and his oil company credit card, confirmed the motel reservations and off we went. Then one year Billy suddenly shot up six inches in height, his voice dropped an octave, and our days of sharing a motel room were over. But what a wonderful opportunity this had been for me! I fished the Beaverkill and the Willowemoc, legendary waters that are among the birthplaces of American fly fishing. I got to meet and to know Harry and Elsie Darbee, legends in their own time, although they didn't act as if they were aware of it. Harry would spend an hour or more at a time patiently answering our questions and giving us advice, treating us no differently from the doctors and lawyers and Wall Street brokers that also frequented his little fly shop.

I was able to attend college at a small school in southeastern Pennsylvania on a scholarship, and although the local trout streams were hardly what one would call blue ribbon, and certainly not in the same league as the Beaverkill, they were far superior to what passed for trout streams around Point Pleasant. When I obtained a used car during my sophomore year it did wonders for my fishing, but didn't help my academic standing any. I'm afraid I spent entirely too much time along Ridley Creek and not nearly enough time studying. Still, the experience that I gained served me well later on. And I did manage to graduate, almost on time, with a degree in biology.

After graduation, I spent nine frustrating months trying to find gainful employment in my field. Finally I took a position as a laboratory technician with the New Jersey Division of Fish and Game, stationed at a fisheries laboratory in the northwestern part of the state. For the two and a half years I worked there, I lived and breathed fish and fishing. I worked with fish all day, went fishing in my leisure time and became active with the local Trout Unlimited chapter, my principal social outlet. There were a number of good-quality trout streams within an easy drive, including a few with some wild trout, and I continued to develop my knowledge and skills.

Then I fell in love with, of all people, a nonfisherman. Having done so, I later passed up a chance to make a play for another man who owned a fly shop and guide service in Montana. Ah, the road not taken. That's what I get for leading with my heart. But there have been twelve relatively happy years of marriage to a man who is tolerant and even supportive of his wife's seemingly eccentric hobbies. He even learned to fly cast and went fishing with me often during our courtship. But once we were married, he went fishing less and less. One day I asked him why, and he looked me right in the eye and said, "Why should I go fishing, I caught the fish I was after." I've been dipping into his unused tackle ever since.

What has it been like being a woman fly fisher for all these years? It's certainly easier now than it used to be, as more women get into the sport. The sight of me on the stream used to literally stop traffic. I'd hear a car screech to a halt on the road above me, someone would get out and stand at the guardrail and say something like, "Jesus, Pete, would you look at this! It's a woman fly fishing! Now I've seen everything." The car door would slam and off they'd go down the road. I was really glad when that stopped happening. I did get a compliment from one fascinated observer, though. A fellow stopped to watch me cast for bluegills on a small New Jersey pond one afternoon. He stayed for quite a while, and as he was leaving, he said, "You cast better than most men I know."

Another problem that affects everyone, but is particularly vexing for women anglers, is the almost universal lack of stream manners one encounters these days. Anglers, and particularly fly fishers, used to take pains to be courteous to others on the stream and for the most part adhered to an unwritten code of etiquette. In the days when someone got into the sport only by having an experienced mentor to initiate them, stream manners were an integral part of the training received. Nowadays, with more and more anglers vying for an increasingly scarce resource, and with the growing commercialization of fly fishing, the atmosphere of privacy, serenity and introspection that was once a major aspect of the sport has given way to crowded streams and a sometimes high-pressure competition for the best fishing.

No one needs to find a fly-fishing mentor these days. Instead there are books, videos and fly-fishing schools galore. These commercial sources tend to go heavy on the technical aspects of the sport and on selling the latest high-tech equipment, giving precious little attention to what they consider peripheral issues like stream etiquette. The result is a proliferation of obnoxious and ignorant anglers who extend common courtesy grudgingly based on what they judge to be the likelihood of physical retaliation by their victims. For some male anglers, a woman looks like a safe target for a hostile takeover of the pool she's fishing. After long and careful consideration of how I ought to handle these situations, I am still at a loss. Although I hate like hell to let them get away with it, I spoil my own enjoyment by getting angry enough to respond. So I usually just leave, sometimes giving a withering stare, sometimes not. I know that there is another good pool around the bend, and it's just not worth raising my blood pressure by jousting with these clods.

Still, the positive experiences I've had in the sport far outnumber the negative ones. And among the most valuable of those experiences have been the wonderful friendships I've enjoyed with other anglers, some female, but mostly male. The gender ratio of my fishing friends has not been a matter of choice, but of necessity. More women are taking up fly fishing, but many of them do it as a way to spend time with a boyfriend or spouse. If I didn't have male fishing buddies, I wouldn't have many fishing buddies at all. Men will most likely continue to outnumber women on the stream by a large margin for some time to come, but I hope to see that change eventually.

One of the most remarkable characteristics of fly fishing is its capacity to become an obsession. I have seen this occur in many others, as well as in myself. I used to fish quite literally at every opportunity. Whenever there was a patch of open, ice-free water, I'd be out there. Like the postman, neither rain nor snow nor dark of night, nor winter cold nor blazing summer heat could keep me from my appointed rounds. I would fish when the temperature was so low that I would have to stop every few casts to break ice out of the rod guides. It seemed to me that uncontrolled shivering helped to impart an interesting action to the fly. If I was having any success at all, I would keep at it until my half-frozen fingers wouldn't work any more and then I'd go back to the car and thaw them over the defroster vent and have at it again. It's a miracle I didn't suffer severe frostbite on such outings. And although I wouldn't set out for the stream in a pouring rain, a little drizzle wasn't enough to stop me. Once I was on stream, a downpour wouldn't dislodge me if the fish were hitting. On more than one occasion I fished in the rain until literally soaked to the skin. I couldn't have gotten any wetter if I'd fallen in.

Then on a beautiful day one spring, I reached a threshold. My chores were done, my obligations for the day discharged, my time was my own. The customary and obvious next step was to gather the tackle and head for the creek. I began to have a little conversation with myself.

"Come on, let's go fishing!"

"I really don't feel like it."

"What do you mean, you don't feel like it?"

"I'm just not in the mood, that's all."

"How can you not be in the mood to go fishing? You're not losing interest, are you? How can this be? Fishing is such an important part of your life; what will you do if you lose it?"

It took me several weeks to come to terms with these unfamiliar feelings, but I finally understood what had happened. I did not love fishing any less; rather, the relationship had simply mellowed a bit. I was no longer driven and obsessed. Once I came to this realization, anxiety changed to relief. Now I could be more selective about when and where I went fishing. I could opt for quality experiences rather than mere quantity. I subsequently developed a theory that once a person becomes obsessed with fly fishing, it takes a certain number of hours astream to effect a cure. For some individuals this comes late in life, for others not at all. I was very lucky to have had the opportunity to immerse myself in fishing for extended periods and thus reached the required level of experience at a relatively young age.

Although being female has had considerable impact on my pursuit of fly fishing, I can't say that it has presented many insurmountable difficulties. Most of the male fly fishers I have known have been intelligent, thoughtful individuals who were open to the idea of women entering the sport. They have been almost universally polite and considerate, sometimes to the point of being solicitous, obviously because I'm a woman. I have never been inclined to make a fuss about anyone extending such courtesies, as long as they know I don't expect it. Once everyone stops being self-conscious about these matters, a comfortable equilibrium is reached. I'm sure I hold doors for the guys as often as they do for me, and any angler, male or female, appreciates a hand up when climbing a slippery bank.

One difficulty I've had to grapple with over the years has been the attitudes of the wives and girlfriends of my male fishing friends toward me. Many women seem to be suspicious of an apparently unattached female (they seldom see my husband around) who chooses to get actively involved with an organization like Trout Unlimited and socialize with a bunch of men. They are sure that there could be only one motive for such behavior, and what they are thinking has nothing to do with fishing in the literal sense. Thankfully this is changing as more women get involved in fishing and conservation. My current Trout Unlimited chapter now has several active female members who are there for themselves rather than for a male partner. I make it a point to get to know the female partners of my male fishing buddies, and as soon as they get to know me, they know I'm a genuine fly fisher and accept that my intentions are honorable, even if they still find them incomprehensible.

There is only one fly-fishing activity from which I have been excluded by reason of my gender. That is membership in The Brotherhood of the Junglecock. The rather peculiar-sounding name does not refer, as one might guess, to Tarzan's private anatomy, but to the male jungle fowl, a rare bird whose unique neck feathers are highly prized for fly tying. This organization was founded around 1930 for the purpose of fostering in America's youth a love and respect for fly fishing and the natural resources that support it so that these things will be preserved for future generations; membership has been exclusively male from its inception. The Brotherhood has several rather lame excuses for not having gone co-ed by now, but none are compelling. Since I have no children of my own, I would very much enjoy being involved in an organization such as this, and having the chance to pass along to some young boys or girls the love of fly fishing and the values and conservation ethic that are mine. Maybe The Brotherhood refuses to admit women simply because they can't figure out a good way to make their name gender-neutral.

A source of tremendous satisfaction to me has been the opportunity to teach fly fishing. I love to share with others a sport that has given me so much pleasure over the years. As an avocation, fly fishing has such enormous potential to fill one's personal needs. It can be pursued and enjoyed in a simple, unsophisticated manner, yet its multifaceted complexities can keep a curious and intelligent mind busy for a lifetime.

I believe that fly fishing will continue to be, as it has been for the past twenty-two years, a significant and deeply meaningful part of my life. It has provided me with intellectual stimulation through its extensive literature and the analytical thinking and creative problem-solving that the sport entails. The art, poetry and prose it has inspired during the centuries of its existence has great aesthetic appeal. It has contributed enormously to my deep love of nature. And through fly fishing I have been blessed with some of the best and truest friendships I have known. I can't imagine what life would be like without it.

FISHING

LINDA HOGAN

Stones go nowhere
while the river rushes them
dark with rain.
Fish are pulled out of their lives
by red-armed women on the banks
of vertigo.

What is living
but to grow smaller,
undress another skin
or scale
away rough edges
the way rivers cut mountains
down to heart.

We already know the history of sand,
and how days pass.
We know water and air
trying to break the spirit of stone.
We know our teeth grinding down
to their pith.

We know flint
all the way down to fire.
Go nowhere, be the fire.
Wait here for a nibble, you fishwomen,

stand where light is pared to a spark.
Be dust
growing to life.

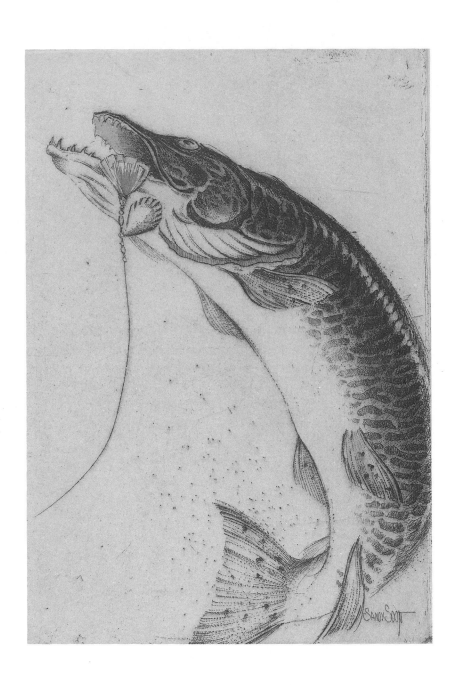

BORDER WATER

GRETCHEN LEGLER

CRAIG AND I ARE ON OUR WAY to the Rainy River to fish for spring walleyes. The Rainy is a great, wide, slow-moving river that runs from east to west, through forests and farms, at the top of Minnesota, separating the state from Canada. Because it is a border water, you can fish the river in early April, after the ice has gone out, a full month before you can fish inland waters.

"It's hard to imagine," Craig says, as we drive along the Minnesota side of the river, looking across at the brown grass and farms on the opposite bank, "that just over there is another country." On both sides of the river there are brown grass and trees and red barns and silver silos. It looks the same. Over there, Canada, rust-colored grass and trees. Over here, Minnesota, rust-colored grass and trees. It *is* hard to imagine. But it is a different country; a place boys rowed across to in rickety boats to avoid being sent to Vietnam. It is beautiful and open and wild along the river. Behind the trees on the Canadian side there is a railroad track, and occasionally a freight train roars by with the speed trains pick up only in the country.

We have purchased Canadian fishing licenses so that we can fish both sides of the river. We have also purchased three dozen minnows and salted them down. You can use Minnesota minnows on the Canadian side as long as they are dead. If you want to use live minnows on the Canadian side, you must buy them in Canada. But you can't cross the border checkpoint at International Falls or Baudette with

live minnows, so, if you want to fish legally with live minnows on the
Canadian side, you must launch your boat in Canada, which means
you must patronize the Canadian resorts, of which there are none on
this stretch of the Rainy.

As Craig drives, I read the fishing regulations. I turn to the fish
consumption advisory. It says that on the Rainy River between International Falls and Lake of the Woods no one should eat more than
one fish meal per month of any size of any species caught there, especially if you are pregnant or plan to be, ever, or are nursing, or plan
to ever, or if you are less than ten years old. For years the Boise Cascade paper mill at International Falls has dumped dioxin, mercury
and other poisons into the river. The large fish in the river taste
slightly metallic. Two decades ago, the river was a slime pit of stink-
ing paper pulp, great pods of which would burp open on the water
and emit putrid gas. Now, at least, old-timers say, the visible pollution is gone, the water is clear and there are fish here again.

"Why are we coming here if all we're doing is poisoning ourselves?" I ask Craig. But, I know why, of course. We are going to be
out on the first open water of the season and to fish. That means sitting still and thinking and maybe reading if I get bored, talking quietly about important things, watching the sky, seeing an eagle fly
over, a few mallards whiz upriver, the brown grass on the bank, the
current bringing big sticks past.

Craig says, "Why doesn't someone sue Boise Cascade's ass? I
don't know how they can get away with polluting like that."

This is a trip Craig and I have taken for four years in a row. "These
traditional things are important," he says. "It's important to have a
history of experience together."

His eyes are on the road, and I watch his profile: a sharp forehead
and nose, cheeks, eyes and lips framed by a closely trimmed gray-
black beard, and a sloppy, sweat-stained gray Stetson. He looks very
young to me, and slightly naive; like a Boy Scout still. I agree with
him about the importance of ritual. We fish rainbow trout in the fall
at Benjamin Lake for two weekends. We walk the logging trails
around Blackduck for grouse. Then there is the season for ducks and
geese near Thief Lake. Then we hunt deer in the woods of northern
Minnesota to fill our freezer for the winter. When it snows we ski,

and when the lakes freeze we fish through the ice for crappies. In the spring comes the Rainy River, then walking in the woods for morel mushrooms, then summer walleye fishing on big, smooth lakes. Our year together is spent in these ways. It is what we do.

But I am uneasy about the trip to the Rainy this time. For one thing, it is always difficult, physically demanding. To load and unload a boat, walk up and down the steep, slippery hill from the river to camp in heavy boots, all is wearing on my body. I get tired. I worry that I am becoming soft and weak. The weather is always unpredictable. One year as Craig and I bobbed in the current, jerking our minnow-baited jigs up and down, snow fell and ice chunks floated past us. Another year it was so warm we fished in shirtsleeves. This year the weather is in the middle. Sunny but cold. But still there is the physical work of it. Hauling. Endless hauling.

But I know my unease has less to do with this, and more to do with the first year we came here. The fishing was so good that year that the river was a solid mass of boats, gunnel to gunnel, bow touching bow, stern to bow, stern to stern. It was sunny, and everyone was having a wonderful time, lifting huge fish from the muddy water, smiling, laughing, weighing the fish, some putting the big ones back, but others keeping stringers of seven-pound fish, whole stringers of fish that would not even taste good, fish that would taste like metal.

At the boat ramp, men milled around, laughing and smoking cigarettes and drinking beer and pop. They were drunken, overloaded, dangerous. The wives and girlfriends of the fishermen stood with poodles on leashes, holding children by the hand, taking pictures of the great catches of fish. The fish-cleaning house was packed, and there was a line outside. The garbage cans in the fish house were overflowing with guts and the orange eggs of the huge spawning female walleyes. Fish heads with shining black eyes flowed out onto the ground. Flies buzzed around. It was a carnival of greed. Hundreds of people appropriating walleye flesh as if it were a right.

I was as giddy as all the rest with our success. Every cast brought in another huge green and gold fish, tugging at my line, twisting and spinning in the water, curved gracefully in the landing net, all muscle. We didn't keep them all, only the small ones. And we only kept our limit: twelve. But we were there.

We camp this year, as always, at Franz Jevne State Park on the river. It is not much of a park: a few dirt pullouts and two outhouses. The roads are winding and muddy, and the park is dark. Our small camp is in the middle of tall evergreens. I feel vaguely gloomy. Surrounded. It is dim and cool, early evening, and the men around us in other camps are lighting lanterns, starting campfires, firing up cooking stoves. I smell fish and onions and wood smoke. I see shadows moving behind the canvas walls of tents. I hear muffled, rough voices. I am the only woman here.

In the women's outhouse I sit down to pee and look at the wall in front of me. There is a crude drawing in thick black marker of a woman's vulva, a hairless mound, lips open wide, folds of flesh deep inside. The rest of the body is absent. There is no head, no face, no eyes, no mouth, no arms or legs. Just this one piece, open and dripping, as if it were cut off with a cleaver and set apart. I imagine it wrapped up in white butcher paper, the kind we'll use to wrap the walleye we catch here. "I want to fill your pussy with a lode of hot come," the writing above this picture says. Cold air is blowing up from the pit below me, hitting my warm skin. My muscles shrink. On another wall is an erect penis, huge and hairless, drawn in the same black marker. The head on the penis looks to me strangely like the head of a walleye with its gills spread wide. There is no body attached to the penis either, just a straight vertical line from which the organ springs. "I want to fuck your wet pussy. Let's meet" is scrawled next to it.

I am suddenly terrified and sickened. I hear a threat: I want to rape you; I want to dissect you. I can't pee anymore. The muscles of my stomach and thighs have pulled into themselves protectively, huddling. Between my legs now feels like a faraway cold world, not a part of me. I yank up my long underwear and wool pants, getting shirttails tucked into the wrong places, and leave with my zipper still down, happy to be outside. As I walk back to our camp I look over my shoulder and left and right into the woods. I wonder if it was that man, or that one, or that one, who wrote this violence on the wall. I am out of breath and still afraid when I tell Craig all of this. I tell him it makes me want to run and it freezes me in place. My voice is wavering. He tells me it is in the men's outhouse, too: a picture of another naked, dripping vulva and the words, "This is my girlfriend's pussy." I ask Craig, "How would you feel if in the men's john a woman had written 'I want to cut your dick off' or 'This is my boyfriend's cock'?" I want to know if this would scare him, too. He says, "I'd watch out."

We are anchored in the current, our jigs bouncing on the bottom of the river. The river is wide and powerful and brown. It smells like cold steel. Craig wonders aloud why in all this water the poison and its smell do not dissipate. We are not catching many fish, but some. Crowded around us are men in boats. This is a good spot, on the Canadian side of the river, and the boats push together here. There are no other women on the water. Only men with other men. Some are drinking Diet Coke and munching on crackers as they wait for fish to bite. Others are swigging beer, cracking jokes, laughing. Cigar and cigarette smoke wafts up into the air. I feel as if Craig and I are being watched. A man and a woman in a boat. We watch ourselves being watched. Craig feels this, too. He says, "All these guys are out here to get away from their wives."

One of Craig's newspaper colleagues asked him once, in a voice that pleaded with Craig to come clean, to tell the truth, to join the club, "Do you really enjoy fishing with your wife?" Every time Craig remembers this he laughs. He repeats it sometimes when we are making love in the tall grass beside a trout stream, or when we are stretched out naked together under the covers in our van. He leans over now and asks, smiling, "Do you really think I can have any fun fishing with my wife?"

We are dressed in heavy wool pants and sweaters and big felt-lined boots. Craig asks me, when I am dressed up like this, if I think anyone can tell I am a woman. The sweater and down jacket hide my breasts. My long blonde hair is under a hat, my face is buried in wool, no one can see my earrings. What would be the thing that would make them know I was not a man among men? What is the line I would have to cross for them to know surely that I was different from them?

"Only when I speak," I say. "Or maybe when you lean over in the boat and kiss me. Then maybe they would think I was a woman. But I wouldn't necessarily have to be."

Until recently it never occurred to me to wonder why I was the only woman I ever knew who walked in the woods with a shotgun looking for grouse, or sat in a duck blind or a goose blind, or crouched up in a tree with a rifle waiting for deer, or went fishing on the Rainy River. It never occurred to me to wonder because I never felt alone, before now.

I used to hate being a woman. When I was very young, I believed I was a boy. I raced boxcars made from orange crates, played football with the neighbor boys and let them experiment with my body, the parts of which seemed uninteresting to me and not valuable. I was with them, watching myself in the light in their eyes, looking at me. I was flattered in high school when someone said to me, "I like you. You're just like a guy." The words I liked best to hear were: rangy, tough, smart, cynical. My father made jokes about women's libbers burning bras. I laughed, too. Throughout college I never knew what it was like to touch a woman, to kiss a woman, to have a woman as a friend. All my friends were men. I am thirty years old now, and I feel alone. I am not a man. Knowing this is like an earthquake. Just now all the lies are starting to unfold. I don't blend in as well or as easily as I used to. I refuse to stay on either side of the line.

In the boat next to ours is a quiet man with a fixed smile who has been catching all the fish. He is over a drop-off, his jig sinking exactly twenty-one feet. That is where the fish are. I ask him where he is from, my voice echoing across the water. He says he is from Warren, Minnesota. I ask him if he knows the boy I read about in the newspaper who got kicked out of West Point and was suing for his right to go back. The boy was his town's pride: a track star, a member of the choir, an honor student, handsome, full of promise. At West Point, too, he was full of promise. With his beautiful voice, he sang solo at the White House for the President. Then, on a tip from one of the boy's high school chums, the military started digging around in his past. Before they found out what he knew they would, he came forward and told them the truth. "I'm gay, sir," he told his commanding officer.

The man in the boat from Warren pushes his baseball cap back on his head and squints at the sun. He says to me, across the water, "I knew that boy really well. He was a model for the community. A model for all the younger kids." He is shaking his head. "It's hard to figure out," he says. "Just so darned hard to figure out why he'd go and do such a thing and ruin his future like that."

"I hope he wins his case against West Point," I say. There is more I ache to add. I want to yell across to him, "What's to figure out? He loves men." But, I say no more and turn away, ashamed of my silence. As I turn away, the man from Warren is still shaking his head. "It's just so hard to figure out."

Craig and I came to the Rainy partly to meet and fish with some old friends of mine, Kevin and Brad, whom I met while reporting for the *Grand Forks Herald* in North Dakota. Kevin and Brad have brought their friend John with them. John is the fishing columnist for the paper and also a professor of English. He is originally from Mississippi.

Around the campfire at night, Kevin tells us about his latest assignment. He is organizing a special section on wolves. The people of Roseau, Minnesota, believe they have a wolf problem and want the Minnesota Department of Natural Resources to get rid of some of the animals.

John is slouched by the fire with his feet straight out, taking long drinks from a bottle of root beer schnapps. Brad and Craig are standing, their hands in their pockets, looking down at the flames and coals. Kevin puts a wad of chewing tobacco behind his lower lip. I squat by the fire, hunched over a mug of tea. John passes me the bottle of schnapps, and I hesitate. For me to drink from it would be to mimic his gesture, to join in, but I am so curious to taste it. I take a small sip and make a face.

Kevin says, "Farmers think the wolf pack is purposely underestimated."

Craig asks, "You mean the government is lying about how many wolves there are so the farmers don't get upset?"

"It's more than the wolf they want to kill," I say. "It's what the wolf represents."

"What's that?" Brad says.

"Lust," I say. They laugh.

"They want control," Craig says. "They want control over nature. That's what management is all about. It's for us, not the animals. Just like with this river." Craig waves his hand toward the dark water.

"It stinks," Brad says.

"Literally," Kevin says.

"Buffalo shit," John says.

We all look at him and wait.

"Do ya'll know how much the rivers were polluted by buffalo shit? Millions of buffalo shitting in the rivers back before the white man came and after?" He's not laughing.

"Why, our screwing up the earth and killing animals, it's as natural as buffalo shit," he says. "We're part of nature, too, hell. If you fuck around with nature—try to clean up the river, protect the wolves—you'll upset the whole balance of time and evolution. Just leave things be."

There is a long, uncomfortable silence. Then Craig says, "The world has had millions of years to get used to buffalo shit. But no matter how much buffalo dung there is in a river, it still will never be as bad as dioxin."

The next day, Sunday, is the day we leave. Craig and I fish from early morning until noon. When it comes time to load the boat and return to St. Paul, one of us has to get out on shore and drive the car to the boat landing. And one of us has to take the boat by water. I want to go by water, to go fast and have the spray fly up around me and the front of the boat rise out of the river.

Craig says, "You take the boat." This is what I want to do, but I am afraid.

"Really?" I ask him. "Really, I can drive it down?" I expect not to be trusted.

"What about rocks?" I ask.

"Watch out for them," he says, very casually. He has no second thoughts. He does not understand my timidity.

Once, in the spring, a friend and I sat on the steps of Lind Hall at the University of Minnesota and watched a group of boys playing on their skateboards, jumping high in the air, knees pulled up, big, orange high-tops hovering off the ground, their skateboards flipping under them, over and over. Then the boys would land safely. Then, there they would go again, taking a running leap onto a cement bench, turning on top of it and coming off again. Graceful and noisy. My friend said, "Guys are brought up to think they can do everything."

I think of this as I pull away from the shore, waving at Craig. I think of my brothers, Austin and Edward, who climb cliffs and fly airplanes. Many women, I think, grow up believing they can't do anything. One of the tasks I believe I never will be able to do is backing the trailer into the water to load or launch the boat. I have tried and nearly every time have ruined something: cranked the trailer around to dangerous angles, smashed a taillight, backed off the edge of the boat ramp, put the van in reverse instead of forward and driven it to the top of the wheelwells into the water. I know that I can learn to do this physical, mechanical task. What I regret is that I do not simply *assume* I can do it. I wish I could launch into it without reserve, full of confidence, free of doubt. Like a man might.

I have learned from Craig that it is not only gender that makes for my insecurity. When we put the boat in at the Rainy River, Craig is always nervous. He believes he is being watched and judged. But, unlike me, he is protected from ridicule. When we bought the van, it came with a bumper sticker, left there by its previous owner. It says, "Vietnam Veterans of America." Craig believes this sticker gives him certain privileges and encourages respect in parking lots and at boat ramps. It prevents laughter. I often think he wishes he had earned this bumper sticker rather than bought it. He was training to be a Navy pilot when the war ended and he was sent home. Sometimes when he meets a man his age and picks up a hint or clue, he asks him, shyly, "Were you in Nam?" Sometimes they say yes and ask him if he was, and he says, almost apologetically, "No. Almost."

I drive the boat down the river, watching out for rocks. I must not hit any rocks. If I hit rocks, I will have failed. I see rocks ahead, but also a spot that looks deep. I go for what I think is the deepest water. Spray comes over the bow and sides. I am bobbing along, zooming, my hair flying out behind me, the shore whizzing past. I am doing it all by myself. My image of my self and my self come together here. I am perfect.

Then the prop grinds against submerged rocks, the motor tilts forward and drags across them, gouging the propeller, ripping the metal as easily as cloth. I crush my teeth against one another. Again, the motor tilts forward, the engine rises in pitch and there is a grating and a crunching. Again and again this happens. I cannot see the rocks. I can't see one rock, I have no idea where they are. I feel defeated. I make it to shore, where men line the banks, and park, hitting one last rock. I pull up the motor to see the damage I have done: the prop is frayed, white paint long gone, twisted silver in its place.

I have fucked up. I never should have been trusted with this boat. I despise myself. It is not my place to drive a boat. It is too big a thing for me. Too dangerous, too demanding. Craig arrives at the boat landing. I start to cry. He says, "Don't cry. Don't cry. Don't cry. We needed a new prop anyway." I expect him to be angry. Instead Craig says, "You need to learn to do this. We should have you practice. You should always drive the boat and back up the trailer, light the stove and the lantern."

I always expect anger and sometimes feel cheated and lost when I don't get it. I expect anger now, with Craig, because that is what I learned to expect from my father. That is the way my father would have reacted if I had failed in this way in front of him.

I learned many early lessons from my father and have carried them with me into womanhood. For my father there is no middle ground between success and complete failure. I learned from him to expect and strive for perfection and to truly trust no one but myself. "If you want it done right, do it yourself," he always said. For my scientist father the world of nature, the world of personal relations and desire, the world of chance and fate, resembles a machine of sorts. Oil it, clean it, take care of it and it will run for you; you can prevent any problem from occurring. As long as you know a thing thoroughly, as long as you have control over it, as long as you command it, it can never surprise you. All of this I learned as a child, each lesson hardening into a code I would adhere to, mostly unwittingly, much of my adult life. Craig is not like my father. Instead of anger from him I get the opposite—laughter!

It has become tradition with us that while Craig puts the cover on the boat, tucks the life jackets away, winds up the stringer, I clean the fish. I take our collection of walleyes to the fish house and see that inside the screen door five men are working, slicing open the walleyes with long fillet knives, talking about their fishing day. "Is there room for another person in there?" I ask. I ask this because they are watching me stand outside the door, stringer in hand, wondering with their eyes what I am doing here. I feel unnatural and self-conscious. Perhaps they think of their own wives, or kids, at home and wonder why I am not there, too. One man, the oldest, the one with gray hair and pink ears, says, "It's kind of cozy in here." I say that I will wait. I am waiting, watching them slice through the fish, peeling off an entire side of the body, then slipping the knife between the skin and the white flesh and separating the two with one or two strokes. It is remarkable to me how easy it is to slice apart a walleye—carving a breathing thing down to two essential fillets that bear no resemblance to the fish alive. The only way for me to do this is to ignore that what I've got is a fish, something that hours ago was swimming, alive. From behind me comes a man with a stringer of fish he can barely hold up. He barrels around me, steps into the fish house and throws his fish on the counter. He is in. I am still outside.

I pick up my fish and march away. Craig sees me.

"Wouldn't they let you in?"

I say, "There's no room for a goddamned girl in that fish house."

I throw down the stringer, the knife, the cutting board, the jug of water, the plastic bags and my orange cleaning tub, fall to my knees on the ground and start slashing at my fish. One, two, three. One, two, three. Three strokes and the fillet comes off clean and smooth. I am angry. I am saying to myself, "I can do this better than any of those bastards. Better than any of them." I feel defiant and confident, proud and suddenly cruel. When I do this, I realize, I am leaping across the line between the fish's life and mine, across lines that divide life into death. And I can do it as well as any. I can move as easily as anyone across this space.

Craig wants to take a new route home. I would never dare. I would simply take the freeway, the safe and easy route. He chooses a curving line that runs through the Nett Lake Indian Reservation. We wind, bump and take twice as long, but Craig likes these roads where you cannot see where you are going. There is one right angle after another.

I am exhausted and sad, but feel safe again. "I should give up and stay home," I say. "The worse it gets the more I see I don't have a place out here." I am looking out the window at the forest bumping past, thinking of the river, the outhouse, the fish house.

Around a sharp corner, a white and brown blur rises from the middle of the road. We see a hawk with a mouse in its claws, a wisp of a tail, four tiny feet hanging down, a little package being carried head forward into the sky by a graceful flapping bird that goes up and up and up and over the tops of the pines. Craig slows down and we both duck our heads and peer out the windows so that we can watch the hawk until it disappears.

Craig sees that I am crying. He asks me, "What are you afraid of?"

"I am tired and afraid of being the only woman. I am so lonely," I say.

He is quiet.

"I'm afraid of the killing," I say. "I'm afraid that I wouldn't know how to live and not murder." I wipe my nose with the sleeve of my sweater. "The line is so thin," I say. "I'm afraid there is no difference between me and them."

Craig is quiet again for a long time and then says to me, "You know, if you don't take your place, then you'll lose it."

"I'm not sure I want it," I say. "Not here. Not like this. Not this place." In truth, *I am not sure.* Not sure at all. But there has to be a space for me; space for me as a woman out here. There has to be a middle ground. A space between the borderlines. A space where we can all learn to be and live and not murder.

FISH

JUDITH BARRINGTON

I AM STANDING at the draining board in our rented apartment looking down at a neat row of fish. I don't know what they are, since the fish market in this small Andalusian village is too noisy for me to hear the names, which probably don't correspond, anyway, to the correct Castilian they taught me at school.

The fish are whole. Each one has a head, a tail and a body, all joined together. And inside, guts. Each head has two eyes, which stare as I wave the small, sharp knife around in the air and contemplate the removal of these guts—a job I have never had to do before, although I am forty-three years old. Something about this gives me pause. I am hearing my mother's voice. Memories of my father hover around too, although I never hear his voice; he visits me in a series of blurred images, always at a distance, and often with a fishing rod in his hand. There was one summer, I remember, when I tried to bridge that distance, a summer when my mother's voice temporarily faded out and my father's image grew sharper. . . .

That summer—1954 I think it was—I tried fishing. Really tried. Before that, I had often gone with my father to row the boat, and I knew how to dip the oars without splashing as we stalked the big trout off the island at Posingworth Lake. I knew, too, how it felt hunched in the bow of the motorboat two miles off Shoreham, as we trolled for mackerel, and how slowly time passed when we sat with our lines out, bottom fishing, while the swell rolled under us with a corkscrew twist that left my stomach hanging. But I wasn't really committed.

My mother despised fishing. She refused to have anything to do with it, although sometimes she would come out to Posingworth late in the day with a picnic tea, and we'd all sprawl on damp needles, where pines stood guard in front of the rhododendron wall. Once, choosing a patch of sun-warmed bracken, I almost sat on two adders coiled like an anchor rope still gleaming from the water.

Even though I admired my mother's tirades against those fools who hung around all day waiting for fish to swallow their hooks, from time to time I would go off with the men—my father and brother, my brother-in-law (under duress) and occasionally our family doctor, a Scot with a deadly accurate cast. My mother had long since given up: she got seasick fishing and sometimes even on a mirror-smooth lake; she hated the smell of wet wool; and it was, she said, *quite dreadful* if you actually caught a fish. The final insult was that she had to clean the fish my father caught, so we could cook them on the campfire and eat them with blackened potatoes in tin foil.

"We're not all that poor," she used to say. "The fishmonger has nice fresh trout, and they come with the innards already out"— my mother would never say *guts*—"and no heads either. I can't stand the way they look at you with those reproachful pop-eyes."

It was my mother who pointed out every year that the trout season opened on April 1st, and what more fitting comment could there be than that. And it was she who turned every mishap into a family story, poking fun at the fishermen. For example, when the three men went out from Brighton beach one freezing Boxing Day and capsized in the surf on their way in again, my mother recounted the event with triumphant satisfaction to all her bridge friends. Could my father really have dived down over and over as she described, surfacing only to yell: "The fish, the fish! Save the fish!" while my brother tried to prevent the boat from being swept out to France, and my brother-in-law staggered around the beach in confusion because he had lost his glasses? I do remember that night, in the dress circle of the Theatre Royal, my father and brother sneezing throughout the play, while my brother-in-law, who couldn't see where the stage was, snored loudly. My mother's expression conveyed her certainty that this was the final proof: fishing was either caused by, or led to, insanity.

More often than not in these early years, I threw my lot in with my mother and sister, who spent a good deal of time playing the piano, the viola and the record player. I joined them with my array of recorders and, later, my clarinet. Until the summer of '54, that is, when, at the age of ten, I temporarily abandoned the female stronghold and joined the hard-core anglers, which had the overtones of a significant choice in a family that was divided along gender lines into two camps: the sportsmen on one side, the musicians and artists on the other.

As usual, my father organized our holiday around fishing, and we went to Scotland, just the three of us, since my brother and sister were old enough to holiday by themselves. The hotel in the highlands was a huge stone mansion, once the seat of some powerful clan with its own tartan, whose crest still adorned the plates and silverware. Seen from the long approach across a heather-covered moor, it made sense of that Scots word *dour:* it cried out for mist and howling dogs—but in vain. That summer the sun shone and the sky was blue, and I was enchanted.

We stayed at Craiglynne for three weeks and the first week was warm, though a cool breeze ruffled the surface of the belfry pool, where "the old preacher," a salmon reputed to weigh at least thirty-five pounds, was believed to live. Inside the hotel's two-foot-thick stone walls, it was cool and dark, and in the library there was always a blazing wood fire, which someone told us they lit every day, year in year out. For two or three days, I retreated to one of the chimney seats and read my way through numerous Agatha Christies and James Bonds. After lunch, my mother would insist that I join her in a brisk walk on the moors with the dogs.

As the weather got hotter and stiller in the second week, I took to wandering on the moors by myself. One day, I sat on a rock high above the river, which cut a path through purple heather and was flanked by bands of lush grass rapidly fading to brown. Two lines of silver birches sprouted from this grass, shading the banks. Down there below the bend, where the current swept wide into a pool, my father stood in his thigh-waders, casting upstream. I watched him for a long time as he moved slowly toward the pool, throwing the line rhythmically, his head shaded by a tweed hat that, I knew, was stuck full of flies, though I couldn't see them from my viewpoint. I

watched him untangle his line from one of the birches, patiently
clinging to a root with one hand while he worked the fly free with the
other. If he muttered, I was too far away to hear; up there on the wide
moor, I could hear only the cries of buzzards and the occasional
chirp of a grasshopper. I watched for a very long time and then decided that this summer I would catch my first salmon.

My father was surprised by my sudden enthusiasm. I demanded
use of the small rod, a supply of flies in a tackle box and my own permit. Waders didn't matter: I simply put on my very small pink shorts
and some old tennis shoes that would allow me to clamber over the
rocky river bottom. This was unorthodox and made my father uncomfortable, but he acquiesced, only too glad of some support in the
family. Indeed his jubilation was such that I later wondered if he battled a few pangs of guilt at dragging my mother and me along on
these fishing trips.

We strode off together in the early morning, laden with canvas
bag and fish basket, landing net and tackle box. At the river we would
separate, each to our own beat, which saved me the embarrassment
of admitting how many flies I lost in the birch trees. I really wanted to
catch a salmon. Surely, if I cast the fly just right and hit those deep
pools under the tree roots, I'd feel the fish grab. But nothing happened. Morning after morning, in between the hours I spent hooking
tussocks of grass, clusters of leaves and sometimes even my own
clothes, I made several perfect casts. But not one of them enticed a
salmon.

I was easily disheartened. It didn't seem fair that perfect casting
did not result in fish. I could understand not catching one when the
line was wound around a tree trunk or the fly was slapping the water
with a huge leaf attached to it, but I couldn't accept that perfect skill
should go unrewarded. It never had before: if I studied, I passed the
exams—in fact, I often passed without studying; if I practiced the piano, I could play Bach preludes from memory. But here was something I wanted badly and was prepared to learn to do right, and it
wasn't working. I couldn't make that large silver fish swirl to the surface and grab my fly.

My father said the river was too low. The hotel proprietor said it
was the heat. The gillie said it was the laird over the hill, who had di-
verted too much water from his stream to irrigate a rock garden. The

only consolation was that nobody else caught anything either. The stuffed fish in glass cases on each landing of the wide staircase seemed to be grinning with delight at all the disgruntled conversations. "Terrible weather," the guests agreed as they passed each other on the stairs in their plus fours or mid-calf tweed skirts, which never varied, despite the eighty-degree weather.

The third week was unprecedented as the thermometer crept toward ninety and the library fire went unlit. I stopped fishing altogether and found a spot where I could lie on the bank under the birch trees and look into one of the still pools. The water was clean and the pebbles on the bottom distinct. Their bluish gray tones reminded me of the beach and seemed incongruous here in this clear brown water flowing between peat banks. The sun pierced the shade like a small spotlight and gnawed into the small of my back till sweat began to run down toward my waist.

I had been lying like this for an hour or two one day, when I noticed what looked like some logs lying in the pool, but it seemed unlikely as the branches of the overhanging trees were much more slender than these hefty objects. Suddenly, one of the logs turned around—not fast, but not pushed by the current either. It turned quite deliberately and faced the other way. Immediately, I saw that the logs were salmon, six of them, basking in the tropical water.

"Only way anyone could catch salmon in that state of mind would be by dapping," grunted my father, when I told him what I had seen. "The river's probably full of the lazy beasts just lying there. You can see them easily in this weather."

For the rest of our vacation, I wandered the river banks spotting salmon. Anywhere the current was not too fast, you could see them, fat and happy. A few fish fell to an illegally dapped fly upstream from the hotel, and the dining room buzzed with the news when the poacher was caught, but mostly they just lay around as if they, too, were on holiday, and I grew very fond of them. My mother and I and the dogs walked as usual, and the men, cooped up in the hotel with nothing to do but boast of other years when the weather was better, fumed. And every day I went to look at the happy salmon, until I knew without a doubt that my mother was right: it would be *quite dreadful* if I caught one.

That was almost my last attempt at fishing and at infiltrating my father's world. My mother never said a word about it, though I'm sure she was glad to have me back. She enjoyed that holiday and always spoke of it with a certain fondness. I'm not sure if it was because the men were frustrated in their foolishness or if it was because of my obvious pleasure at the salmon's refusal to cooperate. . . .

I am standing over the pink-gilled Spanish fish with a knife in my hand, and my mother's voice is complaining: "I do wish they'd sell them with the innards *out.*" In my mind, the fishmonger becomes my father, imposing this messy task on us females. And my father . . . where is he? Has he, as usual, deposited his fish and disappeared until they are cleaned, cooked and sitting on a plate? Why is he so damned invisible?

As I make a neat incision into the belly of the first fish, I remember that the summer at Craiglynne was not, in fact, my last attempt to make sense of my father's world. It must have been '66 or thereabouts, after both he and my mother were dead, when I found myself in Scotland again, touring for a few days with a friend. We stopped at a mill with a little shop. To my surprise, I purchased a tweed hat in soft heather tones. The next day I bought a fly rod and several boxes of flies, some of which I stuck into the hat. Then, armed with a permit and some boots, I strode over the moor to a small hill loch, where I fished in the mist for nine hours without seeing a single trout. My friend thought I was insane, and I hardly knew how to explain, driven by some urge I didn't understand myself. But that truly was my last attempt. To this day, the pleasures of fishing elude me, and my father has not yet emerged from the mist.

Still, slicing the undersides of these fish, scraping off the translucent scales and piling the reproachful heads into the garbage, I am astonished at how familiar it all seems. I know how my mother would have felt about it as the scales glisten on my hands and the knife cuts clean. But I am quite enjoying the task. Somewhere along the way I must have learned there were more than two camps.

WHERE I WANT TO BE

JOAN SALVATO WULFF

THE MOVING WATER OF TROUT and salmon rivers, with all of the life found beneath their surfaces, touches me deeply. I am most keenly aware of being where I want to be when I'm wading a river, fly rod in hand.

Moving through the cool, clear water makes me a part of the river; and the act of casting connects me to what I see and feel with a grace and beauty of its own. Through the artificial fly at the end of my leader, I get a glimpse of another world and can touch another of God's creatures.

It is this beauty, always fresh, and this challenge, always new, that have kept my interest stimulated for a full fifty years. This sport is for me and always will be.

Wading is a vital part of my enjoyment. The flow of the current, forcing a response from leg and body muscles, reminds me that I'm alive and well. As a beginning wader I was fearful, thinking that any next step into dark water would be into a large hole from which I would not emerge. Familiarity is one solution. To women new to the sport, I recommend that you leave your rod on the shore and, with the aid of a wading staff, explore a new stream bottom before actually fishing. Film writer Pat Smith once said of my husband, Lee Wulff, in describing his oneness with the fishing in northern Canadian waters: "Even the rocks under his feet are arranged in a familiar pattern." So it becomes for all of us, over the years, although there are some streams that have obviously been designed for size twelve boots rather than my size eights!

Fishing memories stack up. One that is near the top right now is of my first trip for steelhead on a fly. It was 1986 in British Columbia on the Copper River, a tributary of the Skeena. The Copper is about the size of our Beaverkill in New York, gray-green in color because of its glacial beginnings, surrounded by primeval forest amidst dramatically shaped mountains. A *ten* on any angler's scale.

The basic technique is to cast quartering downstream to the far edge of the current and then, with flies that skim the surface naturally or with hitched wet flies, mend against the current to keep the fly moving *slowly* across the stream.

It was after our lunch break one afternoon that our host, Martin Schmidderer of Exclusive Fishing Lodge, guided me upstream through a log jam to reach a lovely pool. He left me alone in the silence with distant rapids sending a bare whisper through the forest. The current was relatively slow. Although I waded carefully, I felt like an elephant at a watering hole. My slightest movement sent far-reaching ripples dancing on the glassy surface.

I began false casting to extend the fly line, aiming it upstream of the target area until I was ready to make the first presentation at about forty-five feet. The fly line looked as thick as a clothesline moving across the surface; my fourteen-foot leader appeared too short to separate the fly from the line in the eyes of a waiting steelhead. I was using one of Lee's molded-body Surface Stoneflies with a "steelhead snoot," which made it ride high and wake seductively.

The fly traveled at a perfect speed without any need for mending. On my second cast I extended the line by two feet. Nothing broke the stillness of the beautiful gray-green water. On the third cast, as it reached a point directly below me, the head of a steelhead, beautifully symmetrical and seemingly separate from its body, broke the slick surface and in slow motion engulfed my fly.

There have been times, when huge Atlantic salmon have risen to my dry fly, that my feet have lifted off the bottom, adrenalin shooting through me as I made a spasmodic jerk that took the fly out of the fish's closing mouth. This time everything went right. I waited the necessary moment, tightened the line, and he was on! Strangely, he didn't jump or run me into my backing as had earlier fish. It was as if he knew it was a special experience and that he'd be released. (A psychologist would find it easy to tell me why I always call fish "he.") I played him carefully, thankful that the pool wouldn't be unnecessarily disturbed. Finally he came in to me, and I had a lovely moment or two of absorbing his rainbow beauty, measuring him along my rod butt (thirty inches) and releasing him. He was a she.

As I rested the pool, gazing downstream and reliving that great head breaking the surface, a sound like no other—in what it portends—broke the silence. It was the sound of a fish rising. In all of this Copper River experience, steelhead *had* been taken on the surface, but always in a quartering downstream presentation. Now, the sound of this rise told me that my dream of taking a steelhead on a free-drifting dry fly could come true.

With trembling hands I exchanged the Surface Stonefly for a number six salmon-sized Royal Wulff while I pinpointed the steelhead's lie on a second rise. He was just this side of three protruding rocks, and there was a six-inch-wide flow lane down which the fly had to float. My first cast fell a little short. I wanted to snatch it back but patiently let the fly float right on through, hoping it would, at least, whet my friend's appetite. A second cast—this time right on—but again nothing. A third cast. Now I began to have doubts.

Okay, I thought, I'll give him two more chances.

Fourth cast... TAKE! This one wasn't in slow motion. My fish dove for the bottom and then surged upstream with the reel screaming. I took off all pressure. Out of the water he came, all twelve pounds of him, bright and beautiful. And I fell in love again. As the steelhead dropped back into the pool, my fly did a funny thing: it flew out of his mouth. And it was all over, in less than a minute.

Each fish had left a memory—sight, sound, anticipation, the thrill of its strike. The strike is the moment in which the circle comes full. It is why you are there, the reward for your efforts. No devout angler can get enough of it; being alone can make it all the more powerful an experience.

Yes, this sport fits me—physically, mentally, psychologically. Why do I love trout?

For the same reasons men do.

Dame Juliana's Black Leaper (May)

THE TREATISE OF FISHING WITH AN ANGLE *is the earliest known writing on the subject of sport fishing. Written circa 1421, more than two hundred years before Izaak Walton's* The Compleat Angler, *it is widely attributed to Dame Juliana Berners, by legend a nun, noblewoman and sportswoman. In charming detail, the essay offers timeless insight into why fishing is a "good and honorable" pastime. The advice on both technique and the subtleties of fishing etiquette rings true today, and the twelve fly patterns described set a standard that has lasted for centuries.*

The fishing treatise was first printed in the second Book of St. Albans in 1496. The first Book of St. Albans, printed in 1486, contains treatises on hunting, heraldry and hawking. When the book was reprinted ten years later in London, the fishing treatise was added. Dame Juliana's name appears at the end of the book of hunting—the only author name to appear in either edition. In time the whole book became attributed to her, and the romance and mystique of Dame Juliana flourished.

There has been spirited debate about her authorship, and in some cases, even about her existence. Nonetheless, Dame Juliana's standing as an angling heroine endures, and she remains the first and best known female figure in five centuries of angling lore and history. The wisdom laid down in the treatise still touches the hearts of modern anglers and the essay itself is one of the finest ever written on the subject of sport fishing.

What follows is the modernized text of the first printed version of the treatise from the second Book of St. Albans. It is reprinted with footnotes and illustrations from John McDonald's Origins of Angling.
—Editor

THE TREATISE OF FISHING
WITH AN ANGLE

DAME JULIANA BERNERS

SOLOMON IN HIS Proverbs says that a good spirit makes a flower-ing age, that is, a fair age and a long one. And since it is so, I ask this question, "What are the means and the causes that lead a man into a merry spirit?" Truly, in my best judgment, it seems that they are good sports and honest games in which a man takes pleasure without any repentance afterward. Thence it follows that good recreations and honorable pastimes are the cause of a man's fair old age and long life. And therefore, I will now choose among four good sports and honorable pastimes—to wit, among hunting, hawking, fishing and fowling. The best, in my simple judgment, is fishing, called angling, with a rod and a line and a hook. And thereof I will treat as my simple mind will permit, both for the above-mentioned saying of Solomon and also for the statement that medical science makes in this manner:

> Si tibi deficiant medici, medici tibi fiant
> Haec tria—mens laeta, labor, et moderatadiaeta.

You shall understand, that is to say, that if a man lacks physician or doctor, he shall make three things his physician and doctor, and he will never need any more. The first of them is a merry thought. The second is work which is not excessive. The third is a moderate diet. First, if a man wishes to be always in merry thoughts and have a glad spirit, he must avoid all quarrelsome company and all places of dispute, where he might have any causes of melancholy. And if he wishes to have a labor which is not excessive, he must then arrange for himself, for his heart's ease and pleasure—without care, anxiety or trouble—a merry occupation which may rejoice his heart and in which his spirits may have a merry delight. And if he wishes to have a moderate diet, he must avoid all places of debauchery, which is the cause of overindulgence and sickness. And he must withdraw himself to places of sweet and hunger-producing air and eat nourishing foods and also digestible ones.

Now then I will describe the said sports or games to find out, as truly I can, which is the best of them; albeit the right noble and very worthy prince, the Duke of York, lately called the Master of Game, has described the joys of hunting, just as I think to describe it and all the others. For hunting, to my mind, is too laborious. For the hunter must always run and follow his hounds, laboring and sweating very painfully. He blows on his horn till his lips blister; and when he thinks he is chasing a hare, very often it is a hedgehog. Thus he hunts and knows not what. He comes home in the evening rain—beaten, scratched, his clothes torn, wet-shod, all muddy, this hound lost and that one crippled. Such griefs happen to the hunter—and many others which, for fear of the displeasure of them that love it, I dare not report. Thus, truly, it seems to me that this is not the best recreation or game of the four mentioned.

The sport and pastime of hawking is laborious and troublesome also, as it seems to me. For often the falconer loses his hawks, as the hunter his hounds. Then his pastime and sport is gone. Very often he shouts and whistles till he is terribly thirsty. His hawk takes to a bough and does not choose to pay him any attention. When he would have her fly at the game, then she wants to bathe. With improper feeding she will get the frounce, the ray, the cray, and many other sicknesses that bring them to the upward flight. Thus, by proof, this is not the best sport and game of the four mentioned.

The sport and game of fowling seems to me poorest of all. For in the winter season, the fowler has no luck except in the hardest and coldest weather, which is vexatious. For when he would go to his traps, he cannot because of the cold. Many a trap and many a snare he makes, yet he fares badly. In the morning time, in the dew, he is wet-shod up to his tail. Much more of the same I could tell, but dread of displeasure makes me leave off. Thus, it seems to me that hunting and hawking and also fowling are so toilsome and unpleasant that none of them can succeed nor be the true means of bringing a man into a merry frame of mind, which is the cause of his long life according to the said proverb of Solomon.

Undoubtedly then, it follows that it must needs be the sport of fishing with a hook. (For every other kind of fishing is also toilsome and unpleasant, often making folks very wet and cold, which many times has been seen to be the cause of great sicknesses.) But the angler can have no cold nor discomfort nor anger, unless he be the cause himself. For he can lose at the most only a line or a hook, of which he can have a plentiful supply of his own making, as this simple treatise will teach him. So then his loss is not grievous, and other griefs he cannot have, except that some fish may break away after he has been caught on the hook, or else that he may catch nothing. These are not grievous, for if the angler fails with one, he may not fail with another, if he does as this treatise teaches—unless there are no fish in the water. And yet, at the very least, he has his wholesome and merry walk at his ease, and a sweet breath of the sweet smell of the meadow flowers, that makes him hungry. He hears the melodious harmony of birds. He sees the young swans, herons, ducks, coots and many other birds with their broods, which seems to me better than all the noise of hounds, the blasts of horns and the clamor of birds that hunters, falconers and fowlers can produce. And if the angler catches fish, surely then there is no man merrier than he is in his spirit. Also whoever wishes to practice the sport of angling, he must rise early, which thing is profitable to a man in this way. That is, to wit: most for the welfare of his soul, for it will cause him to be holy; and for the health of his body, for it will cause him to be well; also for the increase of his goods, for it will make him rich. As the old English proverb says in this manner: "Whoever will rise early shall be holy, healthy and happy."

Thus have I proved, according to my purpose, that the sport and game of angling is the true means and cause that brings a man into a merry spirit, which (according to the said proverb of Solomon and the said teaching of medicine) makes a flowering age and a long one. And therefore, to all you that are virtuous, gentle and freeborn, I write and make this simple treatise which follows, by which you can have the whole art of angling to amuse you as you please, in order that your age may flourish the more and last the longer.

If you want to be crafty in angling, you must first learn to make your tackle, that is, your rod, your lines of different colors. After that, you must know how you should angle, in what place of the water, how deep and what time of day; for what manner of fish, in what weather; how many impediments there are in the fishing that is called angling; and especially with what baits for each different fish in every month of the year; how you must make your baits-bread, where you will find the baits and how you will keep them; and for the most difficult thing, how you are to make your hooks of steel and iron, some for the artificial fly and some for the float and the ground-line, as you will afterward hear all these things expressed openly for your knowledge.

And how you should make your rod skillfully, here I will teach you. You must cut, between Michaelmas and Candlemas, a fair staff, a fathom and a half long and as thick as your arm, of hazel, willow or aspen; and soak[1] it in a hot oven, and set it straight. Then let it cool and dry for a month. Then take and tie it tight with a cockshoot cord,[2] and bind it to a bench or a perfectly square, large timber. Then take a plumber's wire that is smooth and straight and sharp at one end. And heat the sharp end in a charcoal fire till it is white-hot, and then burn the staff through with it, always straight in the pith at both ends, till the holes meet. And after that, burn it in the lower end with a spit for roasting birds, and with other spits, each larger than the last, and always the largest last; so that you make your hole always taper-wax.[3] Then let it lie still and cool for two days. Untie it then and let it dry in a house-roof in the smoke until it is thoroughly dry. In the same season, take a fair rod of green hazel, and soak it even and straight, and let it dry with the staff. And when they are dry, make the rod fit the hole in the staff, into half the length of the staff. And to make the other half of the upper section, take a fair shoot of blackthorn, crabtree, medlar or juniper, cut in the same season and well

---

[1] That is, soak it in hot water to make it pliable, so that it can be straightened.
[2] A cord used for fastening a net across an open space (or "cockshoot") in the woods to catch birds.
[3] Waxed with wax from taper(?); increasing in diameter like a taper(?).

soaked and straightened; and bind them together neatly so that the upper section may go exactly all the way into the above-mentioned hole. Then shave your staff down and make it taper-wax. Then ferrule the staff at both ends with long hoops of iron or latten in the neatest manner, with a spike in the lower end fastened with a running device for pulling your upper section in and out. Then set your upper section a handbreadth inside the upper end of your staff in such a way that it may be as big there as in any other place above. Then, with a cord of six hairs, strengthen your upper section at the upper end as far down as the place where it is tied together; and arrange the cord neatly and tie it firmly in the top, with a loop to fasten your fishing line on. And thus you will make yourself a rod so secret that you can walk with it, and no one will know what you are going to do. It will be light and very nimble to fish with at your pleasure. And for your greater convenience, behold here a picture of it as an example:

After you have made your rod thus, you must learn to color your lines of hair in this manner. First, you must take, from the tail of a white horse, the longest and best hair that you can find; and the rounder it is, the better it is. Divide it into six bunches, and you must color every part by itself in a different color, such as yellow, green, brown, tawny, russet and dusky colors.

And to make a good green color on your hair, you must do thus. Take a quart of small ale and put it in a little pan, and add to it half a pound of alum, and put your hair in it, and let it boil softly half an hour. Then take out your hair and let it dry. Then take a half-gallon of water and put it in a pan. And put in it two handfuls of a yellow dye, and press it with a tilestone, and let it boil softly half an hour. And when it is yellow on the scum, put in your hair with half a pound of green vitriol, called copperas, beaten to powder, and let it boil half-a-mile-way. And then set it down and let it cool five or six hours. Then take out the hair and dry it. And it is then the finest green there is for the water. And ever the more you add to it of copperas, the better it is. Or else instead of copperas, use verdigris.

Another way, you can make a brighter green, thus. Dye your hair with blue dye until it is a light blue-gray color. And then seethe it in yellow vegetable dye as I have described, except that you must not add to it either copperas or verdigris.

To make your hair yellow, prepare it with alum as I have explained before, and after that with yellow vegetable dye without copperas or verdigris.

Another yellow you shall make thus. Take a half-gallon of small ale, and crush three handfuls of walnut leaves, and put them together. And put in your hair till it is as deep a yellow as you want to have it.

To make russet hair, take a pint and a half of strong lye and half a pound of soot and a little juice of walnut leaves and a quart of alum; and put them all together in a pan and boil them well. And when it is cold, put in your hair till it is as dark as you want it.

To make a brown color, take a pound of soot and a quart of ale, and seethe it with as many walnut leaves as you can. And when they turn black, set it off the fire. And put your hair in it, and let it lie still until it is as brown as you wish to have it.

To make another brown, take ale and soot and blend them together, and put therein your hair for two days and two nights, and it will be a right good color.

To make a tawny color, take lime and water, and put them together; and also put your hair therein four or five hours. Then take it out and put it in tanner's ooze[4] for a day, and it will be as fine a tawny color as is required for our purpose.

The sixth part of your hair, you must keep still white for lines for the dubbed[5] hook, to fish for the trout and grayling, and to prepare small lines for the roach and the dace.

When your hair is thus colored, you must know for which waters and for which seasons they will serve. The green color in all clear water from April till September. The yellow color in every clear water from September till November, for it is like the weeds and other kinds of grass which grow in the waters and rivers, when they are broken. The russet color serves for all the winter until the end of April, as well in rivers as in pools or lakes. The brown color serves for that water

---

[4] The liquid from a tanner's vat, a mixture of tanbark juices, etc.
[5] Covered with an artificial fly.

that is black, sluggish, in rivers or in other waters. The tawny color for those waters that are heathy or marshy.

Now you must make your lines in this way. First, see that you have an instrument like this picture drawn hereafter. Then take your hair and cut off from the small end a large handful or more, for it is neither strong nor yet dependable. Then turn the top to the tail,[6] each in equal amount, and divide it into three strands. Then plait each part at the one end by itself, and at the other end plait all three together. And put this last end in the farther side of your instrument, the end that has but one cleft. And fix the other end tight with the wedge the width of four fingers from the end of your hair. Then twist each strand the same way and pull it hard; and fasten them in the three clefts equally tight. Then take out that other end and twist it sufficiently in whichever direction it is inclined. Then stretch it a little and plait it so that it will not come undone. And that is good. And to know how to make your instrument, behold, here it is in a picture. And it is to be made of wood, except the bolt underneath, which must be of iron.

When you have as many of the lengths as you suppose will suffice for the length of a line, then you must tie them together with a water knot[7] or else a duchess knot. And when your knot is tied, cut off the unused short ends a straw's breadth from the knot. Thus you will make your lines fair and fine, and also very secure for any kind of fish. And because you should know both the water knot and also the duchess knot, behold them here in picture. Contrive them in the likeness of the drawing.

---

[6] That is, the top to the bottom; reverse half the hair so as to make each strand of uniform strength from end to end.

[7] Probably the knot later known as the fisherman's knot.

[Illustration missing[8]]

You must understand that the subtlest and hardest art in making your tackle is to make your hooks, for the making of which you must have suitable files, thin and sharp and beaten small; a semi-clamp of iron; a bender;[9] a pair of long and small tongs; a hard knife, somewhat thick; an anvil; and a little hammer. And for small fish, you must make your hooks in this manner, of the smallest square needles of steel that you can find. You must put the square needle in a red charcoal fire till it is of the same color as the fire is. Then take it out and let it cool, and you will find it well tempered for filing. Then raise the barb with your knife and make the point sharp. Then temper it again, for otherwise it will break in the bending. Then bend it like the bend pictured hereafter as an example. And you must make greater hooks in the same way out of larger needles, such as embroiderers' or tailors' or shoemakers' needles, or spear points; and of shoemakers' awls, especially, the best hooks are made for great fish. And the hooks should bend at the point when they are tested; otherwise they are not good. When the hook is bent, beat the hinder end out broad, and file it smooth to prevent fraying of your line. Then put it in the fire again, and give it an easy red heat. Then suddenly quench it in water, and it will be hard and strong. And that you may have knowledge of your instruments, behold them here in picture portrayed.

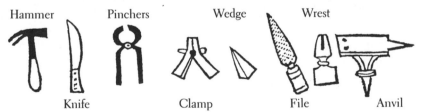

Hammer   Pinchers   Wedge   Wrest

Knife   Clamp   File   Anvil

When you have made your hooks in this way, then you must set them on your lines, according to size and strength in this manner. You must take fine red silk thread, and if it is for a large hook, then double it, but not twisted. And otherwise, for small hooks, let it be single. And with it, bind the line thick for a straw's breadth from the point where the one end of your hook is to be placed. Then set your

---

[8] Probably missing because the printer was unable to reproduce the knots.
[9] An instrument for bending, called a *wrest* below.

hook there, and wrap it with the same thread for two-thirds of the length that is to be wrapped. And when you come to the third part, then turn the end of your line back upon the wrapping, double, and wrap it thus double for the third part. Then put your thread in at the hole[10] twice or thrice, and let it go each time round about the shank of your hook. Then wet the hole and pull it until it is tight. And see that your line always lies inside your hooks and not outside. Then cut off the end of the line and the thread as close as you can, without cutting the knot.

Now that you know with what size hooks you must angle for every fish,[11] I will tell you with how many hairs you must angle for each kind of fish. For the minnow, with a line of one hair. For the growing roach, the bleak, the gudgeon and the ruff, with a line of two hairs. For the dace and the great roach, with a line of three hairs. For the perch, the flounder and small bream, with four hairs. For the chevin-chub, the bream, the tench and the eel, with six hairs. For the trout, grayling, barbel and the great chevin, with nine hairs. For the great trout, with twelve hairs. For the salmon, with fifteen hairs. And for the pike, with a chalkline made brown with your brown coloring as described above, strengthened with wire, as you will hear hereafter when I speak of the pike.[12]

Your lines must be weighted with lead sinkers, and you must know that the sinker nearest the hook should be a full foot and more away from it, and every sinker of size in keeping with the thickness of the line. There are three kinds of sinkers for a running ground-line. And for the float set upon the stationary ground-line, ten weights all joining together. On the running ground-line, nine or ten small ones. The float sinker must be so heavy that the least pluck of any fish can pull it down into the water. And make your sinkers round and smooth so that they do not stick in stones or in weeds. And for the better understanding, behold them here in a picture.

The running ground-line.

---

[10] The loop made by doubling the line and wrapping it.

[11] Something omitted(?).

[12] The carp is omitted here, but mentioned later.

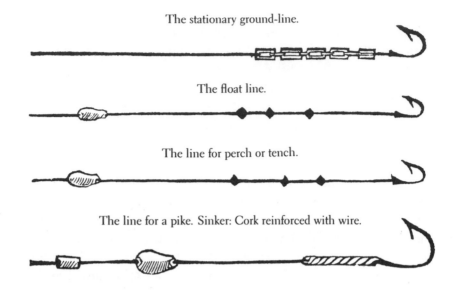

The stationary ground-line.

The float line.

The line for perch or tench.

The line for a pike. Sinker: Cork reinforced with wire.

Then you are to make your floats in this manner. Take a good cork that is clean, without many holes; and bore it through with a small hot iron; and put a quill in it, even and straight. Ever the larger the float, the larger the quill and the larger the hole. Then shape it large in the middle and small at both ends, and especially sharp in the lower end, and similar to the pictures following. And make them smooth on a grinding stone,[13] or on a tilestone. And see that the float for one hair is no larger than a pea; for two hairs, like a bean; for twelve hairs, like a walnut; and so every line according to proportion. All kinds of lines that are not for the bottom must have floats, and the running ground-line must have a float. The stationary ground-line without float.

Now I have taught you to make all your tackle. Here I will tell you how you must angle. You shall angle: understand that there are

---

[13] Perhaps a whetstone, more likely a grindstone revolving on an axle.

six ways of angling. The one is at the bottom for the trout and other fish. Another is at the bottom at an arch or at a pool, where it ebbs and flows, for bleak, roach and dace. The third is with a float for all kinds of fish. The fourth, with a minnow for the trout, without plumb or float. The fifth is running in the same way for roach and dace with one or two hairs and a fly. The sixth is with an artificial fly for the trout and grayling. And for the first and principal point in angling, always keep yourself away from the water, from the sight of the fish, either far back on the land or else behind a bush, so that the fish may not see you. For if they do, they will not bite. Also take care that you do not shadow the water any more than you can help, for that is a thing which will soon frighten the fish. And if a fish is frightened, he will not bite for a long time afterward. For all kinds of fish that feed at the bottom, you must angle for them at the bottom, so that your hooks will run or lie on the bottom. And for all other fish that feed above, you must angle for them in the middle of the water, either somewhat beneath or somewhat above. For always the greater the fish, the nearer he will lie to the bottom of the water; and ever the smaller the fish, the more he will swim above. The third good point is: when the fish bites, that you be not too hasty to hook the fish, nor too late. For you must wait till you suppose that the bait is fairly in the mouth of the fish, and then wait no longer. And this is for the ground-line. And for the float, when you see it pulled softly under the water or else carried softly upon the water, then strike. And see that you never strike too hard for the strength of your line, lest you break it. And if you have the fortune to hook a great fish with a small tackle, then you must lead him in the water and labor with him there until he is drowned and overcome. Then take him as well as you can or may, and always beware that you hold beyond the strength of your line. And as much as you can, do not let him come out of the end of your line straight from you, but keep him always under the rod and always hold him strait, so that your line can sustain and bear his leaps and his plunges with the help of your crop and of your hand.

Here I will declare to you in what place of the water you must angle. You should angle in a pool or in standing water, in every place where it is at all deep. There is not much choice of such places in a pool. For it is but a prison for fish, and they live for the most part in hunger like prisoners; and therefore it takes the less art to catch them.

But in a river, you must angle in every place where it is deep and clear at the bottom, as in gravel or clay without mud or weeds, and especially if there is a kind of whirling of water or a cover—such as a hollow bank or great roots of trees or long weeds floating above in the water—where the fish can cover and hide themselves at certain times when they like. Also it is good to angle in deep, swift streams, and also in waterfalls and weirs, and in floodgates and millraces. And it is good to angle where the water rests by the bank and where the current runs close by and it is deep and clear at the bottom; and in any other places where you can see any fish rise or do any feeding.

Now you must know what time of the day you should angle. From the beginning of May until it is September, the biting time is early in the morning from four o'clock until eight o'clock; and in the afternoon, from four o'clock until eight o'clock, but this is not so good as in the morning. And if there is a cold, whistling wind and it be a dark, lowering day, for a dark day is much better to angle in than a clear day. From the beginning of September until the end of April, angle at any time of the day. Also, many pool fishes will bite best at noontime. And if you see the trout or grayling leap at any time of the day, angle for him with an artificial fly appropriate to that same month. And where the water ebbs and flows, the fish will bite in some place at the ebb, and in some place at the flood. After that, they will rest behind the stakes or pilings and arches of bridges and in other places of that sort.

Here you should know in what weather you must angle: as I said before, in a dark, lowering day when the wind blows softly. And in the summer season when it is burning hot, then it is useless. From September until April in a fair, sunny day, it is right good to angle. And if the wind in that season comes from any part of the east, the weather then is no good. And when there is a great wind, and when it snows, rains or hails, or there is a great tempest, as with thunder or lightning, or sweltering hot weather, then it is not good for angling.

Now you must know that there are twelve kinds of impediments which cause a man to catch no fish, apart from other common causes that may happen by chance. The first is if your tackle is not adequate or suitably made. The second is if your baits are not good or fine. The third is if you do not angle in biting time. The fourth is if the fish are frightened by the sight of a man. The fifth, if the water is very thick, white or red from any flood recently fallen. The sixth, if the fish do not stir because of the cold. The seventh, if the weather is hot. The eighth, if it rains. The ninth, if it hails or snow falls. The tenth is if there is a tempest. The eleventh is if there is a great wind. The twelfth, if the wind is in the east, and that is worst, for generally, both winter and summer, the fish will not bite then. The west and north winds are good, but the south is best.

And now that I have told you, in all points, how to make your tackle and how you must fish with it, it is reasonable that you should know with what baits you must angle for every kind of fish in each month of the year, which is the gist of the art. And unless these baits are well known by you, all your other skill hitherto avails little to your purpose. For you cannot bring a hook into a fish's mouth without a bait. These baits for every kind of fish and for every month follow here in this manner.

Because the salmon is the most stately fish that any man can angle for in fresh water, therefore I intend to begin with him. The salmon is a noble fish, but he is cumbersome to catch. For generally he is only in deep places of great rivers, and for the most part he keeps to the middle of the water, so that a man cannot come at him. And he is in season from March until Michaelmas, in which season you should angle for him with these baits, when you can get them. First, with an earthworm in the beginning and end of the season. And also with a grubworm that grows in a dunghill. And especially with an excellent bait that grows on a water-dock plant. And he does not bite at the bottom but at the float. Also you may catch him (but this is seldom seen) with an artificial fly at such times as he leaps, in like manner and way as you catch a trout or a grayling. And these baits are well proven baits for the salmon.

The trout, because he is a right dainty fish and also a right fervent biter, we shall speak next of him. He is in season from March until Michaelmas. He is in clean gravel bottom and in a stream. You can angle for him at all times with a lying or running ground-line, except in leaping time and then with an artificial fly; and early with a running ground-line, and later in the day with a float-line. You must angle for him in March with a minnow hung on your hook by the lower nose, without float or sinker, drawing it up and down in the stream till you feel him hooked. In the same time, angle for him with a ground-line with an earthworm as the surest bait. In April, take the same baits, and also the lamprey, otherwise called "seven eyes,"[14] also the cankerworm that grows in a great tree, and the red snail. In May, take the stone fly and the grubworm under the cow turd, and the silkworm, and the bait that grows on a fern leaf. In June, take an earthworm and nip off the head, and put a codworm on your hook in front of it. In July, take the big red worm and the codworm together. In August, take a flesh fly[15] and the big red worm and the fat of bacon, and bind them about your hook. In September, take the earthworm and the minnow. In October, take the same, for they are special for the trout at all times of the year. From April to September the trout leaps; then angle for him with an artificial fly appropriate to the month. These flies you will find at the end of this treatise, and the months with them.

The grayling, also known as the umber,[16] is a delicious fish to man's mouth. You can catch him just as you do the trout, and these are his baits. In March and in April, the earthworm. In May, the green worm,[17] a little ringed worm, the dock canker, and the hawthorn worm. In June, the bait that grows between the tree and the bark of an oak. In July, a bait that grows on a fern leaf; and the big red worm, and nip off the head and put a codworm on your hook in front of it. In August, the earthworm, and a dock worm. And all the year afterward, an earthworm.

The barbel is a sweet fish, but it is a queasy food and a perilous one for man's body. For commonly, he introduces the fevers; and if he is eaten raw, he may be the cause of a man's death, as has often been seen. These are his baits. In March and in April, take fair, fresh cheese, lay it on a board, and cut it in small square pieces the length of your hook. Then take a candle and burn it on the end at the point of your hook until it is yellow. And then bind it on your hook with ar-

---

[14] Called "seven eyes" because of its seven pairs of gill slits which look like eyes.
[15] Some kind of blowfly.
[16] A recently borrowed French term. Most of the fish names are native formations, like grayling, or borrowings from Latin, French or Scandinavian.
[17] Many of these baits cannot be identified with any certainty, although we believe that anyone living in the fifteenth century in the place where the treatise was written would recognize them instantly.

rowmaker's silk, and make it rough like a welbede.[18] This bait is good for all the summer season. In May and June, take the hawthorn worm and the big red worm; nip off the head and put a codworm on your hook in front; and that is a good bait. In July, take the earthworm chiefly and the hawthorn worm together. Also the water-dock leaf worm and the hornet worm[19] together. In August and for all the year, take mutton fat and soft cheese, of each the same amount, and a little honey; and grind or beat them together a long time, and work it until it is tough. Add to it a little flour, and make it into small pellets. And that is a good bait to angle with at the bottom. And see to it that it sinks in the water, or else it is not good for this purpose.

The carp is a dainty fish, but there are only a few in England, and therefore I will write the less about him. He is a bad fish to catch, for he is so strongly reinforced in the mouth that no weak tackle can hold him. And as regards his baits, I have but little knowledge of them, and I would hate to write more than I know and have tested. But I know well that the earthworm and the minnow are good baits for him at all times, as I have heard reliable persons say and also found written in trustworthy books.

The chub is a stately fish, and his head is a dainty morsel. There is no fish so greatly fortified with scales on the body. And because he is a strong biter, he has the more baits, which are these. In March, the earthworm at the bottom, for usually he will bite there then, and at all times of the year if he is at all hungry. In April, the ditch canker that grows in the tree; a worm that grows between the bark and the wood of an oak; the earthworm; and the young frogs when the feet are cut off. Also, the stone fly, the grubworm under the cow turd, the red snail. In May, the bait that grows on the osier leaf and the dock canker, together upon your hook. Also a bait that grows on a fern leaf, the codworm, and a bait that grows on a hawthorn. And a bait that grows on an oak leaf and a silkworm and a codworm together. In June, take the cricket and the dor;[20] and also an earthworm with the

---

[18] Possibly a woodlouse or a millepede, both crustaceans. J. O. Halliwell's A *Dictionary of Archaic and Provincial Words* (London: John Russell Smith, 1852) has "*Welbode*. The insect [sic] millepes," and "*Wolbode*. A millepes."

[19] The larva of a hornet (?); more likely a "horned worm" of some kind.

[20] The *dor-worm*, a larva of some sort.

head cut off and a codworm in front, and put them on the hook. Also a bait on the osier leaf, young frogs with three feet cut off at the body and the fourth at the knee. The bait on the hawthorn and the codworm together; and a grub that breeds in a dunghill; and a big grasshopper. In July, the grasshopper and the bumblebee of the meadow. Also young bees and young hornets. Also a great, brindled fly that grows in paths of meadows, and the fly that is among anthills.[21] In August, take wortworms[22] and maggots until Michaelmas. In September, the earthworm; and also take these baits when you can get them; that is to say: cherries, young mice without hair and the honeycomb.

The bream is a noble fish and a dainty one. And you must angle for him with an earthworm from March until August, and then with a butterfly and a green fly,[23] and with a bait that grows among green reeds, and a bait that grows in the bark of a dead tree. And for young bream, take maggots. And from that time forth for all the afterward, take the earthworm and, in the river, brown bread. There are more baits, but they are not easy, and therefore I pass over them.

A tench is a good fish, and heals all sorts of other fish that are hurt, if they can come to him.[24] During most of the year he is in the mud; he stirs most in June and July, and in other seasons but little. He is a poor biter. His baits are these. For all the year, brown bread toasted with honey in the shape of a buttered loaf, and the big red worm. And for the chief bait, take the black blood in the heart of a sheep and flour and honey. Work them all together somewhat softer than paste, and anoint the earthworm therewith—both for this fish and for others. And they will bite much better thereat at all times.

The perch is a dainty fish and surpassingly wholesome, and a free-biting fish. These are his baits. In March, the earthworm. In April, the grubworm under the cow turd. In May, the sloe-thorn worm and the codworm. In June, the bait that grows in an old fallen oak, and the green canker. In July, the bait that grows on the osier leaf, and the grub that grows on the dunghill, and the hawthorn

---

[21] A winged ant, either queen or drone.
[22] Probably a caterpillar that feeds on cabbages.
[23] Probably a green-colored natural fly.
[24] We regret not knowing more about this remarkable observation.

worm, and the codworm. In August, the earthworm and maggots. All the year thereafter, the earthworm is best.

The roach is an easy fish to catch. And if he is fat and penned up, then he is good food, and these are his baits. In March, the readiest bait is the earthworm. In April, the grub under the cow turd. In May, the bait that grows on the oak leaf and the grub in the dunghill. In June, the bait that grows on the osier and the codworm. In July, houseflies and the bait that grows on an oak; and the nutworm[25] and mathews[26] and maggots till Michaelmas; and after that, the fat of bacon.

The dace is a noble fish to catch, and if it[27] be well fattened, then it is good food. In March, his bait is an earthworm. In April, the grub under the cow turd. In May, the dock canker and the bait on the sloe thorn and on the oak leaf. In June, the codworm and the bait on the osier and the white grubworm in the dunghill. In July, take houseflies, and flies that grow in anthills; the codworm and maggots until Michaelmas. And if the water is clear, you will catch fish when others take none. And from that time forth, do as you do for the roach, for usually in their biting and their baits they are alike.

The bleak is but a feeble fish, yet he is wholesome. His baits from March to Michaelmas are the same as I have written before for the roach and dace, except that, all summer season, as far as possible, you should angle for him with a housefly; and, in the winter season, with bacon and other bait made as you will know hereafter.

The ruff is a right wholesome fish, and you must angle for him with the same baits in all seasons of the year and in the same way as I have told you for the perch; for they are alike in fishing and feeding + except that the ruff is smaller. And therefore he must have the smaller bait.

The flounder is a wholesome fish and a noble one, and a subtle biter in his own way. For usually, when he sucks his food, he feeds at the bottom; and therefore you must angle for him with a lying

---

[25] Perhaps the larva of the nut weevil (*Balaninus nucum*), which lays eggs in green hazelnuts or filberts.

[26] Worms or maggots of some kind; cf, *mathe*, "maggot," etc.

[27] Neuter pronoun (!). Fish are generally masculine in this treatise.

ground-line. And he has but one kind of bait, and that is an earth-worm, which is the best bait for all kinds of fish.

The gudgeon is a good fish for his size, and he bites well at the bottom. And his baits for all the year are these: the earthworm, the codworm and maggots. And you must angle for him with a float, and let your bait be near the bottom or else on the bottom.

The minnow, when he shines in the water, then he is better. And though his body is little, yet he is a ravenous biter and an eager one. And you must angle for him with the same baits as you do for gudgeon, except that they must be small.

The eel is an indigestible fish, a glutton and a devourer of the young fry of fish. And because the pike also is a devourer of fish, I put them both behind all others for angling. For this eel, you must find a hole in the bottom of the water, and it is blue-blackish. There put in your hook till it be a foot within the hole, and your bait should be a big angle-twitch[28] or a minnow.

The pike is a good fish, but because he devours so many of his own kind as well as of others, I love him the less.[29] And to catch him, you must do thus. Take a small cod hook, and take a roach or a fresh herring, and a wire with a hole in the end. And put the wire in at the mouth and out at the tail, down along the back of the fresh herring. Then put the line of your hook in after it, and draw the hook into the cheek of the fresh herring. Then put a sinker on your line a yard away from your hook, and a float midway between; and cast it in a hole which the pike frequents. And this is the best and surest device for catching the pike. There is another way of catching him. Take a frog and put it on your hook at the back side of the neck between the skin and the body, and put on a float a yard distant, and cast it where the pike haunts, and you will have him. Another way: take the same bait and put it in asafetida and cast it in the water with a cord and a cork, and you will not fail to get him. And if you care to have good sport, then tie the cord to the foot of a goose, and you will see a good tug-of-war to decide whether the goose or the pike will have the better of it.

---

[28] An earthworm, angleworm.

[29] The sentiment against cannibal fish has been a lasting but not always consistent one among anglers.

Now you know with what baits and how you must angle for every kind of fish. Now I will tell you how you must keep and feed your live baits. You must feed and keep them all together, but each kind by itself and with such things as those in and on which they live. And as long as they are alive and fresh, they are excellent. But when they are sloughing their skin or else dead, they are no good. Out of these are excepted three kinds, that is, to wit: hornets, bumblebees and wasps. These you must bake in bread and afterward dip their heads in blood and let them dry. Also except maggots, which, when they are grown large with their natural feeding, you must feed further with mutton fat and with a cake made of flour and honey: then they will become larger. And when you have cleansed them with sand in a bag of blanket,[30] kept hot under your gown or other warm thing for two or three hours, then they are best and ready to angle with. And cut off the leg of the frog at the knee, the legs and wings of the grasshopper at the body.

The following are baits made to last all the year. The first are flour and lean meat from the hips of a rabbit or a cat, virgin wax and sheep's fat. Bray them in a mortar, and then mix it at the fire with a little purified honey; and so make it up into little balls, and bait your hooks with it according to their size. And this is a good bait for all kinds of fresh-water fish.

Another: take the suet of a sheep and cheese in equal amounts, and bray them together a long time in a mortar. And then take flour and mix it therewith, and after that mingle it with honey and make balls of it. And that is especially for the barbel.

Another, for dace and roach and bleak: take wheat and seethe it well and then put it in blood a whole day and a night, and it will be good bait.

For baits for great fish, keep this rule especially: When you have taken a great fish, open up the belly, and whatever you find in it, make that your bait, for it is best.

These are the twelve flies with which you must angle for the trout and grayling; and dub them just as you will now hear me tell.

---

[30] A kind of heavy woolen cloth.

MARCH

The Dun Fly: The body of dun wool and the wings of the partridge. Another Dun Fly: the body of black wool; the wings of the blackest drake;[31] and the jay under the wing and under the tail.[32]

APRIL

The Stone Fly: the body of black wool, and yellow under the wing and under the tail; and the wings, of the drake. In the beginning of May, a good fly: the body of a reddened wool and lapped about with black silk; the wings, of the drake and of the red capon's hackle.

MAY

The Yellow Fly: the body of yellow wool; the wings of the red cock's hackle and of the drake dyed yellow. The Black Leaper: the body of black wool and lapped about with the herl[33] of the peacock's tail; and the wings of the red capon with a blue head.

JUNE

The Dun Cut: the body of black wool, and a yellow stripe along either side; the wings, of the buzzard,[34] bound on with hemp that has been treated with tanbark. The Maure Fly: the body of dusky wool; the wings of the blackest breast feathers of the wild drake. The Tandy Fly at St. William's[35] Day: the body of tandy[36] wool; and the wings the opposite, either against the other,[37] of the whitest breast feathers of the wild drake.

JULY

The Wasp Fly: the body of black wool and lapped about with yellow thread; the wings, of the buzzard. The Shell Fly at St. Thomas' Day:[38]

---

[31] Feather material, probably from a mallard.
[32] The European jay (*Garrulus glandarius*).
[33] Fibers from the shaft of a tail feather.
[34] The European buzzard, of the hawk family.
[35] The Festival of St. William of York (William Fitzherbert, Archbishop of York, twelfth century) was celebrated June 8.
[36] Possibly "tawny."
[37] With the sections of drake breast feathers set back to back.
[38] Thomas à Becket. This is not the day of his martyrdom (December 29), but the day of his translation, i.e., when his bones were enshrined, July 7.

the body of green wool and lapped about with the herl of the peacock's tail; wings, of the buzzard.

AUGUST

The Drake Fly: the body of black wool and lapped about with black silk; wings of the breast feathers of the black drake with a black head.

These pictures are put here as examples of your hooks:

Here follows the order made to all those who shall have the understanding of this aforesaid treatise and use it for their pleasures.

You that can angle and catch fish for your pleasure, as the above treatise teaches and shows you: I charge and require you in the name of all noble men that you do not fish in any poor man's private water (such as his pond, or tank or other things necessary for keeping fish in) without his permission and good will. And that you be not in the habit of breaking any men's fish traps lying in their weirs and in other places belonging to them, nor of taking the fish away that is caught in them. For after a fish is caught in a man's trap, if the trap is laid in the public waters, or else in such waters as he rents, it is his own personal property. And if you take it away, you are robbing him, which is a right shameful deed for any noble man to do, a thing that thieves and robbers do, who are punished for their evil deeds by the neck and otherwise when they can be discovered and captured. And also if you do in the same manner as this treatise shows you, you will have no need to take other men's fish, while you will have enough of your own catching, if you care to work for them. It will be a true pleasure to see the fair, bright, shining-scaled fishes outwitted by your crafty means and drawn out on the land. Also, I charge you, that you break no man's hedges in going about your sports, nor open any man's gates without shutting them again. Also, you must not use this aforesaid artful sport for covetousness, merely for the increasing or saving of your money, but mainly for your enjoyment and to procure the health of your body and, more especially, of your soul. For when you intend to go to your amusements in fishing, you will not want very many persons with you, who might hinder you in your pastime. And then you can serve God devoutly by earnestly saying your customary prayers. And in so doing, you will eschew and avoid many vices, such as idleness, which is the principal cause inciting a man to many other vices, as is right well known. Also, you must not be too greedy in catching your said game, as in taking too much at one time, a thing which can easily happen if you do in every point as this present treatise shows you. That could easily be the occasion of destroying your own sport and other men's also. When you have a sufficient mess, you should covet no more at that time. Also you should busy yourself to nourish the game in everything that you can, and to destroy all such things as are devourers of it. And all those that do according to this rule will have the blessing of God and St. Peter. That blessing, may He grant who bought us with his precious blood!

PAUL BUNYAN: MY WOOLLY
BUGGER CHUCKING MACHINE

JENNIFER SMITH

BENEATH THE SHADOWS of the rugged Absaroka mountain range near the town of Livingston, Montana, sits a house that looks like it was blown off the movie set of *Gone with the Wind*. Not an unreasonable possibility given the fact that howling wind constantly plagues Paradise Valley year round. The southern-style mansion, owned by the Depuy family, sits near the banks of the famous Depuy's Spring Creek. All who catch a glimpse of the white Grecian columns through the cottonwoods as they travel to and from Yellowstone National Park on Highway 89 weave like drunks as they stare in disbelief at Tara of the North.

As a fly-casting instructor and fishing guide, I have spent many memorable days fishing on my own and with clients on Depuy's Spring Creek near this famous landmark. One client stands out in my memory. He arrived one weekend looking as out of place on the creek as the mansion did. He was built like a football player, broad chest, thick neck—the logging industry could have hired him to uproot trees with his bare hands. He had come to Montana on his honeymoon, and I had been asked by a local fly shop to take the newlyweds fishing. But when I met him in front of Tara, there was no bride in sight. He was Paul Bunyan without his Babe, and I became a bit curious, and at the same time apprehensive about the change in plans.

The newlyweds were staying at a dude ranch thirty miles away. It is the kind of place you would expect to see in Montana. Log cabins house the guests, trail rides and cookouts keep them entertained, and singing cowboys serenade them at dinner. It is a rustic, romantic place nestled in the pine forest above the valley. Guests practice the genteel art of roasting marshmallows over an open campfire and come away satisfied that they have experienced the wild west. Enamored with the atmosphere of the dude ranch, the wife of one week had decided to stay back and rest. I had the feeling I wasn't getting the whole story, but being that it wasn't any of my business I kept my thoughts to myself. My real worry was about getting her groom casting and into fish.

He came outfitted with an ancient rod, patched hip waders, torn vest, dented reel, cracked line and a box of rusted flies—all of his gear generously donated by various dude ranch guests. We donned our waders streamside while the cottonwoods creaked and groaned in protest against the blasts of wind that bent their branches and shook their leaves. The big smile on Paul Bunyan's face as the wind picked up around us assured me he had never been fly fishing before.

Why I started him out on a dry fly I'll never know. It was grasshopper season, and I thought I could get him to drum up a trout or two by slapping a big royal trude on the surface. This way he could see the fly, the fish could hear it, and I could avoid discussing the fine art of matching a hatch that had already been blown into the next county. Mr. Bunyan gave it his best. He held the rod firmly, tried not to break his wrist, punched the cast into the wind and threw off the rod tip into the stream. I scrambled to grab it as it floated by. "Don't worry, this always happens," I reassured him. Rod back in one piece, we continued to battle the elements.

After an hour of tangles and fruitless efforts I felt myself losing hope. This usually doesn't happen. I pride myself on my dutiful patience and cheerful conversation regardless of whatever struggle my client is going through. I have had clients who could not be consoled over the lack of fish, or the fact that their casts spent more time in the trees than on the water. I have had clients take insects that don't hatch and fish that don't rise personally, but I have always managed to stand by, untangle their knots and see them through the end of the day. It takes time to master the sport of fly fishing, and I encourage my clients to keep on trying no matter how difficult it may seem, after all ". . . tomorrow is another day." But on this particular morning, I looked at my watch and calculated a half-day rate. I had planned to give up. I had never given up on anyone before.

I watched my client's line blow in uncontrolled S-curves as he tried to cast. It was exhausting to watch, yet he did not appear exasperated. He kept trying to make it work. Guilt set in. Somehow I had to try and make it work, too. Besides, I had the feeling that Paul Bunyan was enjoying himself.

"I'm going to move you downstream where there are more trees and less wind. I'll put on a weighted woolly bugger. It will be easier to cast. If the wind doesn't let up after lunch, we might have to call it a day," I explained.

He agreed to the plan and we headed downstream.

Despite the limitations being set by the weather and by his skill level, my client proved to be a good sport. He worked hard, asked questions and listened. I admired him for his tenacity. I began to see his potential. I did not want to let him down. It wasn't going to be easy, but I decided I had to get him into one of Depuy's famous rainbows.

I tied on the woolly bugger and reached for my pliers to pinch down the barb.

"What are you doing?" he asked.

"I'm pinching the barb down."

"Hell, don't worry about that. If I get hooked, just rip it out. I can take it," he said with confidence.

"I'm not worried about you, I'm worried about me," I said with a grin.

The moment he cast the woolly bugger weighted with split shot, I knew he was a wet-fly kind of guy. No more match the hatch, it was match the caster to the cast. Wet and weighted was definitely his style. I should have known that something with weight and volume would speak clearly to him. The wind was no longer a problem with this new setup, and soon he really started fishing. Still, an hour later, nothing had tugged on the line.

Paul Bunyan remained friendly and patient. He was determined that nothing would ruin his day. I was determined to see him succeed. Another hour passed. No fish. Eventually he excused himself to go in search of a tree. I stayed on the bank with the unspoken promise to keep my back turned. I have never been able to stand in front of a perfectly good trout stream without throwing a line, so I decided to cast. I picked up the rod and strategically landed the fly right where I wanted. To my surprise and horror, a trout hit it.

Catching fish in front of clients is a big No-No, especially if they haven't caught any yet. I decided it would be a good idea to reel quickly and release it before Paul returned, but too late, I felt his presence at my side. "Would you like to reel it in?" I asked. Immediately I knew I had said the wrong thing. A dejected Paul informed me that reeling it in was what his father let him do when he was a five-year-old. He politely told me it was my fish and stood by as I landed it. Together we admired the bright pink stripe on the seventeen-inch rainbow beauty before returning it to its home down under. "OK, the next one is yours!" I insisted.

Rod still in hand, I was demonstrating how and where I wanted him to cast when I heard the sickening sound of shattering graphite. The rod tip hinged below the third guide and flopped over like a tired rabbit-ear. We had a problem. "You broke the rod!" he chided. I looked at him in disbelief and wiggled the rod back and forth listening to the crunch and crackle of the break.

"I can't believe this," I confessed. Hoping that it wasn't my fault, I asked, "Do you think the woolly bugger hit it when you were casting?"

"Not that I remember," he answered. An uncomfortable silence followed.

"Did you do anything to this rod that might have damaged it?" I quizzed.

"Well, I slammed it in the trunk of the car yesterday, would that hurt it any?"

"Yeah, that would do it," I replied with relief.

We both looked at one another and started to laugh.

"I went to shut the trunk, and it wouldn't close. After two good slams I realized the rod was in the way. I didn't think I had hurt it any." We continued to laugh uncontrollably. Luckily the guy who loaned the rod to Paul told him not to worry if anything happened to it. We both hoped he meant what he had said.

I went to the car and returned with a spare rod, and soon we were back in business. My client began to cast and strip line diligently, minding my every instruction. I had the feeling we were going to get one. I saw the flash and shouted, "Strike!" Paul Bunyan had a fish. I looked to the sky with raised arms and announced, "Yes, there is a God," and then helped Paul steer his trout toward shore. It was a beautiful two-pound rainbow. Photos were taken, praise was showered. I was overjoyed. Paul was overwhelmed by my enthusiasm.

"You're more excited about this fish than I am," he remarked.

"You have no idea," I replied.

Several more trout were caught and released before we stopped for lunch. One poor fish had to sacrifice its jaw upon the setting of the hook. But after all, it was Paul Bunyan we were working with and any lip was going to be a sore lip that came near the fly that day.

Lunch is the time to put away the fly rods and the competitive spirit and relax. It is usually the time I get to answer questions about myself and how I ended up in Montana as a fishing guide. I get to know my clients better, and I enjoy hearing about their lives and what interests them outside learning how to fly fish. As Paul Bunyan and I sat next to the creek eating turkey and swiss sandwiches, the conversation turned to the recent wedding. I was sorry that the bride wasn't there to give me all the details, as I have a fascination with such things, but suffice it to say the groom was delighted with the turnout, the music and the ceremony. He was glad to be on vacation at last and did not want to rush back to work at his auto body repair shop. He owned his own business and talked about how hard he had worked to make a go of it. It seemed to me he worked hard at everything.

During our visit he told me he was glad that he wasn't being guided by a man because he felt less self-conscious around me. He said he felt less threatened by me as well. I was impressed by his honesty and took his comment as a compliment of my abilities to teach and put someone at ease, but as the words sank in, I began to wonder what else he was saying about his experience as a sportsman. Were men always more intimidating and competitive with one another? Are they allowed to enjoy each other's company without being competitive? Are women bringing a less competitive approach to the sport of fly fishing? Because a woman is not seen as a threat, are her skills and experience to be taken as seriously as a man's? I could not help pondering these and other questions that surrounded his statement.

As the last chocolate chip cookie was consumed, I packed up the picnic basket and began to prepare for the afternoon fishing. The wind continued to blow, but not like it had earlier in the morning.

I watched my woolly bugger chucking machine hit the water again and again, but to my dismay the trout would not cooperate. I decided to show him how to cast by quartering downstream and letting the line swing. I moved him onto a new section of stream where the current was faster and proceeded to demonstrate the new technique.

"Here, let me show you how I want you to do this." I took the rod and cast; on the swing a trout hit the fly. By now I knew Paul had a sense of humor, and I started to laugh. Feigning anger, Paul grabbed the rod out of my hands, "Damnit, give me that rod." He proceeded to reel it in himself.

Paul Bunyan had to take another tree break, and again I promised I would turn my back. "Oh no you don't," Paul said accusingly. "Give me the rod." "What?" I replied. "I'm taking the rod with me." And he did. I was left standing on the bank, empty-handed.

We fished until late afternoon and caught several more trout. And if fish could talk, they would express their gratitude at being given another chance at life. Paul Bunyan's strike and retrieve gave the trout the human equivalent of an out-of-body experience. Trout inhaled the fly and reached the surface before they knew what had hit them. Their benevolent captor released them shaken, but unharmed.

At last, evening drew near and the final cast was made. I listened to the click of the reel as Paul spooled his line. We were able to joke about the day's events all the way back to the car. By far it had not been my typical day on a spring creek. A honeymooning groom without his bride, a spring creek without a dry fly fisherman, a client without a rod, a jaw without a trout. But looking at the Depuy mansion, its three-story white columns framed by the Rocky Mountains in the distance, I had to admit there are lots of peculiarities in the world, and strangely enough, somehow, on some days, it all works together.

For a Moment or So

S H I R L E Y   G I L L E Y

In memory of my sister

I CAN SEE A FIELD of corn where the ground should be from where I sit up here on Dad's shoulders. There's where we're headed, past that line of trees. I just love to go fishing. It's early yet and the sun isn't too hot but the bugs are out. I'm glad I don't have to walk. Waking up like this is good because it always seems to take forever to get through this farmer's corn. Already I'm startin' to get excited, but I'll enjoy this ride while I can 'cause Dad's probably gonna get tired of carryin' me soon.

Sometimes up here I think about the Indians and imagine what life would be like if we were them. I sit up real high so I can see all around. And open up my ears so I can hear even the slightest sound. And pretend I'm ridin' on a horse in search of water and a place to camp. I'm gettin' thirsty just thinkin' about it. The further I ride the drier my mouth gets. I think we just have to find water soon, or we'll die.

Maybe the birds will lead us to the river. I watch them closely and see some fly toward those trees. That's where to go. We must go there, I think. I urge my horse on to save us all. Hold on, we must hold on. . . .

I get more desperate with each step Dad takes. He says I wiggle too much. This horse is tired, I can tell. Finally, he just stops. And I climb down leaving my imaginary world behind to stand once again like everyone else.

Even the wind takes a breath while the five of us stand quietly between the rows of corn. "Can you hear it?" Dad whispers. And I
strain with all my face to hear the sound. Only the birds could have
taken us here I think, and I swallow spit to remember slivers of the
dreams I had before. We are saved. We are saved. The words scream
inside my head. We stand for a moment or so to listen for the sound
of the river.

And we're off! I'm chasing my sister, her blond hair hanging
down like silks on corn. She laughs and turns around to see me fall.
Stumbling and scattering little puffs of dirt, I wrestle corn stalks for
the fishing pole I was told I had to carry 'cause it's mine.

Behind me I can hear Grandpa clanking along as he swings bait
buckets from side to side. Sweat trickles down the lines of his face as
he looks up. The sky guides the way like a lantern, leading us through
this tunnel in search of adventure.

Then, with a ball of line rolled up in his hand, Dad catches up to
me. My reel is half empty; a tangle dangles from his net. And for now
the racing halts, as I'm told to stop and take my time.

Walking on. The river, the river, the tide. Stop, take your time. I
repeat the lines over and over to myself in a rhyme. And kick the dirt
on Stop. For the rest of the way I'm lost on the river, the river, the
tide. Stop, take your time.

The banks of the river are steep. My sister and I whoop and holler
restless with freedom. Standing high above the water, we take turns
playing with echoes of ourselves. And send out names of all of us,
Mom, Dad, Grandpa, ourselves. We recognize the voices but in fascination look up and down the river as if expecting to see someone
come out from around the bend.

"Hold on, now watch where you're going." Dad points down toward a muddy slope, dark as black crayola and shiny like a slide.
"That water's swift and it'll pull you under like a fish does a cork," he
says. "Be careful. Remember, we're here to have a good time."

Mom, recovering from the journey, calls us over like a watchful
hen and gathers us around. "You girls stay right here until Daddy and
Papal get the boat ready," she says. "Just look at that big bird up
there. Ain't it pretty? I don't ever remember seeing one like that down
here before."

Part of the fun of goin' fishing is that every time you go there's a surprise. No telling what you're gonna bring up out of that water. And you might even see deer standing along the banks if you're quiet enough. Once I saw an armadillo. And I've often seen squirrels flying and raccoons poking around. I even found a soft shell turtle in Grandpa's overalls pocket once. Just one of those mysteries that keeps me looking in my own pockets, but nothing yet.

The boat bumps against the bank as Mom and Janis and I make our way down the steps Dad dug out with a shovel. I grab a hold of some roots to keep from slipping, but when the roots pull away, I reach for Dad's hand instead.

It takes time to haul everything down and load the boat. Meanwhile, I feel awkward and ugly in this fat orange life jacket that Mom always seems to strap around me too tight. One time, when I was in kindergarten and it was raining outside, Mom made me wear a sweater, a coat and a raincoat with matching bulky red rubber galoshes. I didn't walk up to the school door, I wobbled and tilted side to side from all that weight. The teacher could hardly pull that raincoat off, it was like peeling an orange.

I want a seat of my own, but Mom sits beside me in the boat just in case. We have a John boat. I don't know why it's called a John boat. Why not a Shirley boat or an Ed boat? Oh well, we call the boat Big Blue.

Dad's gonna take us down the river a ways to a place he and Papal caught some catfish last week. It's not far; at least it doesn't seem far to me. Ridin' in Big Blue is like ridin' those horses in front of the grocery store. Only, instead of puttin' in a quarter there's this rope you gotta pull. I've never personally had a chance to pull on that rope, but I think about it sometimes as I watch Dad.

We wave goodbye to Papal. He's got a box full of grasshoppers and hooks and lines in that purse he hangs from his shoulder. If he runs out of grasshoppers, he'll use P&G soap for bait, also in his purse. I swear, catfish will eat anything. Perch are the best though. Especially flatheads, they just love perch. Dad and Papal are saving them for later when they bait out the trotlines. But right now Papal's on his way to set out cane poles along the river's edge.

We have to sit still in Big Blue 'cause if you don't it's likely to turn over. I am reminded of this more than once. Sometimes, I will imagine that the boat does turn over. And when I do, I worry about Mom 'cause she can't swim. And I know she'd do anything to save me. So I remind her to be careful, too.

As we wind around another curve in the river, turtles plop from logs and birds take off. This stretch of the river looks just like the one we just came down. How Dad remembers all these places he's pointing out, I don't know.

"See that big tree in the water against the bank over there," he says pointing as we pass by. "Your Uncle Billy Tom and I noodled a big cat out of there last year. He fought so hard that he pulled me under, and I like to of not come up. He had a hold of my arm clear up to the elbow," Dad says, building up the story with his hands and slowing the motor down.

"What did ya do?" I ask, looking back, my eyes fixed on that place we passed where Dad almost drowned.

"Well sir, I yelled as loud as I could, 'it's got my arm!' And between me and your uncle, we got it loose. But my arm was all chewed up and sure was sore for a while afterwards."

I shiver looking at his arm. "What happened to the fish?" I ask.

"He took off I guess, to grow a little bigger and find another hole in some other log," Dad laughs, moving Big Blue on.

In the spring, my Dad and his brothers go noodlin' a lot. That's when catfish nest to lay eggs in a hole either under a big rock or in some log that's fallen in the water. Usually, you can drop a crawdad or even poke a long stick down into one of these holes and feel a cat moving around in there. But in order to get it out, you gotta dive down and pull that fish outta there yourself. That's noodlin'.

One spring Dad took Janis and me along. We stayed up on the bank watching our uncles and Dad bob up and down among the logs and rocks. We were looking for flat rocks to skip across the water when all at once here they come stepping high across the creek right toward us. Well, something spooked them all right. Leeches. Red bloody ones. Dad gave us lit cigarettes to burn 'em off his back. It was so gross. I think we left not too long after that. And I decided right then and there that I wasn't ever going noodlin'.

We pull the boat up to where we hope the fishing's good and tie it to roots sticking out from the bank. The stories Dad told and I thought of on the way here seem to have kept me from noticing that the rods and reels were getting tangled together. Uh oh. One loose line is all it takes to cause a real mess.

One by one we bait the hooks. I've got big juicy river worms on mine, and between us all, we dangle quite a selection. Grasshopper, frogs and more worms. Now we wait to see what works.

My bobber is red and white, and I have to look away every now and then to keep from becoming dizzy. There's a butterfly waving to me from a branch hanging over the water on the other side. And when the sun peeps in from behind, I can reach out to touch it with my shadow. But I try to keep my eye on my bobber. Already, it's moved from where I saw it last. Any minute now it could go down or take off running. Janis and I have a contest going, each of us trying for the quarter Dad will give to whoever catches the first fish. Fifty cents for the biggest. Janis says since she's the oldest she knows more and therefore has the better chance of winnin'. I say she's full of doo doo. Sometimes she makes me so mad. Mom tells us to be quiet or no one's gonna be catchin' any fish. So, I play with my butterfly and try to concentrate on my bobber the best I can.

Once in a while a bobber will pop under and quickly pop up again. Then, when the line is checked, the bait will be gone. Turtles do this. They're like pickpockets. Sometimes you don't even realize they're there. When you do, they're usually gone before you jerk the hook. It's a good idea to check your hook now and then to make sure the bait is still on. Only problem is, every time you reel in the line, you risk getting tangled up on something below the surface.

Reel in fast, and bring that hook up to the top of the water. I don't know how many times my Dad has told me this. But, remember: my hands aren't so big and capable as an adult's. Still I try but lose hooks anyway. After a while Dad brings it in for me. He's tired of tying on hooks.

Janis doesn't bring her hook in as often as I do. She calmly sits there and has to be reminded to check her bait. I think she's awfully quiet. Too quiet. And I look over to see if she's doing something I'm not. Nope, her line is about as far out as mine. Maybe she's bored and thinking about school or something. I'll just sit quietly, too, and see what happens.

Mom, Janis and I went to the bathroom before we got in the boat. Dad didn't. So now he climbs out of the boat and up the bank so we can't see him.

"Where's Daddy going?" I ask Mom.

"He's going to see a man about a dog," she says.

"What dog?" I ask.

"He's going to the bathroom," Janis tells me and turns to the trees up on the bank.

"Oh," I say and nod my head up and down. So that's what that means.

We sit watching the water again, waiting for Dad to come back, and I'm looking for my butterfly. Then, Mom just starts yelling.

"Grab your pole, grab your pole!" She's pointing crazily over the water.

I look. My bobber is still there, but where is my sister's? "Janis has a fish, Janis has a fish!" I start screaming. "It's a big one, wow, it's a really big one!"

She and Mom both have a hold of the pole, and it's bendin' and jerkin' like crazy.

"Reel it in, reel it in," Mom tells her.

"What is it?" I ask.

The three of us crowd together trying to see what it is. Janis grabs hold of the line, jerks her catch over the side and drops it at our feet.

"It's a snake, it's a snake!" Janis screams and drops the line, shaking her arms toward me.

"Get back, get back!" Mom yells. And we all rush to the far end of the boat screaming. The snake flops around in the bottom of the boat, yanking along with it my sister's fishing pole.

"Edward, come here, help!" Mom yells. "Edward, hurry, it's a snake in the boat!"

Janis and I are standing on the boat seat screaming, and Mom's got her arms around us holding on tight because the boat keeps tilting from side to side.

"Stand still, stand still!" she warns.

"Dad, Dad, help!" Janis and I join in with Mom's cries.

The snake comes closer, causing us all to scream and huddle, and the boat almost sure enough tips over this time.

Down the bank Dad slides. "Stand still!" he yells. "You're gonna fall in. I'm coming!"

Climbing in the boat, Dad grabs the pole. "Betty, hand me that boat paddle," he says. "And it's not a snake, it's an eel. Don't all of you lean over this way or you'll tip the boat over."

Dad holds up the line with this slitherin', fat, grayish, curled-up thing on the end. "An eel," he says, looking as if he's not scared.

"Are you sure?" Mom asks.

"Yes, Betty, it's an eel, we catch one out of here once in awhile," he says calmly.

"Well, kill it and git it outta here," Mom says. "I don't care what it is."

"Well, I gotta git its head down first," Dad says. And every time he hits it with the boat paddle, that thing jumps around and we all go to screaming again.

Finally, Dad picks it up in his hand and holds it over so we can see it real good.

"It's awfully ugly," I say.

"Ooh, will it bite?" Janis asks Dad.

"Not anymore," Dad laughs.

"Well, git it outta here," Mom says. "That thing almost scared us to death," she laughs nervously.

After we all get a good look at the eel, into the river it goes. Part of me is glad that it's gone, but I hold on to the thrill that it caused even though I was really scared. Janis wants to know if there are many eels left in the river. I hadn't thought about that.

We start looking for my pole, but it's nowhere to be found. Dad takes his pole and throws his hook out trying to hook my line that must have gone over the side. We all watch.

In all of the excitement, I didn't notice my own pole. And because of this, I had also missed catching what must have been a really big fish. Dad hooks my line and finds not only my pole but also my hook, which had been taken downstream and gotten tangled up in some brush by something, probably a big catfish. I feel cheated.

Heading upstream, Big Blue takes us back to tell Papal what has happened. I sit here thinking of all the excitement with mixed emotions. On the one hand, I know that the eel will be a moment that I will never forget. But, on the other hand is the fish, my fish, that got away. And as for what and how big it was, I can only imagine. If only I had kept an eye on my pole. I wonder, since an eel is not a fish, will Janis get the quarter?

Coming around the bend, we take our time enjoying the final

stretch of the river. Papal's poles line the banks ready for fish and what will surely be another story. The sun stays behind the trees now, and there's a cool breeze blowing across our tired shadows on the water. I think I see a fish make a wave and hope Dad will carry me across that field of corn on his shoulders.

AHN-KA-TEE

MARYA MOSES

Marya Moses, a Tulalip Indian, was born in 1911 and was one of fif-teen children. She attended Tulalip Boarding School and later mar-ried and had eleven children of her own. Marya fondly remembers traditional Tulalip fishing practices and her many years of fishing in the Pacific Northwest. The following is a transcription of a tape re-corded interview.

MOM WAS EIGHTY-THREE OR EIGHTY-FOUR [when she died]. She had fifteen children and about five miscarriages. We got along real well. We all loved each other. I don't remember fighting even. I suppose it was our mother. I thought from the time I was little until up till I was thirteen [that] she was an angel. The old people would come and spend two, three days with us. And Mom would get out her berries, and then they would tell us Indian stories [around] that long old table. I liked old people. Their values were different. They looked at you for the way you were. They could see—they must have seen what was in you. There's no old people, just me, now. I re-member lots of stuff [from] way back—*ahn-ka-tee*—that's the Chinook for "long ago."

[I can] see that old kettle yet. [Mom] used to cook beans outside on the iron kettle that had three little legs. She'd start ladling it out for us. We didn't serve ourselves; she served us. That way everybody got an equal share. She couldn't read or write, but even townspeople loved her. She was just different than I was. She was just kind and considerate. You would even put your arm around [her]. Not like me; I said I was always different. [Around age thirteen] I started going boy crazy, and she started stopping me, and I got so I didn't like her. Then I think we all kind of started going different ways. But we got along real good, as crowded as we were.

[Mother] had a hard life. [She] had to make sure we were fed and housed and everything, because Pa didn't. We used to sleep four to a bed—feather bed, mind you. We were so poor that we just had a board bed. We lived on ducks, and [Mother] saved the feathers. We all had feather beds and pillows on the floor. She used to get a little bit of stumpage money. There's this mistaken idea Indians get money from the government, which they don't. They were supposed to, but that isn't true. The Bureau of Indian Affairs [let them log] her property, and that forester took 7 percent of that money. So they weren't doing Indians a favor. They were doing themselves [a favor]. They were getting paid plus taking a percentage of the money. She used to get about $50 or $75 a month, which was quite a bit at that time. Everything was so cheap. But I would say *she* made the home, *she* held us together. Even after she was old, she *still* held us together. I don't know if that was good or bad. The only one that broke away from us is my oldest sister. She's in Montana. [The rest of us stayed here.]

My [father] lived to be eighty-three. I think if he didn't drink so much, he would have lived longer. He went on a drunk for three weeks, and then when he come out of it, he had heart failure.

[In the old days] all Indians fished [women and men]. They used to make their own nets [and canoes]. They caught [fish] by the tons. If [a woman's] husband got sick, she'd have set the net, a little net. They'd just have a canoe. They would go out so far and stake it. There was no anchor at that time. Grandpa Moses would make a homemade trap. They made a trap where the fish would go in and couldn't get out. The women did all the work. They caught the fish and cleaned it, they dried it and got their own wood half the time [and then took care of the kids]. Well, that's the old [way. And] them old chiefs sat around and talked about their past glory.

We never wasted anything in that time. They ate nearly all parts of the fish, most parts of it. They told you if you ate the tail of the fish you would marry a chief. They always had little stories. They had hard times long ago. They didn't even waste the spine. You know, when they got through eating the salmon, they'd put the backbone in the basket. Later on, maybe in early spring when times really got tough—you know, freezing—they would make a soup out of that.

[The Indians] lived on fish and ducks. Ohh, the ducks! There were so many that they used to have little traps for them. They'd weave stuff and put it over the marsh. [They'd] clap, and the ducks would fly up and into it. Then the clams—oh, they were plentiful! They watched the moon. [Then] they'd go over to them islands over there [Camano, Whidbey and Gedney]. The women would fix a lunch; then they would go and dry the clams. They'd spend two or three weeks over there drying the clams and preparing for winter. They strung the clams with the cedar inner bark. [There] was just so much around. They dried clams and fish, and they had berries, deers, ducks. The reasons for putting away the clams were for winter use and for trade. They traded dried clams and fish to each other and to other tribes. For example, the Yakima would come down and get dried fish for some blankets, beads and other things. When the white man came they used to go and trade there in Everett. They would holler, "Clams. Clams. Two bits."—that is what my mother told me. They traded to each other, too. They always sold [fish], as far as I know. I mean barter—that's something like selling.

I would say that [for] Indians, since the beginning of time, [fishing] has been important. It was their whole living. The fishing was so important that when the white man made a treaty with us, we asked nothing but to keep our fish, clams and berries. We let all the other, like timber, gold, silver, coal and everything [go]. So you could see how important this fishing was to the Indians here. We asked very, very little in return. Now, it makes me boiling mad when they make it sound as if it is greed when we insist on our fishing rights. The greed is not on our part.

[I have] done a little bit of everything. I would say that Indian women, they all . . . worked at home. Like me, I knit and trade or sell the Indian socks. When I wasn't fishing, I was cutting shake boards. I learned [how to cut shake boards] from working . . . alongside my husband. It was a blessing in disguise, because when he was gone— why, everything turned out wonderful. I got off welfare.

I didn't have a home. Really, I didn't have anything. I had so many children no one wanted to rent to me. After he died, things changed slowly. But I had to work at it. It didn't change by itself. I had to make it change for the good—make a home. I worked in a cannery when my children were little.

[I got into fishing] in '52, I believe. I was left with nine children and two in the service. I got a job cooking for my nephew. [It was] the only thing I could do, because I have no education and all these nine children. Oh, I could start cooking on the beach for them fishermen, and they said they'd give me fifteen dollars each a week. [I was cooking for] a crew, four or five. Oh, they could eat! Oh, criminy! For breakfast, some of them would eat two eggs, some four eggs. One of those guys ate six for breakfast. The crew drank coffee all day long. My children and me, we'd get up four o'clock in the morning and make coffee. Then I had the girls, four of them. They would help do the little dishes and pack water from quite a ways to rinse those cups out.

In about two weeks they didn't catch any fish, and I was supposed to get paid each week. My bill ran up so high that this woman, Mrs. Stiles, told me, she said, "Marya, your bill is $300." I said, "Well, I better look for a job." Mrs. Stiles owned a store on the reservation. She was a kind woman. My bill ran up so high that I said, "I can't cook anymore." Four of them paid me once, and what is sixty dollars for two weeks? So I said, "We're going home." And Tom, my nephew, said, "Hey, Marya, why don't you fish?" He took a little piece of net, about four hundred [feet] and said, "You can have that." So Neil hung it for me and we went home. I was really worried about the bill.

Then, a junkman came along, and he said, "Can I buy your old batteries or anything?" I said, "Sure, help yourself." So he looked around, and I told him my little story, and he was real good. He said, "Say, I got an old boat that got wrecked... in a storm. It ended up over in Camano, and I had to chop off two feet." He said, "It's good, and I'll let you have it for $150." I still don't know where I got the $150. But he took some of my junk and whatever he wanted, and then we kind of horse-traded. Well, I got that little sixteen-foot boat. It had a little teeny engine, [and I had] that little net. So the girls and I [started fishing]; my crew was my daughters. Vicki—she's a nurse now at General [Hospital]—she was the splash girl [and]... she was good. Rachel and April... had the winches. I had a woman crew. They used to say, "Oh, Marya and her all-girl crew." Also, Delbert Moses was bull wincher.

The men used to go way out and drop their net—quite a ways out; they'd drop their net and come in slow. I thought, "Well, gee. They're way out there. Wouldn't take me long to drop in right close."

And I'd come around quick. And here I was corking them in a set. They weren't catching any fish, so they said, "Make a southie." Southie's opposite what the men were doing. So I said, "Southie? Huh uh." And I thought, "Southie? Well, you go south, I guess." But really you were supposed to go the other way. So I made the wrong set, and that's the way the fish were coming—and oh, man! Did I catch the fish! But from there it just kept right on. [When I made the wrong set] they come running out [and] said, . . . "Which way'd you make a set?" I thought, "Hell with you guys. I won't tell you!"

After that they were often kidding me. They'd say, "Let her go, Marya!" and here it'd be a riptide. I didn't know that then. But sometimes it backfired on them. One time at that place over Mission Bay— where them pilings are sticking up—they hollered, "Let her go, Marya!" The tide was running real fast. I really believed them. I went out there, and the net wrapped around the pilings, and my nephew Cecil started cussing. Getting more stubborn, I went out again, and they were laughing. But we caught a whole lot. Boy, you ought to see them move then!

I learned to go way up, enough to compensate for [the tide]. I would be able to make a short set. The men's net was eight hundred feet long. I was able to make three or four complete sets. So, I often corked them three or four times. I didn't know that I was doing that— after all, it's not fair. I made banana sets. I would go right out and come right back in, but I would still catch them. Boy, I started nailing them.

Of course, we worked there. We didn't get rich, but I was able to pay a few of my bills. And then I was able to get off welfare, too. We didn't make that much—like five hundred pounds, where them guys would make tons. But that was a lot to me if I made seven hundred pounds. We only got two bits a pound; we didn't get very much. But them other guys would make tons. But I was so thankful for even that little bit of [fish].

I was very, very thankful. I also didn't think it was my ability or anything out of me. I always thank God for everything. One person made fun of me. "Do you ever watch her? She talks to herself." But I was praying—I'd be saying "Our Father." I never told this, and I'll tell it now. I would say a prayer. I didn't know I'd move my lips. You wouldn't believe it the way I'd also get up there and curse some of them. No kidding. I didn't want them to know what I was doing. It don't matter now. I don't know how [I did it sometimes]; it must've been God that helped me, because my net would be up, but still I'd catch the kings.

Then a man [who had] had a stroke sent for me. [He] said, "I'll sell you my boat and net and everything for $575." He built the boat himself. So I got that [for beach seining], and that's what I'm still fishing with today. It was originally twenty-six feet, but we had to chop it down to about twenty-two. But at that time the price of fish was only eleven cents for chums, and you know, it's quite high now.

I just love fishing. Why, I could be so depressed and be laying there sick with a fever, and I'd start thinking about summer and see the beach and the sea gulls. I could just see it in my imagination. I could see a jumper. Sometime I'd be sitting on a beach having a cup of coffee, and they'd see a jumper. And as old as I am, you'd see me try to run and scramble onto the boat and get out there. To some people, [fishing] might be hard, but to me it isn't hard work. I love it. Even if you offered me a job [that] paid me thousands, I wouldn't take it. I'm not kidding you. I just love it—it's too bad I couldn't be buried at sea.

I like the beach seining. That's my life. I take no part in the gillnet. [It's my boat, but] my sons Gilbert and Danny run it. It's just a twenty-two-foot boat [and they fish] the San Juan Islands, up around there. [The set nets] aren't allowed outside, only in the inner bay [of Tulalip Bay]. I like set-netting, but my bones are—[well], I have to take care of myself. I get cold; my ankle'll hurt, or something like that. It's a lot of fun, and it's a lot of work, too. It's mostly checking your net. You have to check your net, and your hands are in the water all the time. It's too cold to be out there. Beach seining is my life. I love it. It's not so much work to get out there.

[Now, I have] four [helping me with seining]. There's a splash boy, three men on the winches, and myself. I didn't want to pull too much this year. I wanted to mostly relax a little bit, just be out there. I had pulled when it was necessary. Years before, I used to pull right along with the men. I would take the corkline, but I didn't pull on the leadline. This year, I didn't do any of that. My grandchildren are getting old enough. I've got a lot of grandchildren, but I pick out those that really like fishing . . . [and] relieve those that aren't really interested in fishing.

The crew that I pick, they're handpicked. They have to know what they're doing. They've got to take orders. If I say, "Roll it in—fast," or [use] signals [they do it]. They do as they're told. There's four of us. Each one watches for the fish. I've a grandson. He's into it now. Then another little grandson. He will be a splash by next year.

[Here's what I do.] Here's a boat. See, this is a boat now. I go out [from the shore] like that. There's a net now. I'll make a kind of C. I make that bend like that [and the splash], he stays right there and splashes. The fish will come in this way. [Without the splash], they would funnel out like that. But he's right here, and he splashes, and [the fish] come here and they'll go back. He has these paddles—or oars, rather—and he has to keep that up all the time. You hold about five minutes. Ten minutes is the longest you hold your set; that's old tribal regulation. It gives the next guy a chance.

[Now for] beach seining, you have to buy a permit from the tribe. Last year it was thirty-five or fifty dollars. And you get a location—it's six hundred feet—and that's where you fish. I think we are allowed, they said, from mean tide. You know, we own the beach front—all the so many feet there and then so far out. That's where we fish. [The fish will] pass. See, you watch out there for jumpers, or else you could make a blind set; you just go out there and try it. But the fishing hasn't been that good; I don't know what's the matter.

The tribes make their own rules. Each tribe has their own, and the people have a say to that. [At the last general council meeting] the people voted that just a tribal member can fish. But this year, I hope to have it changed so the spouse can fish. They have to be married and live on the reservation if I have anything to say about it. Now, take my daughter that's married to an Oklahoma. She just had a baby, and within a week she had to go and tend to her net, or else have it picked up and she would lose it. Her husband could run the boat, but he could not touch the net . . . and the patrol men were watching, too. This is the first year that I know of them to get that strict. I think they should be. I don't think you should make laws and break them, just because it's your relative. I've always said that. That goes for the white man, too. And, what's the use of having laws if you don't enforce [them]?

I wasn't able to make any money this year [1980], because the damn old state kept shutting us down. Of course, you probably hear them cussing us, too. [I fished] maybe two, three [days this year]. There were game wardens standing right over us, making us turn back the fish—whatever species they wanted. That was hard. If we killed any or caused them to die, they would shut us down. They were right on the fish buyer's boat. If you caught too many [or didn't] follow what [you] were supposed to [i.e., the regulations], they shut [you] down. Why, I'd start out [like] today, and pretty soon they would come out: "It's closed, Marya"—or something like that.

And now I feel as if we are being denied this one [and] only thing that we ever asked, and we are made to sound as if we're culprits— greedy, diminishing it, and all that. Where I feel as if it's just certain people like them sportsmen, you know. I don't know if you've ever seen it. I have. I've hauled in fish with the mouth ripped open, where them fellows get out there, and they'll hook it, [then] they throw it back. Them poor things. Sometimes it's in the eye. No. What gets me is how we've never asked anything. And what is the fuss? Long ago they used to sneer at us "fish-eaters"! It was almost a disgrace, be- cause in them times . . . they looked down at you. Now it's real ex- pensive.

[When I first started fishing, things were different.] The [white] people that lived here all the time, they were real good. They knew what they were getting into. They were living on the reservation, and they didn't mind it. They liked the wild, the trees, and most liked the same things we do. They bought land here years ago for ten, fifteen, twenty dollars an acre. They've made their homes here and they like it here. The third generation—like my daughter's generation—they started selling land, and they sold it cheap. That's what you see build- ing up now. Now, a lot of the [rich ones from Seattle] have homes here. They come here, and they have skis and power boats, and ohh . . . that makes a lot of difference. They could scare the fish right away from you. They know it, too. Some of them [have] even run over my net and cut it. There's no sense to it. Here's a beach like this, and we are allowed out so much. And here's a whole bay, and they come around like that [on purpose], at full speed. You know, them Boeing workers and different ones [with] high-paying jobs have great big boats, and their little brats have them speed boats. And oh, that bay looks like a town, there's so many [boats]. Of course, they could afford it; they're making a lot of money. I hate to see any more of them come here.

There is [money to be made], but you really have to work at it. You have to live and breathe it. You make money, [but it] goes right back into it. Now, you'll notice there's a light on that gillnet boat. We give it a light all night—night and day. . . . [to] make sure she don't get damp inside. Four thousand dollars went right back into that [gillnet boat] for next year. Now I'm down, my money's down again. You can't just go out there and make money. You have to watch your equipment. Last year, I bought nets—over six thousand. That isn't the hanging twine; [so] you pay a man for hanging it—five hundred, some four hundred. You make money, but you put out a lot, and you're thinking about it all the time.

I find my children are coming to it, even the ones that didn't like it. There's one daughter—she wouldn't even eat fish, but now I see she's got her own little boat. She's working up to it. And when they say, "Mom, can I have corks? Can I have this or that?" I say, "Listen, I worked and earned everything I got. If I help you. . . . " You know, it isn't good to give kids everything. Let them earn it like I did. Now that sounds kind of mean, but. . . it's a cold world out there. You have to be able to stand up and can't be fainting every time somebody speaks tough to you and all that. Maybe now [the children] are bragging because they had to work. I think they sound proud.

Two of my [daughters] have gone into it [and two sons]. They even learned to hang the net; they have their own net, and that's something. They got a little teeny boat, and they set net. See, they're just starting out like I did. I don't want to deny them all the enjoyment. [Finding out themselves], that's the best part of it. They'll be so proud when they get old and look back on it.

sapphire sea

CARLETTA WILSON

landscape
like cloud not cloud but smoke
like smoke not smoke but mist
like mist but not mist
clinging rock to rock
black rock/jet rock/jagged night-hued boulder
half-glimpsed and rising
ancient mountainous pools of rock
rock at every side piercing
this farflung vaporish land
i running cast bait into earth clear as cloud
mark them HUNGER FRAGMENT TREASURE
the porcelain fog trembles
the hazy canopy parts
on my line i find fish
large spinning fish
spinning birds of the nether regions
peculiar cyclic beings of the worlds
that lie under the world surging up
striking deep spreading out to form
the unformed girl

yes
i cast my line
my silver thread flew the air
a wire so pure so tried
a web and i the spider
casting bait into open night air
where voices arose glistening
rippling the phosphorous atmosphere
then reeled and fell
that autumn on a black coral night

near the barnacled coasts
before the widening purple water
water as deep as dark
in streams of air
scented kelp/snail/shark/whale

no other night but this
would i stand before you
but this is the strangest memory
this waving water this slippery lake
as the fluid begins drifting
through the vessels of my body
restless against this shell
of skin and bone in a sea red
and covered however bound to its craterous home
i am a ship
another moonscape
a sudden deepwater metallic with flesh
fish-eyed graygreen
a west philly girl in a summerflowered dress
on no other night
but this can i say
how i stood on the shore
and while i stood on the shore
i swam that lake
that while i swam that lake
i stood on the shore
through the air my voice beckoned
from the water my voice called
as men with their rods leaning
tossed their hooks their shining bait
i wanted both
the succulent leaning
the shining bait

til my flesh could take no more
and i shimmered out out of the dark-uneasy

at/once the surface spiked-with-light
startled into circles
every movement flew
pistols of graygreen dashed-dark and pivoted
rays of the open-beneath flashed
within the spray i cried
whole-mouthed/gasping
swallowing the silty shore as sullen sounds swirled
into a clumped/down yawning mood
and the stunning poison
bright/quick/touching sprung alive and i
dove into the deep above while
the late hours stretched away and the living world
the world i was living tumbled away
beneath waves beneath waves beneath waves

no other deceiving beach would receive me
except this this dangerous shore
where i have been caught and cleaned
the flesh of my mouth
pulled back in a swirl of force and my body
my silver lake my sapphire sea
cast asunder tossed and thrown
by fishermen leaning into buckets
scattering my interior vessels my organs my bones
into shallows where schools of fish
swim and turn and women with hands
crimson/stained shake and fan
their damp worn clothes

veiled in sand/hung in crevice
a feast for whatever saunters by

i lie
in the shadows of boulders
beneath the moon's watchful eye
and yet as i am i am consumed
by my own ungarnished hand a hand that flowers
into huge nodding tiger lilies
within whose petals grow gorgeously finned fish
fish with scales like sequins
mouths red as budding rose
for they are pistils within the petals
stamens upon the stalks
swimming towards my beckoning mouth
a mouth as deep as the sea is dark

ONE FOR THE GLASS CASE

LEWIS-ANN GARNER

M Y INITIATION to the gentle art of fly fishing took place at the
tender age of six. A family holiday had been decided. We were
to go to Scourie in Sutherland, Scotland. The hotel there offered
access to more than two hundred lochs to visiting anglers, all con-
taining fighting wild brown trout, ranging from tiddlers to monster
five-pound fish.

I honestly thought my parents were joking when an eighty-year-
old rod, made with wood from the greenheart tree, was thrust uncere-
moniously into my hands. I had already endured a four-mile hike in
the driving rain and wind to arrive at this windswept expanse of water.
Number one on my parents' hit list. At my young age it seemed more
like an endurance test than a pleasant hike over moorland. I was
more intent on finding out what was for lunch and building a harbor
to float heather boats in.

My mother had made up my first cast, which consisted of one fly,
a Greenwell's Glory. My father pointed at my eight-year-old brother,
who was casting further down the edge of the loch. He patted me on
the head and said, "Go and do likewise." My first attempts at casting
were not spectacular—the line was immediately thrown back in my
face by the jeering wind. I persevered though, curious to know what
all the excitement was about.

As a child my bedtime stories had not been of princes and drag-
ons, but of fishing. My favorite was of Miss Ballentine and her

sixty-four-pound salmon, caught in 1922. Unlike most tales, it was
true. She and her gillie father were having a quiet evening's fishing in
a boat on the Glendelvine Beat of the River Tay in Scotland when
the monster took her fly. It is reputed that it took three hours to land
the fish, and in the process they were dragged half a mile downstream
in the boat. A cast was taken of the salmon and placed in a glass case
for all the world's envious anglers to see. Many other fish worthy of
mounting in a glass case have been caught since, but none has yet
matched Miss Ballentine's salmon. I always wondered as a wide-eyed
child if perhaps in some river or loch there awaited a fish like that for
me.

Although I did not catch a monster fish on my first day, I did
catch my first wild brown trout. This was much to the amazement of
the rest of the family, who, I hasten to add, remained fishless that
day. Even more to their utter horror and disbelief, after landing the
fish I carefully dislodged the hook, kissed the fish and returned it to
the water. This was the start of my fishing career. I was hooked. The
sight of that first fish erupting in a boiling eddy of white water will remain a treasured memory. It was the experience of a lifetime. One of
them anyway.

Over the next ten years I visited many remote and desolate areas
of Scotland with my family, which now included another brother
and sister. I moved on to a bigger rod, and the greenheart was sadly
passed on to the younger members; we each caught our first fish with
it.

My last fishing holiday with them all was on Benbecula, a tiny island linked by two causeways to North Uist and South Uist, magical
islands of the Outer Hebrides. I was a rebellious teenager at the time.
All my friends were going to exotic holiday resorts in search of sun,
sea, sand and romance. They would all arrive back at school in the
autumn with fabulous suntans and tales of holiday loves. I would be
seeing sun, sea and sand on Benbecula, but the chances of meeting a
gorgeous suntanned boy who was dying to fall in love with an over-
weight, spotty sixteen-year-old were pretty slim. I consoled myself
that this was the last family fishing holiday and even, in my adolescent fashion, managed to look forward to it.

We sailed from Skye, our faces eagerly turned westward in anticipation. Our vigil was rewarded with the sight of the majestic moun-

tains of North Uist, which rose from the sea in a purple haze. After disembarking at the bustling little town of Lochmaddy, we made our way across the causeway onto Benbecula.

Dying embers of the sun bathed the rugged landscape's blazing carpet of purple heather and warmed the icy waters of the hundreds of lochs and lochans, making them shimmer in the evening breeze. The sight would set any angler's heart pumping. Darkness had not quite fallen when we arrived at our holiday destination, a caravan that must have seen better times. It was standing, sentinel-like, in the middle of a field with guide ropes anchoring it to the ground. We learnt that winds of more than eighty miles per hour are not uncommon. The interior of the caravan was not much better, and it looked as if every earwig on the island had decided to holiday there, too. We settled ourselves in as best we could and retired to bed, each of us dreaming what tomorrow might bring.

On the first morning we were silent as we assembled our rods and tackle. It was a silence demanded by the breathtaking beauty that surrounded us. A fortnight was too short to do justice to all the water on these islands. Perhaps the most beautiful of all the lochs we managed to visit were the world-famous machair lochs on South Uist. These limestone lochs contain some of the finest and most elusive wild brown trout in Scotland, if not the world. The shores were covered with emerald green grass and a riot of wild flowers. Milkwort, bugle, purple orchid, buttercup and speedwell all vied for space. The haunting cry of curlew in the hazy summer skies echoed above the gentle lapping of water. In the mountains lying to the east, golden eagles sought out their prey in the vast wilderness. Our days on the machair lochs were pure magic.

Lochs on Benbecula have their own private beauty. They are strewn across the island like the strands of a spider's web. I still have a date there with some elusive sea trout who came swimming in a shoal into the sea loch where I was fishing. They were barely ten feet from the shore and were leaping and rolling in the water, turning it white. No matter what fly or prayer I used, they eluded me. Only the deepening shadows of Hebridian night forced me to tear myself away. All thoughts of the cold that had quietly crept into my body, tightening its hold with the dipping rays of the sun, were forgotten. The gnawing hunger pangs vanished as the sea trout came laughing and playing into view. With each jump they seemed to taunt, their silver bodies gracefully carrying them through the water. It did not really matter that I had not caught that sea trout to fill my still-empty glass case. I felt lucky enough just to have enjoyed the spectacular show they put on, for my eyes only.

Fortunately, I did not spend the whole holiday fishless. In fact, we all managed a few trout. As our deluxe caravan did not contain a freezer, everything we caught we ate. This was usually breakfast, when we were discussing, or rather arguing, where to go next. Mum and Dad would want to walk for miles to a loch, big brother Blair demanded fishing within easy reach of a pub, little brother Charles wanted to stay with Blair, and little sister Jean wanted easy walks and good paddling. I just wanted to fish. What usually happened was that we would all start at the same loch, and then Mum and Dad would wander off, Blair would soon disappear with Charles in hot pursuit, and Jean and I would spend the day together fishing and playing by the water's edge. Come evening the others would reappear with their catch for the day and stories of the ones that got away. On that holiday I learnt that fly fishing is not all about catching fish. The real pleasure is just being there.

When we returned from that holiday, my boyfriend of the time had found another love. To cheer me up, my father took me fishing on Loch Watten in Caithness. It was blowing a typical Caithness breeze, around force ten. At the end of the evening he had a sore back from all the rowing he had done and no fish to show for it. I had fared slightly better: I had caught two fish, one oar, one nose and one jacket sleeve. His scowling face resembled that of a Nordic invader, especially with the designer bloodstains enhancing his features. The outcome of this was that he decided I should have casting lessons, from him. Two evenings later the wind had dropped, and father announced that it was time for lesson one. The venue, our front field, a vast open expanse of grass. As we climbed the gate, all able-bodied sheep fled to the furthest corner, rabbits raced to the nearest available burrow, moles abruptly changed course and headed for Australia. I ignored all this hostility from the animal kingdom and, clutching my rod, proudly marched to the center of the field. Father huddled in behind me and started working my arms like I was a puppet. Obviously a puppet with its own mind, and object I did to his bellowing instructions as I frantically lashed at the air, grass, his ears, his neck and any other piece of his anatomy that was exposed. Of course I apologized for any damage I'd inflicted on him, but it was not my fault he was two feet taller and had such prominent facial features.

In a huff he stomped off, and I carried on, trying to remember what he had taught me. Once I was sure that no trout would be able to sleep easy again, I headed home. Needless to say the lessons ended as abruptly as they had started. To this day I enviously watch anglers handling their rods with grace and poise, though I have to smile quietly to myself when I hook yet another fish. Father, who has great experience with my casting, calls it luck, as any fish that doesn't hear my flies landing on the water must be stone deaf. I personally like to call it skill. Now if we are out fishing together, he stands well back from me; his only other option is to buy shares in a bandage company.

After leaving home, I married a man as keen on fishing as I was. I well and truly landed on my feet. Not only is he a first-rate companion, but he can also tie excellent casts and still find time to repair the holes in my wellies.

Every angler will tell you a story of the fight they have had, the one that got away, and in those few lucky tales, the one that didn't. Few, including my husband, will confess that one fish they thought they had so brilliantly hooked turned out to be a piece of wood. It was his first attempt at salmon fishing. He had been lucky enough to be asked for a day on the famous South Esk River in Eastern Scotland. Unfortunately, the stretch he was fishing allowed only three anglers a day. We had played cards for the privilege, and he had won. I was to be only a spectator. Leading up to his day out, he had practiced casting with two hands, had equipped himself with innumerable killer flies and had filled his hip flask with Scotland's other famous asset. He at last deemed himself ready for battle with the swirling waters of South Esk.

About lunchtime, his frenzied cry for assistance could be heard all the way up the glen. Knowing him better than most, I realized that he had not fallen afoul but was in dire need of assistance. If he was neck-deep in the water, I should hurry, but if there was a fish on the end of his line, then it was flat out running. By the time I arrived, he was standing, looking rather sheepishly at a four-foot-long piece of wood. I offered to weigh it for him; after all it did take some skill in getting it ashore. Without a backward glance, he started fishing again, and I discreetly withdrew.

To this day I find that nothing can quite match the pleasure of camping by the side of a remote Scottish loch and spending the days walking the surrounding countryside, looking for wild flowers, otters, deer, golden eagle and osprey. And in the quiet evening, when fish come to the surface to feed, casting my line in the hope of catching breakfast for tomorrow. When the curtain of night finally falls, by the light of lamps, I lose myself in the history of the Highlands. I sometimes forget that I am in the twentieth century and not an ardent Jacobean supporter trying to help Bonnie Prince Charlie escape the English and flee to France.

For me there is no finer sport than fly fishing. It does not matter if I don't catch a fish. All that is important is that I am by the water's edge with my rod and nature as companions. Whenever a fishing holiday is over and it is time to leave, a part of me remains forever lost in that heathery mountainous wilderness.

And so, to all anglers, no matter what you fish for, I wish you prosperity and a fish or three for the glass case.

THE FISHING HOUR

BETSY BROWN

THE FIRST TIME I WENT fishing was in May 1967, when I was
ten years old. I have forgotten many things about this important
event, but the one thing I'm sure of is that I didn't catch any fish.

I lived in northeast Philadelphia, in a neighborhood called Fox
Chase. As you can tell from the name, before it became part of the
city, Fox Chase had been a popular vacation place for wealthy Phila-
delphians who liked to hunt.

It was, and still is, an all-white neighborhood with tree-lined
streets and big, brick or stucco houses, most of them dating from the
1920s. My mother was a civilian scientist for the army. The father of
the family next door was a repairman for the gas company (this was
before "repairpersons"), and the guy down the street was a long-haul
truck driver. Mrs. Geyer lived next door on the other side. I don't
know what she'd done before she retired, but I do know that she'd
moved from Germany after the First World War. She thought war
was horrible and was always after me to stop playing with toy guns.

Fox Chase had a legacy from the old country-estate days—two
nice, large parks. Burholme Park was only a couple of blocks away,
but the creek there was too shallow for anything but minnows. For a
creek big enough for real fishing, I would have to go to Pennypack
Park, which was a mile or two from my house.

I'm not sure how I got the idea I wanted to go fishing. Maybe it
was because I knew my dad liked to fish. A little bit of his fishing gear

was in the basement in an old, black, square metal lunch box. My Aunt Libby always used to say I wanted to be a boy because I knew my father had wanted a son—and I always tried to live up to what Aunt Libby expected of me. But as much as I missed my father and wished I could remember him, I didn't want to be like him. No one ever told me this, but somehow I knew that my father had been a weak man, and this was probably why he'd died.

As hard as I wished, it was clear to me that I was not going to turn into a boy. And while I didn't have words for it, it was also clear to me that there was no place in the world I knew for a girl like me to become a grown-up woman. My mother had also been a tomboy, and everyone had been surprised when she'd finally gotten married at the age of thirty-six. But now she said the best years of her life were the nine or ten years she'd been a housewife. Aunt Libby said the same thing would happen to me. I could only hope she was wrong.

The most realistic plan I had was that maybe I could move to Alaska and be a bush pilot. If I didn't have to deal with people, then I wouldn't have to be normal. I loved the outdoors, and I wanted to know how to survive in it. Maybe I wanted to go fishing because knowing how to catch fish would help me survive in the wilderness.

My mom didn't object to any of this. She let me play with toy guns, although she told me years later that this made her nervous. She was one of the leaders of my Girl Scout troop, and sometimes she and I would go on hikes together. And she helped me get my fishing gear.

There wasn't much fishing gear left in Dad's lunch box. So Mom took me to the S&H Green Stamp store, where we traded a couple of books of green stamps for one of those Zebco spin-casting rod and reel sets that came already threaded with fish line. Somewhere else we got sinkers, hooks and bobbers, as well as a little plastic yellow box for bait.

I planned to set out on my first fishing trip very early on a Saturday morning. The night before, I went out in the backyard to catch night crawlers. It had rained earlier, or maybe the grass was just wet with dew, and dozens of night crawlers had climbed out of the ground to breathe. I don't know how I'd found out you could do this, but I took a flashlight and my little yellow box filled with dirt and walked through the grass as softly as I could. I knew that if the worms felt the vibrations from my footsteps, they would disappear into the soil before I even saw them. And I had to be very careful with the flashlight beam. I'm pretty sure that worms don't have eyes, but I remember that once the light fell on them, they'd know something was wrong, and I'd have to grab very fast or ZIP! they'd be gone.

Grabbing hold of the worm was only half of catching it. Or rather, grabbing the worm sometimes meant catching only half of it. If I grabbed it too late, after most of it was back in the ground, and then pulled too hard, the worm would break. Or sometimes the worm would win the tug-of-war and escape entirely. The trick was to squeeze pretty hard and then twist a little bit. That would usually budge it.

Worm hunting was an exciting game, although I regretted condemning the poor things to death. It didn't take long before my container was filled with all the worms I thought I could use.

Then I hurried to pack my lunch and set out my gear so I could get to bed as early as possible. I set the clock radio for four o'clock and went right to sleep. I didn't sit up in bed and secretly read my sister's *Anne of Green Gables* books, as I usually did. When I closed my eyes that night, I still saw worms in the grass.

I think the clock radio was playing Simon and Garfunkel's "Mrs. Robinson" when I woke up on Saturday morning. I shut it off quickly to keep it from waking my mother in the next room. I remember sleepily gathering things together in the kitchen downstairs, but I don't remember eating breakfast. Maybe I was in too much of a hurry.

I almost never got to be awake at four o'clock in the morning, and it was magic. It was much darker than dawn, but it wasn't quite nighttime anymore. It was damp and peaceful and quiet, and it had rained again in the night, because the sidewalks were wet and the sky was a little bit cloudy.

All the cars were parked and the houses were quiet as I walked through the neighborhood. There may have been a light or two on, but I don't think so. As I reached Oxford Avenue, with its darkened drugstores, hardware store, and five-and-dime, I had yet to see a moving car. At the intersection with Pine Road, the traffic lights still changed from green to yellow to red, although there was no traffic to see them. It was like being in fairyland or in a science-fiction movie.

I think I would have waited for the light to turn in my favor before I crossed and headed down Pine Road toward Pennypack Park. My mother had taught me always to obey the law.

For half a mile or so, until I reached Susquehanna Avenue, Pine Road was pretty much like a normal city street. Then it curved down into the woods, which, despite the name of the road, consisted mostly of deciduous trees. I could almost pretend I was in the country. Except that morning, I didn't feel like pretending anything.

When you're a child, your life does not belong to you. Someone else tells you what to wear and what to eat and what opinions (if any) you're allowed to express and when to get up and when to go to bed and when to go to school, where they browbeat you into being as normal as they can make you. And as much as my mother encouraged me to be independent, I still felt my powerlessness. So, in those precious hours when my time was most my own, I often pretended to be someone else, someone who was not a skinny weird little girl who was scared of almost everything. I pretended to be a soldier or a cowboy, like the men I saw on TV, who were powerful and bold and whose weapons never misfired or ran out of ammunition.

But as the edges of the sky started to turn light and as the roosters crowed again and again on somebody's farm outside the city limits, I did not want to be anyone but myself. I would say now that what I had that morning was an intuition of what it could be like to be someone who was not a "normal" girl, and someone who was not out of place, and someone who did not want or need to imitate the celluloid machismo of Vic Morrow or Clint Eastwood. Although it was years before I recovered it, I had a premonition that it might be possible to be a womon instead of a woman. I had a premonition of what it might be like to be a dyke. And for reasons I have never known, that morning in the dark in the woods on Pine Road, I was very excited, and maybe a little bit nervous, but I was not afraid.

I followed the road to the bottom of the hill, took the sharp turn to the right and proceeded the quarter mile or so to the entrance of the park. I do not remember there being any other fisher folk there in the beautiful ghostly gray light. Crossing the footbridge over Pennypack Creek, I followed the main trail until I found a place I wanted to fish. Not that I had the faintest idea of what might be a good place.

It wasn't too hard to bait a hook. I just didn't think about how the worm might feel. I had no idea of how to cast, though. Sometimes I got my hook into the water in kind of the direction I'd intended, though never as far as I wanted. Once or twice I got the line tangled in a tree. It didn't matter. There was no one to make fun of me.

Eventually, the sun rose high in the sky, and I got bored and sleepy, so I let the rest of the worms go and walked home. I'd snagged on the bottom a couple of times, lost a couple of hooks and thought perhaps I'd had a couple of nibbles. But I hadn't caught any fish, hadn't even gotten a definite bite. I think I may have been surprised to discover that I didn't care about that, either. Now I'm grateful that I didn't somehow get a fish out of that creek. I think factories dumped waste in it upstream, and the water was pretty rank.

In my mother's retirement apartment in the Lutheran Home at Germantown, on the bureau in her bedroom, tucked into the corner of the frame of my high school graduation picture, is the picture my girlfriend took of me holding up the biggest fish I've ever caught—a nine-inch bluegill taken from a duck pond off the Willamette River in Eugene, Oregon.

Mother and I have discussed my first fishing trip, and neither of us can figure out why she would have allowed a ten-year-old to go out to Pennypack Park by herself at four o'clock in the morning. My mother thinks she made a mistake. If so, I'm glad she did.

Thoughts from a Fishing Past

JANNA BIALEK

IN MY FAMILY, a thirteenth birthday decided not whether a child was an adult, but whether he or she would become a fisherman. At that age we were allowed to accompany our grandparents on their annual trek to southern Ontario, joining that mysterious fraternity of fishing people that only an adolescent could covet with such romantic imagination.

Although my grandparents had seen to it that we were not strangers to the water (I will admit to actually having swum in the Ohio River) or to fishing (strictly small-time pond stuff), none of us could anticipate what was in store on the fishing trips we had waited twelve years to take. Logic told us that there must be some exotic, inherently adult secret about fishing that our family was keeping from us, or else they would not have denied us this experience until we were "old enough."

It has been eighteen years since I last went on one of these trips. I have been fishing many times since, but it is not the same. These Canada summers were not typical family vacations; to my grandparents it seemed almost incidental that other people were along. We were there to fish.

It is hard for me to imagine the kind of person I'd be were it not for this experience, or even to fully understand what all those fishing summers gave me. Many of my strongest memories are of sensual things: smells, sounds and feelings that touched me in some way.

Like the feeling of being sunburnt, of letting the sun warm my skin until it was hotter than my blood and would goose-pimple at the mention of a shower. The nearly audible sound made the first time I punctured a hook through the skin of a rockbass. Or the sweet, oily smell emitted from our Johnson motor. Clothes, too, carry special remembrances. Bracing against cold summer mornings required dressing like a coat rack, layer upon layer, a bathing suit underneath. Donning a certain nylon one-piece suit even today gives me a momentary subconscious chill, anticipating the sweaters, flannel shirts, shorts and sweats I would need to be warm again.

But my most striking memory is, of course, that of taste: of freshly caught pike, lightly dipped in cornmeal and fried gently in butter. Of sun-warmed blueberries gulped down by the handful. The "tastes" of being sunburnt, exhausted, starving and pleased with yourself, combined with the freshest and most delicate culinary experiences nature can offer.

Our guide on these trips was always Cecil, a handsome Indian with white hair and only one leg. Although after thirty-three years my grandfather knew the waters of northern Lake Huron in his sleep, he would not go fishing without Cecil, would use no other guide in his absence. This strong man was mysterious and slightly sexual (I suppose that anything mysterious is sexual during early adolescence), yet also a comfort against my grandfather's impatience and inflexibility. For long hours Cecil would sit in our boat, watching the water, never giving advice but always knowing exactly the right thing to do if asked. He was part of the machinery that kept us fishing, but more than that, he made what we were doing seem somehow very old and important.

There was a pattern to our fishing days, one which probably had changed only minutely over the decades my grandparents had spent making this trip. I was a Dr. Spock baby, unused to day-in and day-out rituals that carried no spirit of negotiation, no intrinsic flexibility or democracy. Looking back, the sameness of this routine had a timeless beauty, like a blueprint designed to offer maximum resistance to the forces of change. My grandfather had a genius for the routine, for putting together what was needed to make an experience memorable.

So every morning we packed the boat, drove to the shallows for minnows, which we caught with a big net and oatmeal, then under the little low bridge to a cove for rock bass, perch and other bait fish we were not legally entitled to use. By eight o'clock we were out into the open lake for four or five hours of pike, muskie and maybe walleye fishing before lunch.

Lunch was a short break on one of the thousands of tiny, rocky islands, eating bologna sandwiches and maybe finding a windfall blueberry patch for dessert. Early on I learned to use this time to give my legs sufficient exercise to withstand another four hours of sitting in the boat.

Of course within the sameness of this routine were a few diversions: stories, water fights, being thrown off the boat for no reason. Each of us at one time experienced a lost fish, occasion for communal grief and penetrating silence as we considered the foe which was at the same time so much bigger yet also smaller than each of us.

One of my grandfather's gifts was knowing when to quit, knowing when we would get too sunburnt, knowing the instant before we were ready to hate fishing forever. Although the summer sunset was a few hours away, the quality of the light, of the water and air, was laden with the end of the day. Thousands of sea gulls would accompany us, anticipating a feast of purple and red entrails as we stopped on a small, rocky island to clean our catch. Everyone begrudged them this meal; they were the thieves who took our bait, who warned our catch that we were coming. But sea gulls, too, were part of the scheme, a shared enemy and subject of story, a clean-up crew that reminded us that they, too, required fishing to live.

Evenings had their own small excitements: the itchy tingle of a shower against my sunburnt arms; the feel of clean, soft clothes and the earthy, wonderful smell of dirty ones. The recognition and prestige earned by a good day's catch. Being with people I not only loved, but with whom I had now shared something exhausting and important and fraternal. I was never eager to go to bed; for this I paid with ridicule about my inability to get up in the morning.

The simple rhythm of these days was one of the things my grandparents lived for, something I did not appreciate and for which I now long. But at the time I felt that my presence, as the first female grandchild, had altered this family tradition somehow. Perhaps I overheard, or just felt inside, that "It was only fair that I be allowed to go." Simple justice, not some grand scheme, brought me on these trips. That my joining these trips could be controversial saddened and confused me; since I saw no difference between my interests and capabilities and those of my male cousins, I was shocked that others would.

But as much as I hate to admit it, my presence did cause some changes. My grandmother, as loyal an angler and good a sport as ever was, could now (with the right amount of urging) step away from this hard day's fishing, ostensibly to watch over and protect me from an overload of male bonding and fish guts. I have often wondered about her motives for patiently accompanying my grandfather on these trips every year, making the arrangements and the sandwiches, cleaning the boat, doing the thousands of things that made our vacation so effortless. Certainly she loved fishing, loved it as much as anyone, my grandfather included. Certainly she loved my grandfather. But it took more than love to make such a trip, to put in so many hours of work with so little appreciation given in return. During those long hours of sitting on the boat, while the guide and my grandfather and cousins and I fished, she fished, too, but also cleaned the fish box, kept track of the mountains of clothes stripped off as the day got warmer, parceled out lunch, stowed away gear and did countless other things the rest of us were too selfish to notice. Looking back on vacations I have taken with only my husband and child, the logistics of packing and planning and organizing such a trip seem a minor miracle, like an art that seems deceptively easy when demonstrated by a genius.

In truth, the intense level of fishing my grandfather practiced often *was* too much, not more than I could take, certainly, but rather more than I was willing to take. The incredible beauty of the Georgian Bay, of totally solitary wilderness, offered too many opportunities. Together, my grandmother and I would collaborate on schemes to break away, to spend a lizard's afternoon casting off the rocks on one of the tiny, empty islands. Or stealing up a hillside for the joy of the climb and the view. Hours later, waiting to be picked up from an island, we were not the least remorseful about spending the day, as my cousins termed it, "doing nothing." The teasing I took for such indulgences reminded me of my different status, that men and women had different rules for play.

Although I liked fishing as much as any of my cousins, I did not like their exclusive, deny-yourself-any-other-experience version of it.

Too much was missed: the little village where great sailboats stopped and the store owner wore a kilt, the onion sandwiches and blueberry cobblers and the perfect aloneness of a rocky hillside where a mink could crawl around unafraid. Maybe my male cousins wanted these things, too, but were too boxed in by my grandfather's expectations to allow themselves the joy of any other experience. My grandfather approached a day without fishing as some sort of lunatic idea; he had come 750 miles to fish, and that was what he did.

When I think about it, though, there *is* something about fishing that promotes the kind of exclusive passion my grandfather felt. Too many hours of sitting under the hot sun, my mother would say. Sitting, for hours, is part of it. Long thoughtless and thoughtful hours with no guaranteed reward require that only the serious need apply. What other pursuit would demand so much and give so little back? But fishing seems like being in the arms of a beautiful mother, the gracious solitary event when you find out that you are alone in the world, but it is all right because your mother is there, too. It is not really the kind of thing you learn while fishing, but rather only in retrospect as you grow older and have only rare opportunities to fish.

Fishing people are different. They are outdated and yet know exactly where they stand in the world. They take away life, yet are generally the most gentle people I know. Perhaps those long hours of standing alone in a trout stream, or surrounded by water in the middle of a lake, or digging into the ocean's great depths teach a lesson about boundaries, about where your world ends and a larger, unknown one begins. Nature gives those who are willing to listen, to put in the hours, a lesson in humility. People who fish know that life is a morality play in which you are sometimes the victor, sometimes vanquished. It is all of life's lessons in the space of a morning. Only an extraordinary person would purposely risk being outsmarted by a creature often less than twelve inches long, over and over again.

In their wisdom, my grandparents passed on to me a fishing experience that was either to be loved or hated, a day-in and day-out early rise, late return, nothing but fishing summer. They did it that way because that was what they loved and wanted us to love, too. So we fished until it was in our blood, until for days after we would gently rock back and forth as we slept, our blood coursing in waves instead of spurts. We fished until we reached that fusion of mind that extends beyond hand and rod, line and bait. We fished until we learned that fishing is not about killing or competing or even appreciating nature. Fishing is about being alone on the other end of a stick plunged into eternity, into primordial life.

As I think now of passing on these experiences to my daughter, I am saddened. The things I learned about life while fishing were not lessons to be taught, they were conclusions made because I was given the freedom to learn my own lessons. They were things learned in the comfort and safety of an extended family and in the glorious gift of a world seemingly without boundaries. But time has scattered my daughter's cousins, grandparents, aunts and uncles into impossible places and schedules all around the country. Our family no longer takes vacations like the ones from the past; it would require a gargantuan degree of commitment for everyone to spend the summer the way I used to, year after year. And the little village of Whitefish Falls, I'm certain, has either been lost to progress or developed beyond recognition.

Fishing with my daughter, while wonderful, is not the same. The wilderness has been tainted; I know that I will never be able to leave her alone in the same way that I was left alone. I am not sure whether there actually are more dangers today than in the past or if this fear is simply my reaction to the fact that there is no longer anyone to protect *me*, and my failure to accept that I am now the parent.

The last time my grandparents made the trip to Canada, my baby sister, the last grandchild, went along. She was an unheard-of age, only eight. Although I was grown, old enough to understand, it hurt to see this tradition seemingly so casually broken. If the rules of my childhood could change so carelessly, so could just about anything. I now feel guilty for such selfishness; my grandfather passed away shortly after and would have left his last grandchild without this great experience, this great opportunity, had he stubbornly stuck to his rules.

The lessons I learned about fishing were lessons I learned about life. They were gleaned from a lifestyle, a set of priorities, that today seems at best antiquated, at the worst, elitist. The great reaches of unexploited nature are almost beyond us; the vast resource of time seems no longer vast; indeed, must be spent carefully and constructively. My grandparents were part of an age where the things that we long for so desperately were taken for granted: family, vacations, working hard with a guaranteed payoff. Although it is not necessary to have these things to go fishing, what I did in summers past was not simply "going fishing." For these two weeks, and other times in between, I fished, had a fishing life, one unmarked by anything but the need to communicate with some being totally foreign, yet totally part of myself. And for that privilege I am eternally grateful.

CUT AND PASTE

JEAN RYSSTAD

I NEVER TRIED TO stop her. My little girl. She was twenty-five when she started going out on that boat—not just any boat, you know—these last years it was the *Pacific Sun*. She'd been going out the last seven years on a fishing boat almost as big as a freighter. The *Pacific Sun*. Imagine.

I'd try to imagine Kerry on the *Sun* and end up shaking my head, wondering at it, at her. And she'd say, "Mom, you'll never, never understand." She'd laugh. It wasn't a mean laugh, not what you'd call a superior laugh. I didn't hear it that way, though I think some others did. Not just women, who I think have a tendency to be jealous of a girl like Kerry, but men, who wanted to see her as something like a token on that boat, a toy. Well, Kerry was no toy. She was a strong-minded girl, and she knew her worth. She got to know her worth, unlike some . . . Well. That's enough.

The crew on that boat, those six men, were here with Kerry one night. They were in high spirits. They'd had a big trip. I thought, oh, I see what she likes. But I never told Kerry that. There was something in my heart afterwards, some wondering—more not less—about how it was for her out there, sometimes twenty days at a time.

Kerry wanted me to be happy for *her* happiness. She'd come home after ages away, and she'd say, "Mom, the rougher it gets, the more I love it." She'd say, "It's the only time I feel alive. Except," she'd say, "it's really weird how separated you get from people and ordinary things." She said it got like being on land was the "at sea part."

She used to talk like that all the time, and then, oh, the last year or so, she quit. She didn't mention "separations" anymore, and I didn't ask. I wish I had. It would give me more peace if I were more sure of her thoughts and her spirit that last year or so. I think the more sure you are that something's right for you, the less you need to talk about it. I think that was the case with Kerry. And for myself, now.

She was a smart little thing. She always was. She looked as dainty in a plaid flannel shirt as she did in a skirt and blouse. She favored that gauzy stuff, the flimsy stuff the hippies used to wear. Oh, all the kids went through their stages. They all pass through their stages. And sometimes the places they have to go, to get back to what they are, are disturbing. But what can you do about it? Can you put up a road-block or a chain or invent a storm warning? They have to go their ways. And if you don't see that when they're born, you see it later.

She had eyes like a seal when she was born. They were black and unblinking, and she looked around. She had this black thatch of hair, and the nurses, they'd tell me she was the cutest baby in the nursery. One of them said, "I just love her, but she has the personal-ity of an alligator." She *was* a cross little thing for the first few months. She didn't cry much, but she was, well, cross. I've thought about why.

I had one trip with Kerry. I mean a holiday, not a trip like they call a fishing trip, "going out."

Kerry was always asking me to go somewhere with her. Every time she came in, she'd say to me, "I'll take this trip off—where do you want to go?"

And I'd say, "Kerry, you save your money," and she'd laugh. She always laughed about money, at least she did after she got on that big boat.

And then one time she came in the door happy as all get out and she says, "We're going *somewhere*, so you might as well say where you want it to be."

She pestered me till I said, "I always liked that Mexican music." She was out the door as fast as she came in, away downtown for tickets. It's a mystery to me how that girl got me packed and on the flight that same day and how I felt the years dropping away from me and this gladness to be in the air with Kerry, flying to a country with a foreign language.

Oh, she looked so lovely when her skin was tanned. And she enjoyed those boys who'd come around the little huts where you'd get a fancy drink and watch the sun sink into the ocean. I couldn't get over the color of the water down there. It was enough, I said to Kerry, to be there on the beach. I didn't need to do anything else.

It was surprising to me the number of people from home that we met in Acapulco. Not that I knew them, but Kerry'd explain who they were. Fishermen, their wives or girlfriends, baking the rain out of their skins, they said.

I didn't want to be a nuisance, a weight on Kerry. I told her to have fun, to go off with her friends when she wanted, and she did. She kept opposite hours to mine. I'd get up early and walk the beach, and I enjoyed that so much. I sometimes walked with other old ladies. I was going to say, like myself, but they weren't. They were much more elegant than I was. But there was a kind of complaint from them, perhaps boredom, that I couldn't join in on that I didn't share. And I think if I go back there, if I went to some other place now, began to travel, I would get up earlier and take my walks alone.

My eldest son, Jim, wants me to move.

Well.

That boat went down, and they were all lost. The *Pacific Sun*, that great big boat, those six big strong men, my little Kerry, all, they say, lost. Imagine. I said to Jim: "Lost! I lost my wallet, I lost my head, I lost my way, but to lose a big boat? Lost is a *land* word. It's a word for traveling on foot. It's a word you kids all used when you didn't want to look for something."

And Jim heard me out a hundred times before he finally said, "Lost at sea. Lost means the boat sank. The boat, the crew, including Kerry. Lost. Gone down. Disappeared." He raised his voice, poor Jim. I don't blame him.

Jim's a realist, he says. And he is, I guess. He's done very well for himself. A teacher, and his wife, Janna, a teacher too, and they have their two children, my grandchildren, Rachel and Carl. The kids come here, and Rachel asks me, "Grandma, how come your house is so messy when it's only you here. You have way more stuff than us." The boy, Carl, he's such a dazy little putterer. He asked me, "Grandma, do you have some things to make a bridge?" And I asked him did he want toothpicks or kindling. That made him smile.

I think Kerry would have enjoyed children. Her own, that is. I think, given time, she would have had them and drawn as much from them as she did from her time at sea. But you couldn't say, "Kerry, you're thirty now . . ."

"But *isn't* it strange that nothing, nothing was ever found?" I couldn't help myself, and I said that to Jim a week ago when he was over to visit. He said, "Mom, don't get yourself worked up." He brought me brochures, a seniors' complex at Sherbrook Gardens. I asked him if there's a view of the water, and he said there were apartments available with inner courtyards, benches, gardens, fountains. That there was a waiting list for the ocean views. He said, "You'll see what peace it brings you."

I have good kids.

They care about me.

Jim, he comes as often as he can. Don stays away as long as he can, and they both think they're doing it for me.

The boys never wanted to fish with their dad.

Their dad had nothing like the operation that Kerry was on, nothing like that. He had a troller that he built himself. A family boat. Enough for a living. A good life, trolling.

I used to go with Gordon when we were first married. The summer before Jim was born, I went a few trips. I couldn't say I liked it. I didn't like going to the bathroom in a pail, and I never got over that. Of course, Kerry's boat, that boat had everything a house could have and more. A sauna! Imagine that. On a boat!

Gordon, come trolling time, he'd get the boys to go out, alternate ten days, from the end of June till September when school started. The boys didn't take to it.

Gordon would holler and holler up the banister for them to get out of bed—it would be four o'clock in the morning—and they'd just burrow down deeper in their covers. And you know, at that time of the morning, I'd have liked to, too. I did until my conscience got to me, and then I'd get up and fix a breakfast and pack the cookies or whatever I'd made to start them out. Sometimes a chicken or a roast.

One morning when the boys weren't rousing to Gordon's calls, down the stairs comes Kerry. She was around five then. She said, "Take me this time, Dad." She wasn't even buttoned up right, her little green wool jacket sitting on her crooked. That's how little she was. After that, she was away with her dad every summer. He never had to call her twice.

Gordon admitted she was as good as the boys. He wouldn't say better, but she was his favorite because of her love of the life. He never spoke about it, and I suppose it hurt him somewhat that his sons didn't have the love. It wasn't ever mentioned.

Don. He and Gordon never got along. If they had, I don't think Don would feel so lost, so much loss. He and Kerry were very close. When Don last came to see me, he had just started managing a donut franchise. And you know what he told me? He said, "Mom, guess what I do with the stale donuts?" He was grinning, but he was watching me. He said that he saves them up for a few days, and then he drives out to the beach past town and tosses them one at a time like horseshoes into the sea.

"What do you think of that?" he asked.

I said, "I think she'd laugh like crazy if she knew." If she knows, I *thought*, but didn't say.

He said, "I sometimes think I hear her."

And I said, "Yes, I understand."

Kerry never lorded it over the boys about how she was on the boat with her dad. She kept it to herself as if, if she talked too much, she'd lose her birthright. No. Now that's not the right way to put that. Anyway, Gordon passed away before Kerry got her chance on that big dragger, the *Pacific Sun*.

This happened in March, last year. That boat, five men, the captain, Kerry. Never seen again. They had the largest search party in Canadian history for that boat. By sea and air. And they found nothing. No sign.

They said the explanation, the most plausible explanation, was a freak wave. Waves, they said, run in a pattern, a series, and, oh, maybe every fifth wave is a big one. But a freak wave is something else. They happen when these series of waves join up, or "get into step" and they become a mountain of water, a hundred-foot wave. They say one took the *Sun* by surprise.

Oh, I don't know.

"They" say, "some" say, that the *Pacific Sun* crew were a maverick crew. Maverick. That they fished the high seas, out of boundaries, that they explored and opened new grounds for years, and that they didn't call a mayday because they were in illegal grounds. That they hoped they wouldn't founder, that they had a huge load of fish, that the load shifted. That they went down struggling to stabilize, went down not believing that the boat wouldn't come back like she had so many times before.

But there's another thing. There was a logger working in an inlet, grounds the *Sun* often traveled past.

He said he heard the call: South Harbour... South Harbour... This is the *Pacific Sun*... The logger reported hearing the call once, on his radio, but never again. The transmitting station had no record of that call, and the logger, after reporting what he heard, could not be found again.

"They" tell me, Jim tells me, that it is normal, not unusual, for people to report having heard distress calls shortly after a boat's gone missing. They say it is a psychological trick the mind plays. A wish to hear. A wish to help.

"Your imagination," Jim said, "is getting away on you." Kerry gave me a picture of the *Sun* not long before she was lost. I hung that picture in the kitchen by the window. Just last week, a wet spot appeared on that picture, and I showed Jim. It was "evidence," I thought. "Jim," I said, "that's Kerry. She's saying something." Jim said it was the kettle that made the spot appear, but I don't plug the kettle in by the window because it steams the window and I like to see out, of course. More so than I ever did. Jim asked if he could have the picture. He looked so worried that I agreed, and when he asked me if I was going to take the apartment at Sherbrook, I said yes.

I know what I know. Having or not having a picture doesn't take it away. Having or not having a water view won't change it either.

I used to clip all the papers for Kerry when she was at sea. I cut and saved papers, articles from magazines. Anything I thought might interest her. I kept a scrapbook.

She'd plunk her bag at the door when she came home and give me a kiss and head straight for my desk by the sunporch window.

Every time I saw something—a cartoon—oh, she liked *Garfield* when it first came out and then *Larson, Off the Wall, Bizzaro.*

I didn't clip everything, just the ones I had some idea that she'd appreciate. It gave me an interest and a kind of double pleasure, imagining her enjoyment and then seeing it, hearing it when she came home. We knew each other through that scrapbook even though she was away so much. And to quit this clipping, this cutting and pasting for Kerry was the hardest thing. And then it dawned on me that day Jim left with the picture of the boat and my word that I'd move to the Sherbrook soon. It dawned on me that cutting and pasting was the thing I should never quit. It was something between Kerry and me that Jim never knew.

The last time I saw Kerry, the last time she was home, she was herself, or seemed to be, right up until it came time to leave. "Mom," she said, "C'mere and sit on this suitcase for me." She always crammed so much into that old case of hers.

I went to the bedroom closet, and I brought down that beautiful soft purple leather bag Kerry'd bought me in Mexico. I said, "Kerry, you take it."

And she said, "Mom, that's yours."

I said, "My traveling days are over, and yours are in full swing."

She took it, but there was a look passed over her face. I swear there was a look.

I told Jim that, and he said, "Mom, it's easy to think all kinds of things." When I told Don, he said he thought that Kerry had wanted me to travel. That maybe she knew she wasn't coming back and she wanted me to have that bag to travel with. That she didn't want it lost.

So you see the difference between these boys. Don gets too excited if you give him a link, an inkling of what's in the air. It is a problem.

She was standing in the doorway with the door open and that lovely bag slung over her shoulder and that big old suitcase heavier than her, almost, and she took a look. It seemed she looked for a long time at everything in this house. I won't forget that looking: at the spines of books, at the burled coffee tables the boys made one year after the other in shop at high school. She was taking a picture, all right. She was taking the house and everything in it. My, she was loaded down that day. I felt her heaviness, and I had to sit down.

She said, "I don't think..." And then she stopped.

I couldn't stop myself, and I said, "Kerry, won't you please let that boat go without you this trip." I hadn't said that for years.

She said, "Mom, I've got to go."

I said, "Of course you will..."

She came and kissed me—I don't think she heard me at all then; I would say she was floating then. I would say she was stepping aboard the *Sun* . . .

I have been packing my things. I'll be moving in a week or so. I am ready for the move because she came to me.

I had been wavering about my decision to move, wavering about my secrets, about my judgment. I thought: You silly old woman. Stop this papery-thin communication between yourself and Kerry and get on with the real stuff between your sons and your daughter-in-law and your grandchildren.

I'd refused to paste the stories of the *Sun*'s disappearance into any scrapbook. So I thought: There's the sane thing. The start of it. I'll begin to put the story in its place. The news of the disappearance, the search, the failure to find, the sympathy cards, the minister's letter. And I thought, once I've done this, I can carry on with the other scrapbooks and it won't be so strange.

I sat down at the desk and began to trim the papers. I cut columns and began to scissor out each family's hopes, their statements: Cautious. Loved the sea. Respected the sea.

There's a sound that scissors make when you cut into paper, and it came to me that the scissors were an engine, a boat, a bow cutting through water. I had such a strong sensation of being on water, traveling toward them as long as I kept the scissors moving. I knew enough to know that I was at my desk, but I also knew I was moving into some other place where I'd never been. Some might say—Jim, he would say—that I was removing myself from the final cut, resisting. But I know I moved closer into what happened. I thought: If I could only keep cutting, I could reach them.

When I'd cut all there was to cut, it panicked me: Stupid, stupid, I thought. Crazy.

I opened the scrapbook and picked up the glue, and at that moment a bird—like a missile soaring straight to its target—rammed the glass. The window rattled in its frame. The glue crashed to the floor, and my tears came in that same instant. They sprung.

I can recall that springing sensation, the surprise of tears, very clearly. How quickly, like the first spurt of blood from a cut.

I came back into myself, bit by bit, the self I've lived with every day, but with something else, a kind of joy, or freedom. That bird was Kerry and we will meet again.

FISHING FOR EEL TOTEMS

MARGARET ATWOOD

I stood on the reed bank
ear tuned to the line, listening
to the signals from the ones who lived
under the blue barrier,

thinking they had no words for things
in the air.

The string jumped,
I hooked a martian / it poured
fluid silver out of the river

its long body whipped on the grass, reciting
all the letters of its alphabet.

Killed, it was a
grey tongue hanged silent in the smokehouse

which we later ate.

After that I could see
for a time in the green country;

I learned that the earliest language
was not our syntax of chained pebbles

but liquid, made
by the first tribes, the fish
people.

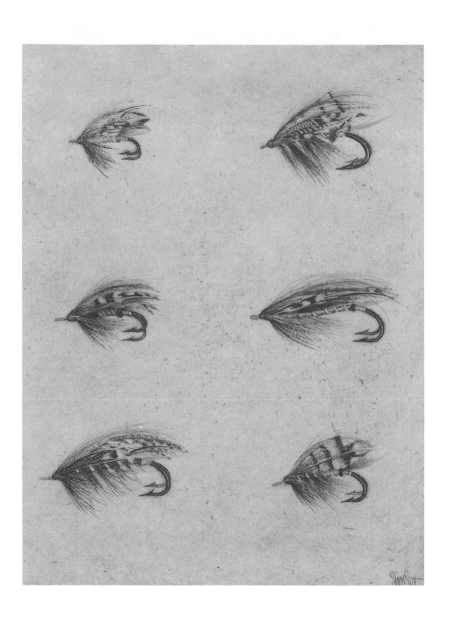

WITHOUT A BACKWARD CAST:
NOTES OF AN ANGLER

KATHARINE WEBER

TROUT ARE MYSTERIOUS. *They're quiet and graceful, the oak trees of the fish forest. Mackerel, on the other hand, are noisy fish, tough and clever. They fight like hell. I've had a one-pound mackerel bend a fishing rod practically under the boat in waters off the coast of Maine. Between the two lie bass, who are middle-of-the-road fish, noncontroversial. Sunfish one catches intentionally only if one is under the age of twelve; they're stupid and weak, a very lower-class fish. I have never met a sturgeon, but I have a hunch that they are downright intellectual (perhaps a bit dark and Russian, too). Salmon are without a doubt, the most intelligent of fish; they also have an excellent sense of humor.*

Why this excursion into fish personalities? Knowing what and who is on the other end of the line is as important as knowing the rules of the game. This is the heart of it, the essential lure: the one-to-one challenge between angler and fish.

The first time I ever held a fishing rod was at a stocked lake in Minnesota when I was seven years old. I don't think I cast the line or landed the fish, but the rod was put into my hands for a few minutes after a trout had been hooked, and I remember the thrill of the tension and pulse of the struggling fish. My family was not athletically inclined, and I think this was not so much a sporting occasion as it was a diversionary way of finding something to eat. I hung around the table where the fish were being cleaned and was given a lump of quartz that I had spotted on a low shelf next to some discarded fishing nets. I treasured the snowy cluster of crystals, which seemed to me much purer and more desirable than the fish flesh it resembled.

The next time I fished was even less authentic. My grandmother paid three dollars at the World's Fair in New York for me to have the privilege of dangling a baited hook in front of some pathetic-looking trout that were milling around in a two-foot-deep plastic pond. I think I was entitled to fifteen minutes. (Three dollars for fifteen minutes' worth of opportunity to hook an anemic trout was absurdly steep, and this was 1964).

I hooked a fish and had absolutely no idea what to do next, but the fish, which had probably been through this several times that day, gave only a few feeble attempts at shaking the hook, and I finally hauled it out of the water, where it flopped in the air on the end of my line. The man who ran the concession offered to wrap it up so I could take it home, which I was very interested in doing, but my grandmother, conscious of ninety-degree August heat and an entire day still ahead of us at the fair, briskly declined and told me that I would rather put the dear, dear, cunning little fish back, wouldn't I? I looked back over my shoulder as I was led away for some nice Belgian waffles and saw my fish swimming again in the tepid water with the other fish, some of whom were swimming backwards and upside down.

At this point in my life, fishing held no real fascination for me. I was not to become a fisher for another ten years.

When I was twenty, I met Nick. After a few months it was clear that we would be married and spend the rest of our lives together. We went to Ireland for our honeymoon. We took along a spinning rod, just in case, and ended up spending almost every day of our two weeks wading in freezing rivers, casting for salmon. The underbrush grows very close to the water along the Ilen River, and most zealous back-casts ended up in a tangled line and a lost lure. The rivers were all flooded and swollen that autumn, and we never caught a thing. But I acquired a respect for the salmon of Ireland. One chilly afternoon we saw a couple of salmon just larking in a pool—our casts were probably a source of amusement for them—and one fish jumped clear out of the water, danced on his tail and nipped away. We were enchanted. We spent more time sliding in cow dung across farmers' fields, finding a clear spot where one could cast with impunity, and we warmed up after cold mornings on the rivers at the West Cork Hotel in downtown Skibbereen, where the dinners (lunches to you) consisted of wondrous heaps of roast pork or mutton or beef and four or five kinds of potatoes, piled in mounds on your plate by red-faced young women too shy to look you in the eye. Eating was an exercise in excavation.

I think I had not been happier than during some of those moments standing in my new wellingtons in some marsh waiting for my turn to fish—to cast and cast and cast. That's mostly what fishing is. We cast our arms off, developed strategies, talked to the fish, lied about what we'd seen to other fishermen and planned out routes with the primitive map issued along with the fishing license by the wizened little man who perched behind an official litter of rubber stamps at the license office in Skib. We had one rod and one license between us.

You don't see many women fishing in Ireland, and the ones you do see are usually English or German. We saw one other couple fishing, and they had fixed up a strange rig with sand eels and several hooks, which seemed rather joyless to us. They caught many trout. We preferred our system. We caught nothing. But I developed a certain amount of skill in casting, although I still to this day, because of the undergrowth along the Ilen, tend to throw more of a side-arm than an overhead cast.

A year later, we moved into the eighteenth-century Connecticut farmhouse where we live today. One of the features that attracted us to this bit of countryside is the small lake on the adjoining property, which while not exactly teeming with fish does allow one frequent glimpses of ducks, geese and resident herons, depending on luck and time of day.

What one sees is, of course, one of the main attractions of fishing. Fishing takes you to some incredibly beautiful locations and then gives you the excuse to stand there all day and enjoy yourself. You would never fall asleep while fly casting; in fact, wading and casting are vigorous forms of exercise. It's also a game of skill, not a game of waiting, as polefishing must be. The rules of the game are that you are a person who can't see beneath the surface of the water terribly well and you can't use any equipment that isn't sporting (no submachine guns, X-ray devices, drag nets, dynamite and—with a finer calibre of sportsmanship in mind—no multiple hooks and no unfair techniques such as jig-hooking, which is a nasty way of getting a hook into any part of a salmon, without the salmon's cooperation). The fish have their fish sensibilities and the advantage of home territory. The object of the game is for you to make the fish think that your lure or fly or bait is a delicious little morsel swimming free and clear, and if he goes for it you have to have the skill to outmaneuver and land him. The object of the game for the fish is not to be fooled. For him, it's a matter of life and death.

Three summers after Ireland, Nick and I felt ready to move on to more serious fishing. We learned of a fishing camp in northern New Brunswick, Canada, and decided to spend five days there in mid-July. To get to Jim Black's fishing camp, you fly to Presque Isle, Maine, where someone from the camp meets you, and you are then driven a couple of hours north. The Tobique River, a tributary of the Serpentine, flows past the camp, and most of the outlying wilderness is owned by big paper conglomerates; the only traffic is huge logging trucks that go by empty in the morning and come out of the woods in early evening piled high with tree-length logs.

We were in for a bit of culture shock. The Blacks' television set was on every hour of the day. Their daughter possibly never went outside the entire time we were there. (And we ended up spending ten days there.) At the edge of civilization, these people were closer to suburbia than we were, living just outside New Haven.

Our lodging consisted of a log cabin with a sagging double bed and a wood stove. It had the luxury of its own spring-fed sink and toilet. This meant that occasionally a tiny fish would find its way into the toilet bowl, which can be very disconcerting, for both you and the fish, first thing in the morning.

The first afternoon conditions were all wrong for catching a fish, but we were impatient and it was a good time for me to learn how to fly cast. Nick quickly recalled most of what his father had taught him about casting on a memorable father-son fishing trip to Lake Parmacheene in New Hampshire. And I was eager to move on from the known, safe waters of spinning into the more subtle, cerebral currents of fly fishing. I was given some hip waders about four sizes too big, and with a slow leak in one knee. But with four layers of socks, there was so little room for water the leak never became more than a nuisance.

Careful not to wade any deeper than within a couple of inches of the tops of my waders, I slowly learned how to lay the fly down on the water. In fly casting, you pull out line from the reel with your left hand and hold it bunched in a loose loop, while with your right arm you whip the rod back and forth overhead, from eleven o'clock to two o'clock. As you whip the rod, you let it take more and more line, which you unreel and feed with your left hand, until you have thirty or forty feet of line in the air, in constant motion. With all this line whipping back and forth over your head, you are now ready to make a cast. You throw the line forward in a smooth, continuous sweep so that the line travels forward in a perfect horizontal unrolling, and with a little flick, the fly is laid down on the surface of the water without a splash. When an expert fly fisher casts, it's a beautiful thing to watch. It seems effortless and perfect, and it can be hard to believe that this process is human invention and not a natural occurrence.

Even on that bright afternoon, I felt the tension and alertness one feels in the presence of the possibility of a strike. We fished both dry and wet flies, the dry flies sitting on the surface of the water, the wet sinking an inch or so. One casts slightly upstream, floats the fly and then lifts it off the water with a quick, splashless flick before it reaches the end of the floating line and begins to drag. A dragging fly or needless flailing in the water discourages the salmon.

Salmon, we learned, don't strike at flies because of hunger, but out of irritation or sport. They don't eat at all in fresh water, and any salmon killed on a river will have a clean gullet. Apparently, Atlantic salmon gather under the ice in the Davis Straits and gorge themselves on shrimp and not much else, which would certainly account for the unique flesh of a salmon. When salmon return to their rivers, it is only to spawn. Salmon invariably find their way back to the river in which they themselves were spawned, and some guides swear that they even come back to the same rock pools in the river, year after year. Stocked salmon have a piece of back fin clipped off for identification. Their spawn, obviously, have complete fins. When Jim's wife

Nita landed a naturally spawned fish on our fourth day there, she looked at its back fin and declared, "This here is God's own fish," with evident satisfaction.

Our routine was to get up at five-thirty every morning, before sunrise, have a preliminary breakfast, and then fish from six until about nine-thirty, when the mist would have burned off completely and it would be too bright to fish. We would then go back to camp, have a more serious breakfast, usually with eggs from Nita's chickens, and then go back to bed. At one we would have lunch. In the afternoon we played cribbage, read, bicycled down the road to look at the same three pairs of handknit socks made by the church ladies and offered for sale in the only store in town, or visited with members of Nita's voluminous family, who were perpetually dropping in. My favorite was her toothless brother Murray, about whom it was darkly hinted that he tied salmon flies made from his own pubic hair.

One afternoon, after yet another fishless morning, Jim and Nita took us on a hike into an area with mountain streams. We hooked dozens of very small rainbow trout, on worms, feeling no guilt because Jim felt they were trapped in a pool created by a new beaver dam and that there were too many fish to survive. The trout were delicious pan-fried in bacon fat, eaten with fried eggs and bacon and toast.

One late morning, Jim poled our canoe over the rock pool we'd been fishing, and we could count seven fat salmon. We knew they were there. We fished with greater determination.

One afternoon we saw two baby bobcats tumbling together across the path in the woods.

Jim demonstrated excellent moose calls.

Our five days stretched into ten, and we never hooked any salmon.

We were back the following summer, in August this time. My mother, a bird-watcher, joined us. Jim had aged visibly, and Jim Jr. was our guide. On the third of our eight days there, we went trout fishing on the Serpentine, on a stretch accessible only after an hour of driving on dirt followed by a strenuous hour of climbing. Trout flies are smaller and lighter, and it was a windy day. I had cast a few times, standing in deep midstream. (Nick's Christmas present to me had been chest waders with felt soles, and a fishing vest.) A gust of wind took my fly in mid-cast and carried it back into my left eye. I yelled for Nick with what must have been a terrible voice; he was at my side in seconds. He gently took my hand away from my eye and saw that the fly was just barely caught in the skin of my eyelid. He freed it, and then the two of us clung together shaking. We both knew that because I am blind in my right eye, that little trout fly had come very close to changing my life. My one piece of advice to all who would fish: wear sunglasses. We retrieved Nick's rod, which he had flung in the bushes on the bank, and waded upstream around a bend where Jim Jr. and my mother were waiting. They didn't hear my scream over the roaring current. We never told anyone about what had happened.

Two days later I killed my salmon. (I don't know why, but one says "killed" with salmon, just as one rides with the "hounds," never the "dogs.")

Choosing a fly at any given moment, is, I suppose, a science, but as with picking horses at the track, whimsy can be as successful as any more consistent method. I would generally change flies after a few casts; my selections were based on intuition and what I thought I might be in the mood for if I were a salmon. On that morning, the fog lifted early, and we were discouraged and ready to quit.

I felt as though the salmon had defeated us, as though it was Us and Them. When they refuse to engage, the relationship between we who fish and those who are fish remains entirely theoretical. What we want—and I include in that "we" anyone who has ever dangled a worm on a bent pin off the side of a bridge as well as aristocratic sportsmen flailing elite waters for thousands of dollars a day—is the one-to-one engagement. The I and Thou of it all.

That morning on the Tobique, I was restless and bored. It wasn't happening. I changed to a brown fairy, a handsome wet fly, for my last few casts of the morning. I knew the salmon were there. Coaxing one to strike had become an urgent, almost archaic wish to attract, to compel. I was sending signals to a distant planet.

Three casts later I felt that unmistakable surge of something alive on the line. Salmon, when hooked, have been known to try anything to get off the line: for every two fish hooked, only one is landed. The reel was singing as the fish took off downstream. As soon as I felt a slack, I reeled in like crazy, keeping a tension without pulling in too sharply, which would break the line. Then the fish would run the line out again, and I could see that I was getting near the backing on the reel. There would be occasional pauses while he changed direction or rested, and I would reel it all back in. I felt the fish tiring. Way upstream, I thought I saw another salmon jumping clear of the water, but it was my fish trying to jump the hook. I tried to keep the line taut. Suddenly I felt a strange new tension on the line. The fish was rolling over and over on the line. "That dirty fish!" declared Nita, "You bring him in and tell him to stop those games."

I reeled the fish in closer, and Nita warned me that if he went near the rocks he might try to saw the line between two ledges. We could see the fish clearly for the first time; it was much bigger than I had realized. The fish went out for one more weak run, and then I reeled in as tightly as I dared; Jim Jr. made a deft pass with the net, and we had our fish. It weighed a little over ten pounds. I saw that I had hooked the fish, a female as it turned out, solidly in the lip. But there was only one turn left in the knot I had made to tie the brown fairy, and I had used five. Another few minutes and the fish would have been off the line with the fly. The fish could then have worked the fly out of its lip by scraping along the river bottom. Jim Jr. killed the fish with one blow with a rock. It was awful. Inert, solid, the salmon was transformed forever. But, still, I had earned it. We would eat it, smoked, and I would salt her sacs full of eggs, too, for delicious caviar. When a salmon dies, it's a death far more profound than the last fierce flappings of a mackerel in a bucket. I was both appalled and elated. Nita broke the spell when she pointed out the cuts in the tail and back fins, caused by the line when the fish had stood on its tail and rolled. Nita said, "You did real marvelous."

Fishing *is* marvelous: there is the challenge, the tuning of a skill, the aesthetic. But mainly there is the irresistible urge to tangle with the mysterious and unknown, to rely on intuition and hunches. You do it for those moments of casting your thoughts beneath the surface of the water to see if you can conjure up a fish.

When I was little, I thought there were actual fish in the sky after rain, and I would always strain my eyes to see them between a rainbow's bars of color. The swimming spots in my eyes that resulted were, I convinced myself, what people meant by "rainbow trout."

My mind still makes that leap when I fish for rainbows—a particularly brilliant fish can make me believe again that water is not its only element.

CURRENTS

SABRINA SOJOURNER

1/25/91 7:06 p.m.

Y OU'LL FEEL BETTER once you're at the cabin," Marsha said.
Everyone has said. I've never had so many people encouraging
me to get away. At least they had some place for me to get away to.

I'm at Marsha's cabin. I've been here for three hours, and if Feel
Better is around she hasn't discovered me. Of course, I wasn't expecting miracles. I know I still have a lot of grieving to do and that I'm
ambivalent about doing it. I still can't believe Edna is dead and that
she was murdered so viciously. She was one of the nicest and most
generous people I had ever met. I will miss you, Edna. I do miss you.
There are things I want to say to you, but I don't know where to begin. The sadness of your death just sits on me. It just sits on me.

9:30 p.m.

I'd forgotten how much I like puttering. Feel Better found me while I
was puttering around the kitchen and on the back porch. Found
some cans of veggie chili and some frozen bagels. Had that for dinner. Checked out the fishing gear on the back porch. Marsha must
not have been up here in a while. The tackle boxes are a mess! Decided I didn't have it in me to clean up both, so only did one. I had
forgotten how fanatical Marsha and Dee Dee are about fishing.
There was a lot of stuff to sort through. Found lures and floaters I'd
never seen before. It will be fun trying them out.

It will be good to be out on the lake tomorrow. If it's not too brisk, I may take the hobie out instead of the skip. Actually, I have enough warm clothes I could do either. If I take the hobie, I can sail over to my favorite cove without warning the fish of my presence. It would be nice to bring something home. Being here alone I'll have to do my own gutting and scaling. Scaling I don't mind. But my stomach may need to settle after gutting.

I think I'll stop at the bait shop and get some stink bait. I can leave two lines out back for catfish. Yes, I am really thinking about putting my own two hands in stink bait. What choice do I have? Marsha and Dee Dee are not here, so I can't plead with them to take care of it for me. Anyway, it's only slimy blood and who knows whose guts. In the cove I can catch trout, if I'm lucky. Mostly I want the time to relax and be with myself.

Yes! Feel Better has actually found me. I'm looking forward to tomorrow.

1/26/91 8:30 a.m.

Awoke before dawn. Stayed in bed and snuggled with myself. Allowed myself to feel all the different feelings I've had over the past month—good and bad—and let them move through me. I love that place of semiconsciousness. I could hear the wind outside playing with the chimes. I had a vision of being in the cove and settling myself on one of the boulders that juts out from the water. I was getting my line ready. Trying to decide on which lure, how many weights, when this big trout came close enough to the surface for me to see her clearly. She looked to be about four feet long, as big as some salmon I've seen. She stayed in the water with her head slightly turned so she could see me. I felt like she was trying to tell me something. But when I knelt down to get closer to her, she darted into the deeper part of the lake. After that I floated back to consciousness.

As I write this, I remember fish often represent one's intuition in dreams. Perhaps the big trout's elusiveness represents my disconnectedness to my own intuition at this time. Being able to almost, but not quite, hear what I need to say to myself.

I'm beginning to think this fishing trip is much more timely than

I thought. It's been too long since I last indulged in fishing. Some people may think it funny for me to call fishing an indulgence. How many other activities allow so much room for one to be outdoors and alone and quiet? As much as I like hanging out with the girls on Dee's boat, or being in the skip with just Marsha, I relish the times I get to fish by myself. I love the sense of being at one with my surroundings, delighting in the sense of this being a perfect moment in time.

It looks like the day will be pretty, even if it isn't warm. And I'm ready to get out in it!

1:15 p.m.

Since I needed to go to the local baitshop/grocery/deli, I decided to drive over to the cove instead of sailing or motoring.

It feels to be around fifty. Just warm enough for your breath not to fog. It's definitely colder, though, in the shade. I set two lines here in the cove. One in the sun close by and one in the shade on the far end. I didn't stop back by the house to put the catfish lines in the river. I'll do that this evening when I get back to the cabin. I built a fire and am glad I brought this sleeping bag to sit on. It feels good out here. It was a nice walk down from the road.

The morning has been wonderful—aside from having to deal with an asshole at Betty's store. There are several things about the North Georgia mountains on which you can depend: beautiful, luscious green forests (except in the fall when all the golds, oranges, scarlets, crimsons and yellows come alive); clean, clear lakes and ponds; and running into at least one red-neck cracker wanting to make your life miserable because you're black. Fortunately, Betty runs the store in the mornings and likes having "self-sufficient women" coming through and doesn't let the men fuck with us no matter what color "we" are. If Gabe, her louse of a husband, had been there, no telling what would have happened. But that's why I go in the mornings. Allows time to have a cup of coffee with Betty. She's always glad to see me, and this morning was no different. It was after our coffee chat, while I was wandering through the store to get what I needed, that I realized this asshole was following me. When I got to the produce and was picking through the vegetables, he actually said, "Don't be puttin' yer hans all over ma food!" Betty yelled from across the room, "Michael Paris! Are you plannin' on buyin' all those veg'tables?"

"I wuz goin' ta buy some til she pu' her hans all over 'em." Arms folded across his chest, he was rocking on his heels, trying to intimidate me.

"Well," Betty drawled, "I was goin' ta sell ya some til you opened up yer dang mouth! Sabrina's ma friend. She's up here all the time. And if she gits so much as a hang nail, I'm poin'in' the authorities in yer direction!"

He slunk toward the door. "I'll be back ta git ma veg'bles after you've had a chance ta wash 'em off."

"Send Peggy, then. I don't have time for such foolishness!"

I couldn't see the look he gave Betty as he passed her on his way out. Whatever it was caused her to stick her tongue out at him. As soon as the door closed behind him, we both broke out laughing.

As she was ringing up my groceries, I asked her if she was going to be all right.

"Oh, darlin'," said Betty, "These crackas 'round here know better than to truck with me or anybody I care 'bout. I can't protect everybody. But I protect who I can. You hear anythin' atall strange around the cabin, you give Gabe 'n me a call, ya hear?"

Yes, Betty. I hear. I hear what you said and what you didn't say.

The bell!

8:30 p.m.

The bell turned out to be a false alarm. But the day was not a total loss. I pulled in the line that had been in the shade, and there was a trout hanging off the end looking quite perturbed because it had taken me so long to "rescue" him. Since he was puny but healthy, I unhooked his jaw and threw him back. Hitting the water startled him for a second, then he flopped his tail and was gone.

For curiosity's sake, I added a couple more weights and baited the hook with stink bait. Yes, I put my hands on it. I think I hate the texture more than I hate the smell, if that's possible. But the point is, I did it myself. Not just once, but four times in one day. It does get easier.

I baited that hook, put it back in the water, took the rod that had been in the sun and climbed up onto the higher boulders. I cast my line from there. That was fun! Since there was no one else around and no tree limbs on which to get caught or tangled, I got to play with casting, something I hadn't done in a long while. The currents in the cove are misleading. They run deep and are different from the signs that appear on the surface. In one place, the current will take your line out. Twenty feet either side of that spot, it will bring it in quickly or just let it hang there.

I caught two nice-sized perch from atop the boulder and a larger trout on the line in the shade. I was surprised either liked stink bait. I said something to Betty later when I went to her house to let her take her pick. "Chil', the fish in North Georgia are ornery enough to eat anythin'." She winked at me as she pulled out all three fish and started gutting the trout. I scaled and filleted them. Left her one of the trout fillets and three of the perch. She offered to cook my share for me. My heart went out to her because I could see she was hungry for company. I asked her if I could have a raincheck and she, of course, said yes. Maybe I'll invite her up to the cabin for dinner tomorrow night. I'd like an evening with Betty; it's Gabe I can't stand. He's so mean to her.

While we were cleaning the fish, Betty started telling me stories about a great old trout in the lake. I had forgotten about those stories. She said one of the old men had seen this trout in a cove a little further north of where I like to fish. Betty says the men refer to the trout as Big Ben, but she calls her Selena "because very few men outlive their wives, so she's more likely to be a female." I asked Betty where she got the name Selena. "Because she once told me in a dream that was her name." Then she asked me if I thought she was crazy for dreaming about talking fish.

"You're crazy only if Michael Paris is sane," I said. We both laughed. I asked her if she knew what the name meant.

"I think Selena's some kinda goddess."

"A moon goddess," I said.

"That makes sense. If a fish is goin' to come to you in your dreams, she ought to have some kinda mystical name."

She's right. I didn't tell Betty I dreamt about Selena. I'm not exactly sure why. I just didn't.

I'm excited, though, that the fish in my dream might actually exist. I think I'll go out the farthest cove tomorrow.

My favorite thing about fishing is being able to just be. Being able to get myself as quiet inside as it is outside. When I am quiet, amazing things happen. Today, a squirrel came up and shared my lunch with me. I was quiet long enough to be able to spot birds I often hear but rarely see, including winter wrens, a hermit thrush, a covey of bufflehead ducks and a broad-winged hawk perched on a boulder about twenty feet from me.

Being quiet also allowed me to touch the deeper parts of my grief for Edna. And I found myself thinking about how much I miss having a family. I was actually able to release some tears. There are times when I get tired of "growing" and becoming "enlightened." Times when I'm in need of a plateau. This weekend—fishing, walking in the woods, sailing on the lake—is a kind of plateau. An opportunity to take a time out: to reflect, meditate.

Fishing is a means of meditating for me. Twirling the hook around and sending it out into the world, my thoughts go out into the world with the hook. I place my sadness on the hook and let the weights pull it down into the deep parts of the lake. When I pull the line back and find the bait gone, I thank the unseen creature who ate it and hope it nourishes it. I re-bait the hook. Again, I twirl the hook, once, twice, three times for luck and send it out into the world. The good thoughts I had today rewarded me with dinner. I wonder if there are any Zen fishing books written by a black lesbian feminist femme?

Noon 1/27/91

Got up early and sailed the hobie over to the cove, set two lines and went on to the cove Betty described. It's a good thing I decided to bring an anchor with me at the last minute because there is no place to comfortably go ashore over here. I'm also glad I brought a thermos of soup and coffee. It was very cold until the sun came up over the mountains.

I've already caught two nice-sized speckled trout and a perch. There's lots of carp in this part of the lake. They've been coming up to the keels but have avoided the line, which is fine by me because I don't care for carp, anyway.

No sign of Selena, though. I have to laugh because I really don't know if she exists outside of the stories and Betty's and my dreams. I dreamt of her again last night. This time, we were able to communicate. I understood I was listening wrong before. I was trying to listen with my real ears when I needed to be listening to my inner self. The message was still foggy, something about peace and believing. And she seemed to be saying something about letting go, but I couldn't understand what it was I needed to let go. I asked her if she was talking about letting go of grief. I'm not sure if she ignored the question or didn't hear it. She just repeated herself. Perhaps I didn't communicate the question . . . a tug!

A carp!?! Betty will enjoy it, and I will gladly give it to her.

So, what is it I need to let go, release?

Old hurts and pains.

Which old hurts and pains? There's so many from which to choose and I thought I *had* been letting them go. There's always the daily assaults to my humanity, and now there's Edna. What do I need to let go?

Expectations that can't be fulfilled; the childhood hurts that can never be undone.

At thirty-eight I'm still recovering from my family relationships. These last two years of being single I think have helped, though the first year or so was shaky. It's hard not putting a relationship first. And there's little support for being happily single in the lesbian community. I don't think there's much support for being a happily single female in the straight community, either.

So, where am I now around all of this? I believe, I know, I am taking better care of myself. I am more accepting and loving toward myself. I'm not sure I'm more secure unless staying present with myself long enough to figure out what's going on with me counts, and I think it does. It's okay that it takes sometimes as much as a week for something "hard" to fully impact me. That's much better than it taking months or years, which it has in the past. I'm letting myself cry more, and I don't get as freaked out about crying alone. I've been letting myself go to bed and hide in sleep when I feel real bad, which has been a lot lately.

I'm still hurting because Edna was murdered. I hate that she—or anyone—has to be ripped out of the world. It's okay that I'm still hurting. I need to continue working through my grief for her. I need to recognize this depth of pain will always touch the scars and the remnants of old hurts.

Well, time to head in, the afternoon breeze is coming up.

6 p.m.

The most amazing thing happened when I went back to my cove. When I pulled up the line I had dropped in the shade, there was Selena. The line was so heavy, I just assumed some old debris had gotten caught on the hook. Truthfully, I was expecting the classic old fishing boot filled with water. But there she was. I didn't know whether to laugh or cry. She was beautiful! Absolutely beautiful.

There's a shallow pool close to that part of the ledge, so I placed her in it while I checked her out. From the scars around her mouth, I was clearly not the first person to have caught her and thrown her back. She even had a hook that had healed into her skin. Who knows how long that had been there. My hook was embedded in the roof of her mouth, but she was patient while I first tried to work it out, then cut it off at the roof. Not knowing how badly she was hurt, I wanted to wait until the bleeding at least slowed before putting her back in the water.

I splashed her and stroked her while I was working on the hook and then while I was waiting to make sure she was going to be okay. It was during the latter that I finally got what she had been trying to tell me in my dream about peace. We peace-lovers need to believe in peace as much as the war-makers believe in war. In this time of war we cannot afford cynicism, for we will only victimize ourselves. I was reminded of an essay by Alice Walker in which she talks about how the "Universe responds." She points out that the militarists and the scientists have a better understanding of this phenomenon than we who want peace and love to prevail. It's not about being blind to the pain and anger and hurt in the world. It is about, in the face of those realities, being able to hold onto our belief in the way of goodness. Dhanyi Ywahoo calls this "Walking the Beauty Road."

We need to remember there is truth in the old adage "Love will find a way." I know in my heart peace will come when we no longer believe in war. Bigotry will die when we are collectively ready to embrace differences.

As I placed Selena back in the water, I thought about the vision in which she first appeared. This time, in the light of day, as I knelt on the ledge, Selena did not run away. Only when I nodded my understanding of her message did she rise up out of the water, flip her tail in the air and fall back into the water to return to its depths.

As I gathered my belongings and prepared to go back to the cabin, I realized I had given her some of my old sadness to take with her. There is now more room in my heart for peace.

THE BASSING GAL

SUGAR FERRIS

THE SUN'S FACE PEEKS THROUGH the branches of the pines surrounding the cove, creating dancing ribbons of color on the smooth surface of the water.

On the deep side of the shallows, hidden in the water's murky depths, is a brushpile. Suspended in the brushpile is a large female bass. As the sun climbs higher and the water begins to warm considerably, the bass's metabolism begins to climb, but she doesn't dare venture too far from her trusted lair. After all, she knows the loonies will be on the lake soon and she doesn't want to be in open water when all hell breaks loose.

Warm rays hop across the lake and the bass begins to see a little more clearly. She's slowly making a move to descend into the deeper water when she feels a strong vibration pulsating in the thin vertical bars that run along her left side. She is aware that the pulsation is far too strong for anything that might swim in these waters. But she also realizes that it's not quite strong enough to be one of the loonies up top.

Turning slowly she catches a glimpse of a flashing silver minnow as it streaks across the surface of the water, and watches a frightened green frog leap from the bank. A dragonfly flutters too close to the surface. She wonders how a minnow that big can swim away so quickly. It occurs to her that something isn't right. As she begins to move even deeper into the brushpile, there is a plop on the surface, just in front of her. She suspects that one of the loonies is behind it all, for the flashing minnow is gone before she can react.

A sunbathing water turtle rolls off a log and scatters a shoal of bluegills moving by her. The bass weighs close to seven pounds and could have inhaled any one of the bream that suited her fancy. Her stomach is empty, and the warming water quickens her digestive rate. Instinct tells her it's time she busted something, but her laziness is no match for the bluegill's quickness.

The bassing gal lets her boat drift across the quiet cove along the shores of the ancient tributary that is now covered by the waters of the impoundment. She arrived at the brushpile too late. The bassing gal knows that a large bass is in the brushpile—or down on the ledge—but two other anglers are already anchored where she wanted to fish.

"Rats!" the bassing gal mutters as her boat continues to drift away from the brushpile. She reaches into the rod box and pulls out her favorite fishing rig. She watches the two anglers, still sitting on the brushpile, from some distance away. She knows they don't have a prayer and begins plugging the drop-off about one hundred yards away.

The bass flexes her gills a few times and is ready to move out to the main body of the lake. Suddenly there's a plop directly above her. It's a worm. A small dark, wiggler that drifts down the ledge and settles. The bass watches the small creature as it begins to gently lift off the rock bottom.

With the coldness of a ruthless killer, the bass flares her gills and explodes at the worm as it jumps upwards. It doesn't descend but leaps a few feet beyond the bass's deadly lunge. Blowing air and water through her gills, she quickly turns her heavy body.

Her contracting stomach reminds her that she is in dire need of a meal. An underwater current breaks some forty yards down the ledge. A good place for baitfish but an unpleasant place to be when the loonies hit the water. Strong instinct tells the bass to follow the ledge to the current. She begins to make her move toward the area when a thrashing vibration wakes through the water. It's coming from where the earlier vibration stopped—right over her. An awful grinding sound is powering overhead and the water—even at twelve feet—is rolling her around.

It's a loony. The bass waits, suspended, as the water rolls back to normal. She decides on the spur of the moment to forego following the ledge to the current and moves back in the direction of the brushpile. Her trusted habitat beckons and she moves in, hoping for something edible to venture her way.

The bassing gal sighs as the two anglers at the brushpile move away. She wants the big bass that lives in that brushpile, but the two fishermen really ripped the water when they left. The bassing gal knows the roar of the outboard spooked the big bass into very deep cover. No matter—she likes a challenge. "I'll just flip a hard-to-resist appetizer right on top of that old bass's nose," thinks the bassing gal.

Safely back in the brushpile, the bass feels, then hears one of her kind splash the water in a feeding try. She takes an ambush position. Something plops into the water about twenty feet away. It's a tasty looking worm, longer and lighter than the one she'd encountered before. But it was moving away slowly, barely lifting off and then falling gently to the bottom. Of course it would have been a good meal, but it was too far away and in dark water. The bass would rarely search that far no matter how tempting the meal.

The bassing gal was off the mark with her first cast to the brushpile. She'll fish it slow, for the bass might be suspended just off the cover. On her second cast she would flip right into the thick of the brushpile.

The bass turns a little and faces ahead. There are no loonies roaming yet, but there are no baitfish either. The bass becomes increasingly restless and hungry. Again she senses, then hears, one of her kind splash the water in another feeding try. The action triggers her body, and she comes awake with the alertness of a predator. That shoal of bluegills best not come close now.

Just above her, on the surface of the water, something splashes. The bass's body remains perfectly still. Only her eyes shift slightly to inspect the sound. A worm, just like the last one, floats directly in front of her, wiggling ever so slightly. She senses food. Wasting no time she explodes. Her cavernous mouth opens, and the worm is soon deep in her gullet. She closes her mouth to ingest the little worm into her gnawing stomach. Realizing a moment too late that it's a bad worm, she tries to blow it out. The worm tugs like nothing she has ever felt before. At that precise moment the bass feels something sharp drive into her upper lip.

The angler has her!

Fear plagues the bass, and she quickly speeds for deep water, searching for the safe hiding place. The tension in her builds. Bursting into what has always been a safe haven from all intruders, the bass races in a straight line, just as a fingerling would race from her.

Anxiety increases as the bass feels the small brown worm, one thousand times smaller than she, pull her away from the brushtip. In vain, she tries to smash the worrisome thing against a limb, but is once again pulled into the open water.

The bassing gal plays the drag, keeping a steady pressure on the old sow bass, tiring her out.

The bass decides she'll go for broke and streaks straight upward, breaking the water like a missile. She thrashes, twists and tail dances across the surface of the water just before she plunges back into the depths to head for her haven of safety.

Instinct summons the last of her strength, and with a valiant effort she dives. But the bass's energy is gone. It's too late.

Something, not the worm, has grabbed her lower lip, and she is lifted out of the water. Her lower jaw is held with a steady grip that seems to paralyze her entire body. Ah! So this is what a loony looks like.

The bassing gal looks at her prize for a few moments, realizing this is her best ever. A real trophy. As she releases the hook from the bass's mouth, the thought crosses her mind that she should release the fish. The bassing gal doesn't want to, but she will.

Leaning across the side of the boat, she casts a longing glance at the bass. "If I take this fish home, I'll be the envy of all my angling buddies and every member of my bass club." With that one last thought she quickly eases the bass back into the water.

The bass lies just beneath the surface for a moment, flexing its gills. "Rats!" screams the bassing gal just as the bass begins her dive into the murky depths, "Why didn't I take a picture of her?"

The water feels wonderful to the bass. Her metabolism is soaring, but her frenzy has subsided. Free from the loony, she turns slightly, pauses, then darts toward the brushpile. It takes a few seconds for her to reach the thick center limbs of home where she'll hold as tight as she can.

In half-an-hour she'll feed again!

FLY FISHING FOLLY

AILM TRAVLER

FLY FISHING TWISTS fate like a dream and together with wildness, makes anything possible. Wildness dances at the edge of
nonsense and catastrophe: a thunderstorm comes out of nowhere on
a high alpine lake, and snow follows heat lightning; a forest fire
sweeps a hillside and new shoots sprout green in spring; a searing
drought sucks creeks and rivers dry that just last year were home to
hundreds of spawning trout. Fly fishing both nurtures wildness and
transforms it.

When I go fishing I deliberately go to a place I don't know yet. It
would be easy to fish the same waters week after week, to drive to a
place where I could catch "stockers," those predictable rainbows
dumped out of steel drums for creel addicts. But that's not the idea. I
want to make it hard for myself, mysterious, a shape-shifting journey
to another world where I can turn into a wild trout.

Journeys to the world of wild trout take me to places where survival hangs in the balance. Wild trout depend upon a yearly and sea-
sonal life cycle of thousands of insects, and they can survive only in
clear, cold streams recharged by snows and rains, streams that are not
overly acidic. And wild trout are endangered by those who dam rivers
for profit, turn mountainsides into board-feet and use radar screens to
catch fish.

The loss of pristine trout waters makes fishing hard. Fly fishing
makes fishing even harder by demanding an attention to minutiae

that is archaic. It requires an intimacy with bugs, birds, weather, water and fish that sticking a worm on a hook never asked of me.

I have to squint at a tiny fly of feather and fur pinched between my cold fingers; I get a headache trying to tie the fly onto a piece of hair-thin gut. Then I am forced to slide on my stomach through thorny gooseberry bushes, step into the ooze of a bog or over sharp rocks and boulders so that the trout won't see me. For what?

To touch something primordial and strange. To catch a glimpse of trout feeding in a pool beneath a waterfall, watch them dart out from a shadow to sip an emerging nymph or struggling caddis fly. To become water and stone, current and foam; to find myself alone at "the beginning," the time of creation, when animals, fish, birds and fir trees spoke the same language.

Fly fishing is a way of hooking into the world, being part of the swirling current and riffle patterns on a river, the tall grasses bending down into pocket water; the chill, the sun, the quiet or the screech of hawks. You become what you fish: a vulnerable cutthroat in a brushy, steep mountain stream; a sly brown hiding deep in the roiling waist-high waters of the Rio Grande; a skittish brookie in a meandering meadow creek; a wary golden trout in a deep alpine lake.

I do not have to fish in order to survive. Eating off the land is really possible only for those who have access to thousands of acres of wilderness year round. Surviving off the land is a rarity these days, and only a handful of indigenous peoples know how to do it.

The truth is, fly fishing is folly: useless, unreasonable, irrational, and without purpose. Fly fishing is folly precisely because it makes survival harder than it already is, and by doing so, turns survival into art.

Like poetry, fly fishing is evocative beyond thought—the rings of water after a rise.

Poetry may not be "useful," but its form obeys primordial laws of meter and rhythm. To utter the ineffable, one must retrace a journey to the beginning when meter and rhythm were born, the source of "a little language such as lovers use, words of one syllable."[1]

The same is true of fly fishing. Just as poetry obeys primordial

---

[1] From *The Waves*, Virginia Woolf.

laws, there is a canon of law in fly fishing: how to cast, what a fly should look like, how to read the water and so on. You have to learn to snap or flip the line in the air so that your fly lies perfectly on the water; you must know your knots, your entomology and the proper tippet for the proper leader.

But these are just the mechanics. The real requirement is to learn to think like a trout who, in a split second, sorts out a bunch of shape-shifting elements in order to survive. In that moment, gazing at the air above the water for whirring insects, parting stickling willow branches, peering at a glistening riffle for a shadow or in the tailspin smooth water behind a rock for a disappearing fin, the rules vanish and there is only a dream. Flip Splash. The hesitation after the trout strikes. You raise your arm to set the hook.

When the trout leaps out of the water to take the fly, there is silence. You don't know how you got there, standing half in the water, brush scratching at your cheek. A dream. The trout hits the water. The hush breaks, the leaves rustle again, the water flows again. A bird calls. The trout is tugging at your line, and you are transformed.

Like the heroes of great mythological quests, fishermen like to boast of the "big one" that got away and, more often, the big one that they caught. The fish's proportions are heroic, and as the fish is pursued, its size increases. In "fish stories," not only are the fish huge but the waters are teeming with them as well.

Back in 1947 me and Bill hiked up an old trail and fished this creek. We must have caught 110 fish!

July 12, 1890. Ralph and Grandfather went up to Shingle Bridge and brought back 240 trout.

The trouble is, those waters no longer exist. They've been sucked dry for irrigation, dammed up for electricity and silted into nonexistence by mining and logging. And if streams and lakes manage to escape this pummeling, they are overfished.

I was guilty of it. In the beginning I wanted to catch as many fish as possible. I even had a worm farm so that I would have an unlimited, free supply of worms in order to catch an unlimited amount of fish. A weighty knapsack full of trout wrapped in mint grass in a plastic bag and sputtering, crisp trout in the frying pan were the objectives of "going fishing." I'd break the rules and smile when I opened the freezer and saw all of those neatly wrapped packages of trout.

Then something happened. One spring I decided to get a fly rod. I don't know why. It was a feeling, a vague image of something that teased at me, drew me in, like the hexagram Youthful Folly in the I ching, "It is not I who seek the young fool, the young fool seeks me."[2]

My desire to catch as many trout as possible didn't change in one season. It was when I started tying my own flies the following winter that I began to notice a transformation.

When I am sitting at the tying vise the world is focused on the space in front of me where dubbing furs, feathers, thread and ribbing materials are spread out: deer, hare and muskrat fur; rooster and hen hackles; peacock swords, pheasant tails; gold and silver tinsel; red and yellow floss; brown, black and cream thread. Everything else vanishes.

The hook in the vise represents the water the insect I am imitating hatches from, swims around in, flies out of or falls into. The type of fly I tie chooses the weather, the shore, the stream, river, lake or pond, the wind, sun, clouds and, ultimately, the trout I want to catch. Once the fly is tied onto the tippet of my leader, it is more than an imitation insect, it is my guide to another world.

The idea behind fishing with a fly is to trick the trout into thinking your fly is a real insect. You get so tricky that pretty soon you forget why you are spending so many hours bent over a hook no bigger than a lettuce seed, and hours more retrieving the nicely camouflaged hook from brush, branches, and beaver dams. Expending that much effort at creating something elegant only to lose it on the underside of a boulder buried in the river or the top branches of a nearby juniper might be considered pain in the service of beauty. To do it week after week, season after season, is folly.

The spring which followed my fly-tying winter, I came full circle and found myself at the beginning of my journey, but now with folly as my guide, I knew "the place for the first time."[3]

Besides tying flies, I had also studied maps of northern New Mex-

---

[2] From Hexagram four, Meng/Youthful Folly, *The I Ching or Book of Changes.*
[3] From "Little Gidding," *The Four Quartets,* T. S. Eliot.

ico and southern Colorado, looking for places where nobody went, where I might find pristine waters teeming with fish all to myself. I located a protected wildlife area crisscrossed by two streams, inaccessible to all but mountain bikers and hikers with a lot of time.

One weekend, in the midst of a vicious drought, a friend and I put our bikes in the back of the pickup and drove a couple of hours until we came to an unassuming barbed wire fence and gate in the foothills of the Rockies. Before us lay a landscape of brown, stunted grasses, shriveled bushes and leafless trees. Blue-green mountains loomed in the distance.

It was suffocating, hot. We biked a few miles on a dirt road and then cut north, overland, bumping our way along overgrazed meadows and cow paths, in the direction of the first stream shown on the topographical map. We crossed a pitiful, dribbling sluice of warm water and headed for the forest, where the map showed a lake with a stream running into it.

When we got to where the lake was supposed to be it wasn't there. We pulled our bikes over fallen trees and up some ravines. We rode further, climbing steadily, in and out of aspen glades along the edge of pine and fir trees where we surprised elk napping in the shadows. Soon we were biking along a small creek flowing in the darkness of dense underbrush and willow thickets.

When the trace of a trail began a steep climb, we gave up and stopped. I had long ago lost the thrill of the bike adventure and wanted to fish. I put together my fly rod and tied on a small-sized parachute Adams I had tied that winter. I walked downstream a ways and then, crouching and crawling, fought my way through a tangle of willows and gooseberry bushes. When I finally reached the mossy banks of the creek and saw the crystal pools stepping their way upstream, I was entranced.

I moved closer, trying to stay invisible in the brush, and bent toward the first pool. The water was so low that the native cutthroat trout were bunched in the pockets of deep water formed behind fallen logs and cairns of mossy rocks. I tossed the fly onto the surface of the pool and with a splash and tug I had my first fish. It had been so easy that, after flipping out the hook, I gently let the cutthroat with its red-orange gills slide back into the water. It swam away in fright, but there was nowhere to go because the water was so low. Seconds later the trout was back in position behind the log, darting for food floating down the current.

I went to the next pool. The same thing. I lobbed my Adams gently onto the surface and strike! I released another speckled cut-throat. Trout after trout. I let them all go. I was excited. Success was coming so swiftly and easily. I reached a point near where my friend was reading under a tree. I waved her over, and we both crept into the brush upstream to a pool. I cast my fly into the current and a trout leapt out of the water to take it. My friend watched me let the fish go with amazement. I caught another. She congratulated me and went back to her book.

I scrambled upstream through the brush and peered down at the tailwater above a small waterfall. A bunch of cutthroat were holding in the deep water, waiting for a morsel. I put my rod aside. I took off my boots and rolled up my pants. Cautiously I stepped in the cool water. I splashed some on my face and sat down. The trout swam next to me unperturbed, treating me like a rock, a place to rest and wait for unsuspecting insects. We sat there. They finned, I was still. I watched them fish for nymphs and bugs. I was content.

I learned something that day, something about myself and the natural world and the fragility of ecosystems of which we humans are but a small part. It is not we who are the heroes with our fish stories, it is the trout themselves. They have managed to survive drought, selfishness and greed.

I yearn for rivers and streams teeming with fish because I would love to be able to catch fish and bonk them on their heads without a care in the world. But even if those places did exist, and a few still do, I would let the trout go anyway. Catching and releasing wild trout is not just a sport or game, it is *letting the cycle continue.* Not trying to stop the wind or rain but letting it *pass through.* Success for me lies in wildness and wonder—the folly of releasing wild trout back into their cold, clear waters to grow old.

FISHING THE WHITE WATER

AUDRE LORDE

Men claim the easiest spots
stand knee-deep in calm dark water
where the trout is proven.

I never intended to press beyond
the sharp lines set as boundary
named as the razor names
parting the skin
and seeing the shapes of our weaknesses
etched into afternoon
the sudden vegetarian hunger for meat
tears on the typewriter
tyrannies of the correct
we offer mercy   forgiveness
to ourselves and our lovers
to the failures we underline daily
insisting upon next Thursday
yet forgetting to mention each other's name
the mother of desires
wrote them under our skin.

I call the stone   sister   who remembers
somewhere my grandmother's hand
brushed   on her way to market
to the ships
you can choose   not to live
near the graves where your grandmothers sing
in wind through the corn.

There have been easier times
for loving   different richness
if it were only the stars

213

we had wanted
to conquer
I could turn from your dear face
into the prism light makes
along my line
we cast into rapids
alone   back to back
laboring the current.

In some distant summer
working our way farther from bone
we will lie in the river
silent as caribou
and the children will bring us food.

You carry the yellow tackle box
a fishnet over your shoulder
knapsacked
I balance the broken-down rods
our rhythms pass through the trees
staking a claim   in difficult places
we head for the source.

A LITTLE SHORT
OF THE RECORD

ELIZABETH ENRIGHT

THE GUIDE'S NAME was Captain Len Baker. For the first hour or two the people in his fishing parties called him Captain Baker, but pretty soon they called him Len, though he went on calling them Mr. or Mrs. Whatever-it-was.

Gregg had been calling him Len all morning, but Celia still called him Captain, or just "you." They had been out on the flats since eight o'clock stalking bonefish, and so far had had no luck, though several times they had seen little regattas of silver triangles as the fish "tailed" in the shallows.

"They feed like that, snoot down," Len said. "Anyways, they do in the warm weather. In winter seems like they don't even want to get their tail ends out where it's cold."

He stood in the prow of the skiff, poling the boat stern forward; he was a young man, thirty-two or -three, burned to a deep red-brown. He wore dark glasses and a shredded straw hat; around his lips was a circle of white zinc oxide, and as he poled evenly and quietly his trained eyes roved over the flat, thin water. If there was anything worth seeing he would see it.

"There's a fish there," he said. "But it's a country mile away. Over close by that mangrove bush. Watch."

The mangrove bush, like all its kind, stood up out of the water on a lot of hooped legs. Whatever fish had stirred there was gone now. It was nearing noon, and the water of the keys was a new color. In the early morning it had been milky-blue and brown; later it had looked yellow, and close by it still looked yellow but in the distance it was green as jade. Pilings from the old railroad trestle stood up in a line between mangrove humps, and every piling was topped with a bird, a pelican or a cormorant, even a gull or two. Some of the cormorants were drying their wings; they held them out, open from the shoulders.

"They remind me of those jackets traveling salesmen hang up in their car windows," Celia remarked.

Gregg said nothing; whimsey bored him. Len said nothing as he had not listened.

The pole dipped quietly into the water, and the boat breathed forward. Reflections of cloud glazed the water with white. They could hear the traffic brushing along the mile-distant highway.

"Nurse shark there to the left," Len said, pointing with the pole; a ragged shadow slipped over the marl and weed, and far out on the shallowest flat a Ward's heron stalked with the villain's step and the fanatic stare of a mad professor.

"Well, where's all the fish?" said Len, after a long lulled silence. "They oughta be tailin' good. Water's about ten inches, just right. Weather's just right. Might be it's gointa be a storm tonight or tomorrow. They always seem to know, and then they duck down somewheres out of sight. You folks want to eat now?"

"Might as well," Gregg said, taking off his beaked cap and blotting his forehead with a handkerchief. He was an extraordinarily handsome man; his black hair, barely skimmed with gray, rippled back from his brow in deep, perfect waves. In his sun-dark face three things always struck a blow in the solar plexus of any woman who met his direct regard: the even blackness of his eyebrows, the flawless light blue of his eyes, the white, white teeth. As he grew older he grew handsomer, and in this Celia was well aware that she would not be able to keep pace with him much longer.

The guide poled to a little channel between two mangrove islets. On a silvery old knock-kneed platform there was an assemblage of lobster pots and a dry seine. Len moored the boat there, and they sat in the strong light and ate their lunch. It was now the very middle of noon; everything seemed stilled, held in suspension. The old tough birds on the trestle pilings were motionless as gatepost birds.

But in the deep little channel below them, shadows curved and flitted.

"Snapper down there," Len said, through his sandwich. "Big one's a snook. Caught me plenty of good tarpon here, too, after sundown."

Gregg carefully extracted the lettuce from his sandwich and dropped it overboard, where it wagged away slowly on the current.

"Best tarpon I ever got was off the coast of Cuba," he said, without looking at Celia. Then he took a bite, chewed and swallowed it. "Ninety-seven pounds."

"Man, that's a big fesh!" said Len.

"Sure gave me trouble," Gregg said. "We were fishing off Batabanó when we contacted this baby. Felt as if a pile driver had struck. I swear. And then the fun began; it took me five and a half hours—*five and a half hours*—to boat the bastard, and every time I got feeling like I might conk out, the skipper would douse me with a pail of sea water. After a while the other fishing craft around quit what they were doing and closed in to watch the circus, and when we finally boated this baby they cheered; I'm telling you they really cheered! Ninety-seven pounds."

"Man, that's a big fesh!" Len repeated approvingly.

"Don't know if I'd care to meet another one like that one," Gregg said with a laugh.

Celia was silent. The story was not true. The tarpon had been caught by Jates Wellington, a friend of Gregg's whom she disliked and who disliked her. It had taken him three hours to land the fish, not five, and Gregg had told the story so often as happening to himself that he probably believed it by now. It was the same with the story about how he had won a packet at Santa Anita in 1949. Actually he had lost a packet. And there was the account of his excellent advice to the Secretary of Defense, and how this advice had been praised and acted upon, when in reality he had once sent such a letter to the Secretary and it had never been acknowledged.

When he told these harmless, ornamental lies Celia hated and despised her husband. The fact that he told them in front of her, aware that she knew they were false yet would permit them, both hurt and shamed her. Then began the argument or the explanation to that imaginary third person whose all-seeing eye could never be deceived.

Where is your integrity? inquired this observer. There was no real reply. There were only glimpses, concessions, memories: Gregg teaching Stevie to pitch a ball; sitting up with a colicky baby in the night;
his tact and patience with the children in their adolescence (more
than she herself could give); his silent fortitude long ago when he had
lost his job; his occasional gay drunkenness at parties. There was the
way he looked, and there was their bed. Who can stand like a light-
house, immovable throughout a marriage, glaring toward integrity?

"If you've finished congratulating yourself about that tarpon for
the thousandth time, maybe we could continue our search for these
measly little bonefish," said Celia sharply.

Gregg laughed. By ignoring her anger he avoided the danger of
bringing its cause into the open; he was very good at that. But Celia
could feel a sudden startled attention in the attitude of the guide.

The light of early afternoon was flat and all encompassing and
seemed as it always did to her, the only light of truth; hope and illusion were equally bleached away with other tender colors. The thin
waste of water, the gentle movement of the boat, the figure at their
backs poling them forward, all gave the scene a flat, timeless quality
as if this moment separated from the context of their lives might last
forever.

"Was Charon old or young?" said Celia, too dazed with light to
keep her anger. "I can't remember. I think he had a beard."

"Well, it's a question. How old *is* an immortal?" Gregg's firm
hand came down on her dry nervous one.

The guide drove his pole deep into the marl and lashed the
painter to it. Swiftly and quietly he baited the hooks.

"Where?" inquired Gregg. "I don't spot them."

"Shh, you gotta be *quiet*," whispered Len. "They're shy. I seen
them scatter for a butterfly's shadow. Over there. Yonder."

In the patched water to the stern they could see a quirk, a tipped
sail flashing like mirror, a triangle, a splash. There was another; two,
three, many of them.

Line hissed through the air, the bait made a tiny splash far away.
"Here, give this to the missis," whispered Len. She took the rod,
warm from the sun, and held it tensely. Gregg's line curved to the left
and a few yards away from hers. The little sails, capricious, turned

listing and flashing, approached the bait, left it, came back. Celia's heart rolled over in her chest.

Gregg's bait was hit first. She could feel his sudden startled wince; the jar of the boat as he whipped his rod back fiercely. "Got one!" He stood up unsteadily and his cap fell onto the floor. The rod in his hands arched like a bow, and the line was drawn straight, straight as a wire . . . and then it slackened, tossed loosely in the wind.

" I lost it," he said despairingly.

"You didn't set the hook right, sir," Len said, with patience. "See, you have to let them take it in their mouth, feel it around, kind of taste it and start to go off with it; *then* set it. They got superstitious mouths, those fish. I thought you knew."

"Goddamn," said Gregg.

"Well, he's not the only fesh on these keys. Reel in now, sir, I would. There's some after the missis' bait still."

Celia's heart rolled over again. She felt excitement out of all proportion to the cause, and was close to prayer. She watched the little tails turning and tipping, heard the faint flicker of their movement, and when she felt the first tentative, testing of the bait disciplined herself to wait the short moment before the assertive pull, the grab. Then she jerked the rod up.

Line whistled from the reel.

"Just let him run," sang Len gently, as if these were words to a lullaby.

Far away the water rose up in a wind as the line cut it, and the fish rushed in a great circle around the boat.

"A good seventy-five yards he's took," Len said. "Now, missis, pump him e-easy and start to reel as you go down."

"Good girl, Celie," said Gregg. "*You're* doing it right."

Another thing about him was that he was generous.

Her arm and wrist ached from the pumping and winding, and there was a sore spot on her diaphragm where the rod handle was braced. Every time she brought the fish close enough to see it, dark and fleeting, it would take fright and fly with the line again. Sweat fell from her forehead, and she was in real pain as she worked, but at last she had it close enough to the boat so that Len could reach out with his net and ladle it from the sea.

"Son! That's a beauty! Go better than ten pounds, I reckon."

"Congratulations, darling," Gregg said, patting her shoulder. As for her, she was trembling, her right arm almost palsied, and she sank to the seat, laughing weakly.

The great fish, armored in silver, lurched and strove in the net; with all its struggle of motion its eye remained unmoving, fixed in a bright hard stare.

Len hooked the fish scale under its gill and held it up.

"Twelve pounds and a little!" he exclaimed. "That's a *fesh*. The *record's* only fourteen, missis! He's hooked good, too. You want to keep him? The weight would justify keepin' him."

She touched the cold, slimed scales with the tip of her finger. "No, let him go."

He put the fish over the side, held it there in the water teasingly for a moment as it struggled in his hands.

"Go on, then," he said. "Go tell the folks."

Off went the shadow, darting and swerving, safe and dignified in its element.

The afternoon wore on slowly; there were no more fish. Celia sat quietly, secretly reliving and reliving the glory of her catch as though she had really performed a deed of unusual skill and valor.

At five o'clock when they returned to the dock of the fishing camp they were sun beaten, spent and yawning.

"Good-by, Len, and thanks."

"You sure caught a beauty, ma'am. Good-by."

"So long, Len, see you next year maybe," said Gregg. "Coming to the bar, darling?"

"No, I think I'll sleep till dinner."

But after her shower she felt refreshed and wide awake and decided to join him. As she walked along the path from their cabin to the main building she was aware of a great feeling of well-being and peace. The sea was now a pure delphinium blue, and overhead the coconut palms bridled and rustled like large, dry birds.

Len was coming from the boat dock, sunburned, bowlegged, amiable.

"Come and have a drink with us," said Celia.

"Why, thanks, I'd like to, ma'am. I sure could use a beer."

"Only a beer?"

She thought of the occupants of the bar with whom she and Gregg had become familiar in the past two nights after their days of Gulf fishing. There was the elderly man whose face up to his eyebrows was dark and clotted, but above them, where his hat had been, his great bald head was as pale and polished as an Episcopal bishop's. He had sat drinking zombies in silence, staring at Celia. There was the woman who had once been very pretty, still trying to be pretty, still hoping for a miracle, pursing her pleated lips and twitching at her scalded curls. As the evening wore on, her voice rambled and deepened, a flush darkened her cheeks, and there was the glimmer of gold in her constant laughter. Her husband was one of the heehawers that collect in the bar of any fishing camp, and so was the man from Michigan who was obsessed with the idea of Amar'ca and Amar'cans (a narrow band of people holding his own views; the rest were pinkos, eggheads and slack thinkers).

None of these people went in for beer. And she and Gregg, too, after their rocking, sun-dazzled days, downed their share of harder liquors and went tipsy to bed to sleep the total sleep of children.

"Well, I might make it a dry Martini," said Len, after serious thought. "Bout once a year I might take *one*."

"Good."

The screen door sucked shut behind them, and they crossed the empty dining room silently on their rubber soles. The waiting tablecloths flapped at the corners, and the rustle of the palm fronds sounded, now, like rain.

As they neared the bar they could hear Gregg's voice. "What a fight he gave me!" he was saying, beginning to heehaw, too, like the others. "Twelve pounds, a little over; not much short of the record! Well, we'd almost given up, nothing nibbled, not even the crabs, and all of a sudden I see these little tails begin to wave, and I wait. I feel this soft little nibble, and I wait. And then when I *strike* it, the line spins off the reel so fast it smokes! I swear. Seventy-five yards before I could draw a breath—"

Automatically Celia and Len had stopped short of the swinging door.

"Look, Mrs. Hanson," said Len in a low voice. "I gotta go home. My wife, I just remembered, she's got her aunt comin' to supper and I gotta get back. She'll have everything fixed."

"Oh. I see. Not time for even one?" But there was no persuasion in her words.

"With her aunt there already, prob'ly . . . Oh, no, look, ma'am, if I went in there now I'd just get into an argument. Into a fight, I reckon. Heck, it was you caught that fesh; we all know that. I better go."

"All right, Len, I understand. But Len—"

"Ma'am?"

"Do me a favor and don't talk about it, will you? Leave it the way he says it was."

She watched the esteem ebb from his face.

"If that's the way you want it, ma'am."

"Yes. Thank you."

When he had gone she pushed open the louvered door and went over to the bar beside Gregg.

"Why, Celie, I thought you were asleep." His look was startled, even alarmed. Perhaps this time—

"Your hubby's just been telling us about the whopper he caught today," said the former beauty, her hand cupped lovingly around her glass.

"Whopper is right," said Celia smoothly. "Yes, wasn't he fortunate?"

The bartender placed his hands on the bar before her; his forearms, below his immaculate, rolled-up sleeves, were tatooed. On the right arm there was a blue and red picture of a girl in a bikini; on his left there was the bleeding heart of Jesus and a cross.

Celia fixed her eyes on the girl in the bikini, and said: "Give me a Martini, please, Lou. Very dry." (When had she absorbed the fact that his name was Lou?)

"Darling!" said Gregg, his voice solicitous with guilt. "You know you never drink Martinis! You know you can't, darling."

"Make it a double, Lou," said Celia. "I'm drinking for a friend."

THE SEARCH FOR THE SWORD

ALBIA DUGGER

I DOUBT IF ANY SINGLE experience influenced me to make sport fishing my career. It came about more as a synthesis of events that evolved slowly over the course of fifteen years, coalescing into a hybrid career of fisheries scientist, fishing captain and fishing writer-editor.

Becoming a fishing person wasn't an easy process for me, but it was a natural one, since I had worked as a marine biologist since I was sixteen. I can't say I started at the bottom and worked up, nor could I actually say that I started at the top and worked down. It was more like starting somewhere in the middle and then wandering in circles, picking up on opportunities as they presented themselves.

However, the ups and downs of my fishing career were definitely held together by one special goal, my desire to capture a swordfish as an angler.

Miami, Florida, 1976

I had graduated from college, pre-med, and finally admitted to myself that I was not cut out to be a doctor. The closest thing I had to a job was part-time photo-modeling for ads and catalogs, but as far as a career went, I hadn't a clue.

So there I was at age twenty-four, playing at modeling, with long, sculpted fingernails and a photographer's warning against getting sunburn marks during the vacation to Mexico I was planning with a girlfriend whom I had met while sailing in the Bahamas.

At that point, if someone had told me I would go back to marine biology, study fishing and become a licensed merchant marine officer, I would have told them they were nuts. But something happened on that trip to Cozumel that changed my outlook. I almost caught a swordfish.

Cozumel, Mexico, 1977

My friend Karen had grown up in a fishing family in Fort Lauderdale, whereas my fishing experience was limited mostly to casting from bridges and seawalls as a kid. So, when Karen introduced me to the elite American crews fishing in Cozumel, I was, in a way, starting at the top. They explained to me in terms I didn't understand that there was a special type of fishing they did at night. That seemed perfect for me—no sunburn.

Although I had worked on research vessels, shrimp trawlers and sailing vessels, the thirty-one-foot Bertram was the first sportfishing boat I had been on, and as we left the dock at sunset, I explored every nook and cranny, touching the impressive Penn International 80-wide offshore reels and studying the heavy fastenings and hardware of the massive Lee's fighting chair. The long, spidery outriggers stretching into the darkness, the tuna tower bristling with radar and radio antennas, all were strange and intricate puzzles that widened my eyes with wonder.

Karen sat in the fighting chair and showed me how the harness was adjusted so that the weight of a big fish was taken by the angler's legs working against the footrest of the chair. The mysterious preparations in the offshore darkness, in a world circumscribed by the perimeter of the blue pool cast by the tower's isolated spotlights, made the whole setting seem unreal.

Suddenly the vibrating roar of the engines and the pounding from the invisible seas were replaced by complete silence. We were over the deep-water edge, in pitch blackness, somewhere offshore of the midnight Yucatan jungle, ready to drift with the current. Soft, tentacled squids were fastened to the hooks and marked with eerie-green chemical lightsticks that glowed like balls of fire as they sank through the crystal clear depths of the Yucatan Channel. All other lights were extinguished. We rocked and drifted with the current, speaking with hushed tones in respect for the greater silence of the night.

The click of the reel when it came sounded like a shot, and Karen jumped to the fighting chair. As she buckled in, I was instructed to steer the chair to keep the nearly invisible line straight off the rod tip. I gasped as Karen was suddenly pulled physically out of the chair by a huge tug on the giant rod; she was suspended like a marionette in midair, straining against the strings of an invisible puppeteer.

The force of the strike took me by surprise. The biggest fish I had ever caught was a snapper. The idea of an ocean creature large enough and strong enough to exert that kind of pressure was frightening. As the fight raged in darkness, I was caught up in the intensity of the struggle against the unknown adversary. I saw the pain and effort of retrieving every inch of line after many swift and powerful runs stripped the reel lower and lower.

But finally the tide turned, and line began appearing on the spool. Excitement mounted and urgent instructions were issued as the glow of the lightstick was seen rising from the depths, pulsing with the unseen tailbeat. Suddenly the double-line was at the rod tip. Briefly I saw a fierce, wide-eyed black animal with a strong broad sword like the horn of a dark unicorn rising from the water, thrashing angrily at its tormentors, as the mate reached out and sank a heavy 8-inch piece of steel into its side. Even then it took all the strength of two large men to subdue the huge, violently thrashing creature and pull it through the door in the transom. One crewman pinned the long, heavy sword to the deck with gloved hands, and the other grappled with the sleek muscular form as its last throes were exhausted. Finally it lay dark and silent as the night on the wet and rocking deck.

My heart was pounding. This was my first sight of a great oceanic predator, the broadbill swordfish. I was awed by its strength and size, its dangerous sword and its giant, mysterious eyes that glowed like prophetic crystal balls.

When they put the lines back out and said it was my turn, they may as well have said it was my turn to be an astronaut and we were in countdown to blast off. I was terrified. It was 3:00 a.m. in pitch darkness far offshore, and we had an armed prehistoric creature lying there under our feet. I had seen it try to beat two husky men into the deck after an hour of trying to pull Karen overboard into the black thousand-foot depths. When the clicker went off again, I sat in the chair and was buckled in, but with the dread of something happening that was totally beyond my control or ability to cope with.

I followed instructions stiffly, in slow motion. They backed the drag off in consideration of both my inexperience and the odd way the fish was acting—instead of making the strong, deep runs typical of a swordfish, it was swimming along fairly close to the surface.

They were right. The fish came to the boat easily; it was a small shark. I was relieved that nothing terrible had happened, but somehow incredibly disappointed, too. The more I thought about it, the madder I got. I was like a kid on her first roller coaster ride, dreading the unknown beforehand, then disappointed afterwards because it was over so fast.

Florida Keys, 1977

Most normal people, I assume, would have said "Well, that was fun" and gone on with their lives. But I had been looking for a direction, and that experience convinced me that I was still a marine biologist at heart. Swordfishing had taken a firm hold on my imagination and lit a fire under my ambition.

I moved to the Keys and learned to fish. I got introductions to some of the best professional fishermen in Florida, who taught me with skill and patience. I went out on the charterboats and worked my way around the cockpit and up to the bridge, learning everything from catching live bait and chumming with sandballs to gaffing kingfish and reading fathometers to identify prey.

But I didn't stop at just learning fishing techniques. I went to the University of Miami and enrolled in its prestigious graduate school for marine fisheries. The department head was studying swordfish, and I walked into his laboratory and told him I was going to help.

My project was to meet commercial swordfish longline boats when they returned from fishing and to take data and examine the swordfish stomach contents to find out what they ate. I soon learned considerably more about swordfish, and about fishing in general, both in class and on the docks.

But then I got sidetracked. Living in the Keys, I was immersed in fishing of all sorts. To pay for my schooling, I had taken a job doing recreational fishing surveys, which involved visiting docks all over Florida and the Keys and talking to fishermen. I got involved with fisheries management debates, giving public lectures and even representing the local charter boat association as an expert witness to the state legislature.

Because I had studied fish and was also willing and eager to listen to an unending stream of fishing stories, I was gradually becoming accepted in professional fishing circles. Soon I was lucky enough to hook up with an established fishing team and really started traveling and fishing.

Havana, Cuba, 1978

Cuba had opened its doors to the United States for the first time since the revolution in 1958. Not to tourists or politicians, but to fishermen. We were invited to the Hemingway marlin tournament held outside Havana. I was excited about experiencing Cuba: the culture, the politics, the fishing. But Cuba was also reputed to have some of the world's greatest swordfishing, and secretly I wanted to try my luck there.

We soon found ourselves drifting off the sea-walled and bastioned high-rise metropolis of Havana. We put in our time marlin fishing, with the result that our angler, Billy Pate, achieved the honor of catching the world's first blue marlin on fly rod. During the ten days it took to accomplish that feat, we survived a series of ordeals. Our boat was shot at, and we were literally starved, restricted incommunicado to a chain-linked compound and placed under constant armed guard while we were at the dock. This was all before the other American boats showed up, since we had fished alone during that time by special dispensation.

Once the rest of the American fishing boats arrived, our Cuban hosts suddenly turned extravagant, sparing no expense to entertain their wealthy capitalist guests in fine style with exotic foods, drinks, stage shows and nightclubs.

After a month of trolling for marlin off Havana, we were finally allowed to spend a night out on the drop-off drifting for swordfish. I stood patiently by the chair, waiting for the telltale click. The only other fishing boats visible were Cuban longliners, their burning smudgepot-buoys sending flickering threads of orange smoke into the night sky.

It was peaceful, and we were tired from trolling in the blistering tropical-summer heat all day. One by one, as the night progressed without a bite, we nodded to sleep at our posts.

I awoke with the sun in my eyes and a large automatic weapon in my face. A menacing-looking naval vessel was alongside our small sportfisherman. The Cuban gunship had been sent to look for us, no doubt because we were overdue and had neglected to check in or report our position. They had seen our boat drifting with no crew visible, and we had failed to heed their radio signals in Spanish. Even worse, we were running our radar illegally. We were obviously spies. Having had some preview of the food and living conditions we might expect to be offered as spies, we were immediately very apologetic.

The gunboat escorted us back to our slip with a lecture, and the machine-gun-toting guards posted outside the boat were doubled for the rest of our stay. We were granted no more permission for nighttime swordfishing.

Despite the rude awakening, my first thought at seeing our boarding party had not been fear, but disappointment that we hadn't gotten the swordfish bite. If we had, it would have been worth it.

Cozumel, 1979, 1980

My trips to the Yucatan each year were rewarding. We fished in daylight for sailfish, marlin, dolphin and wahoo. At night we drifted for swordfish. The swordfish were abundant, and the unique, slow-motion strikes came regularly, sometimes three or four times a night, but not for me. These swordfish were caught by the paying customers. Every time I got in the chair the wheel of chance came up empty.

Montauk, New York, 1981

The following summer I found myself in New England, fishing for giant bluefin tuna, those swimming Volkswagens weighing nearly a thousand pounds each. We fished the Canyons, forty miles off-shore, often leaving the dock at three in the morning and returning at midnight to offload and refuel.

It was exciting to see those huge swimming machines feeding in the chum slick, especially considering how much money they were worth. Like everyone else, we sold the giant tuna we caught. Because there were no buy-boats to take the catch from us offshore at that time, we often made landfall at the nearest convenient spot to offload and sell the fish.

One day while we were at the dock in Montauk, a sportfishing boat we knew came in with three swordfish, the biggest I had ever seen. One was over nine hundred pounds; its sword, more than three feet long. The eyes seemed bigger than grapefruits. I stood on the dock and stared, quizzing the boat's crew, who looked inordinately pleased with themselves as they posed for photos with rod and reel.

They told us they had caught the swordfish while drifting at night and showed us a spot on the chart. We took what we thought was special information and headed offshore.

That night, after tuna fishing, we didn't return to the dock, and this time I was the one and only angler. We drifted in the dark, sixty miles offshore over the deepwater canyons, fully expecting to be eaten up by numerous giant swordfish.

Nothing.

When we came in the next night, there our friends were again with two more swordfish. Baffled, we went out and tried again, with the same result.

On our next return to the dock, we discovered the problem. Our friends had been secretly trading with the Japanese tuna longliners, exchanging cases of beer for swordfish that, legally, the longliners were supposed to be discarding, and making top dollar at the fish markets with their "catch."

The dockmaster asked me to examine their swordfish to confirm that they had died on a longline before they were boated. I was glad to do it, because what they were doing was illegal, a breach of interna-tional trade agreements. Also, I had been getting pretty demoralized by their apparent success when viewed against my own dismal fail-ure. I thought of all those nights I had slept out in the cold and the wind to be near the fishing rods when I could have been in a warm, stationary bed. We never did catch a swordfish in the Canyons at night.

Nantucket, 1983

By this time I had fished around the world, in Hawaii, Australia, the Mediterranean and the Caribbean, and seen more swordfish caught than almost anyone other than a longliner. But, after eight years of trying to catch one myself, the swordfish still eluded me. So, one calm, sunny day in Nantucket, we set out to find a swordfish just for me.

In Nantucket they sight-fish for swordfish, not at night as I was accustomed to fishing, but during the day, because the water is so cold that it forces the deepwater fish to come to the surface to warm themselves in the sun.

I was seated in the fighting chair when I heard the lookout's voice shouting from the tower above, "There he is," and saw the twin sickles of the dorsal and tail fins of the basking swordfish. It was a big one and it was beautiful. Its black back glistened with iridescent shades of purple, blue and gold as the fish finned lazily along the surface.

They baited the swordfish from the tower as I held the rod ready in the chair. The huge fish struck the bait on cue and dove, pulling line from the freespooling reel. I waited for the signal and locked it up. There was a jerk on the line and for one exhilarating second we were connected. Then the line went slack. The fish was gone.

I thought it was over, but a minute later the fish resurfaced and with redoubled determination I resumed the position in the chair. But instead of the expected signal to ready the bait I heard the dreaded words, "Ready on the harpoon." The captain guided the boat up and over the fish's back, and in a second "my" long-awaited swordfish was buttonholed by the "lead mullet."

It was the closest I had ever come to catching a swordfish. Words failed me as the nearly five hundred pounds of valuable fish was hauled ignominiously over the gunnels. In sympathy the captain presented me with a small gold swordfish as a memento.

Miami, Florida, 1984

I had nearly forgotten I was working on my master's degree to become an educated fisheries scientist. I had been faithfully performing my interviews everywhere I went, from Pensacola to Gloucester, but the university was starting to get curious about exactly when I intended to finish.

Before wrapping it up though, I had to make a slight detour back to Cozumel, just to keep track of the swordfish situation there. What I found was calamity—no swordfish! There had not been a swordfish caught on rod and reel all season. No double-sickle fins broke the surface during the day. Nighttime drifts were fruitless. I was despondent.

Without swordfish to distract me, there was nothing left but to apply myself to my master's degree. I went back to Miami, installed myself in the cubbyhole student office overlooking Biscayne Bay, surrounded by hundreds of labeled jars of pickled, partially digested swordfish dinners, and diligently submerged myself in statistics and the scientific method, resulting in an original thesis analyzing the value of different fish species to Florida sport fisheries.

Each spring, for the next few years, I returned to fish in Cozumel, but conditions never improved. Longliners moved into the Yucatan Channel, and sport-caught swordfish became a thing of the past.

Miami, 1987

With no great fishing causes to distract me, I finally completed and received my master's in fisheries science from the University of Miami. I had promised myself that when I had finished my master's in fisheries I would take the time to sit for my captain's license, the Coast Guard's master's certificate. I documented my sea time, studied hard and received my license to become a merchant marine officer.

Hawaii, 1988

Now that I was an official, functioning marine biologist, one of my first projects was to attend the prestigious International Billfish Symposium in Kona, Hawaii. This meeting of the top billfish scientists from nations around the world, including Japan, New Zealand, Australia, France, India, Great Britain and many others, was the most important scientific and political event in billfish history.

The news concerning swordfish was dismal across the board. Atlantic swordfish had been overfished by commercial nets and longlines and, without regulation, were possibly in imminent danger of stock collapse.

A war of words raged between management and commercial interests, but the international nature of the problem combined with a lack of sufficient "scientific" evidence left the question unresolved. The final result was that swordfishing would remain unregulated.

As a recreational angler, I took that attitude as a personal affront; as a scientist the evidence of the rapidly shrinking average size of Atlantic swordfish was enough to convince me that something was wrong. Swordfish were disappearing from the oceans, and something had to be done about it.

Miami, 1989

What could I do to influence the world to stop overfishing our valuable oceanic fishes, in general, and billfish specifically? I was in the unique position of having "mastered" both sportfishing and fisheries science, and there was obviously a looming communication gap between the two. I began writing about fishing, relaying scientific data to the fishing public through the major sportfishing magazines. The more I wrote, the more demand there was for conservation information. Suddenly I found myself with a new full-time job, not catching billfish but writing about them.

Cozumel, 1990

Everything seemed to be going right. It appeared I had finally found my niche. But there was one important thing that remained to be done. I had to have that swordfish I had started out to catch fifteen long years earlier. Through four career changes, and more than the usual number of ups and downs, that one quest had remained constant. If I could only fulfill that one, long-standing goal, it would confirm that my life was finally on the right track. It was spring, so I flew to Cozumel. I had come to the island in the spring each of the last fifteen years, hoping to catch a swordfish. For the past half-dozen years, there had been no swordfish available there for anyone to catch. But maybe this year would be the lucky one.

Unbelievably, the first thing I heard when I stepped on the dock was the crackle of VHF sets from the bridges of the sportfishing boats lining the marina, reporting an unusual sight offshore: swordfish! Great, stout, black billfish with huge eyes, tailing and free-jumping in the Yucatan Channel for the first time in years!

It seemed like fate when the crew of the boat I was standing next to commented that they would love to catch a swordfish, but that they didn't have an angler. A match made in heaven, I thought, and we agreed to try. In the gathering dusk I boarded the fifty-seven-foot Viking *Jasmine,* and we headed offshore.

Above the thousand-foot drop-off, the sportfishing boat rocked gently in the darkness. The nearly full moon swinging overhead was the only visible point of reference. I talked about swordfish with the mates, Randy and Gary, as they adjusted the fighting chair for me, measuring the footrest, adjusting the straps of the fighting bucket and safety lines, soaping the seat and removing the backrest.

Randy measured the lines overboard by arm's lengths. Phosphorescent Cyalume lights in green and red marked the three rigged squid with balls of colored fire as they drifted down and away: one hundred, two hundred, three hundred feet to staggered depths. The eighty-pound Penn reels were set as I requested, with just enough drag to keep the breakaway weights from pulling line with the swell.

Finally the lines were out, the cockpit prepared. It felt strange and exhilarating to be a part of the first-time excitement again. None of the young crew had ever fished for swordfish before, but they were ready.

Around us, black sky engulfed black water, swallowing the invisible horizon. To pass the time I dipnetted tiny fish and squid, looking for the miniature billfish that are sometimes attracted to the lights. Kenny, *Jasmine's* captain, watched the depth sounder from the bridge.

Suddenly, over the radio came a report of another sportfishing boat hooked up to the south—they had boated a small swordfish! We cheered for them as our anticipation heightened.

We waited. One two-hour drift passed in silence, then another. Soon the two other drifting sportfishing boats were headed home. It was 1:00 a.m., and Randy was looking disappointed: Nothing had disturbed our lines yet. But I knew it wasn't over. The dozen sword-fish I had seen caught after midnight during the early years in Cozu-mel had taught me patience.

Then, tick-tick, and a silence. We were all on our feet, eyes glued to the reel. The deep-line started to go out.

Randy turned to me for instructions. I decided to leave it in free-spool while Gary and Randy started clearing the other lines. I moved the rod to the chair and buckled in.

Now it was up to me. How long to wait before setting the hook? I had learned from experience not to rush it. I made a slow count as the other lines were cleared, then I started winding—and winding—would there be anything there?

Suddenly the line came tight. "He's on!" Randy shouted to the bridge, and the sound of the engines roaring to life split the long, dark silence.

"Does he feel heavy?" Kenny wanted to know from the bridge. No, not very, but strong. The first run pulled me to my feet against the footrest—then again, and again—four long, strong runs against twenty-four pounds of drag to lean against and rest between pumping and winding.

The fish had eaten the deepest squid and gone straight down. There was no thumping and shaking, and the mono leader was still intact, so, combined with the classic broadbill strike, I was pretty sure it was him, but I was nervously anxious for visual confirmation.

There was nothing for us to look at but darkness and the brown-white swirl of propwash tinged with smoke as Kenny worked the engines back and forth to keep the line centered and the fish made strategic moves to port and starboard, hunting for an angle. Gary and Randy stood on either side of the chair like sentinels, eyes straining into the darkness to keep the line in sight.

They murmured words of encouragement, but I didn't hear. I was having my own monologue with the fish and the night, rating the fish's movements against tunas, sharks and billfish I had fought. It was definitely different; it felt right.

The fish wanted to pull and was making slow but steady headway against the drag. Time and again Randy asked if I could take line; I just shook my head and pointed to the slowly ticking spool.

To gain leverage, the crew worked the boat to an even steeper, but more dangerous, angle over the fish. Now I was able to work the rod: pull, bow, level-wind, pull, putting all the strength of my legs and back into the bucket, straining my fingers to get an extra quarter-wrap of line on the reel.

Finally we were rewarded. After what seemed an eternity, the fish was coming up. For an instant there was a flash of light in the darkness of the depths, not the brown of shark or the gold of tuna, but the pure silver-blue of swordfish gleaming in the crystal Yucatan depths. I glowed with exultation.

Randy yelled excitedly to the bridge that this was it, and the tension of the end-game mounted. Randy donned double-thick wiring gloves as Gary readied the gaff and moved into position low against the gunnels. The double-line came up once, just out of reach of Randy's outstretched glovetips—then was gone as the fish made a last desperate lunge for freedom.

When he finally spent himself, I renewed work. Suddenly, double-line appeared again, and the fish broke the surface twenty feet behind the boat, head and purple back out of the water, brandishing its sword for all to see.

Randy's gloved hands reached for the leader and kept him coming, sword-first over the gunnels, giant round eyes staring. He wasn't big, only 112 pounds, but he was beautiful.

In all, only seven swordfish were caught in Cozumel that year, and all during one week. Afterwards, the swordfish disappeared as mysteriously as they had arrived. What made the swordfish come to the Yucatan after so many years' absence? What inspired me to be there during that one particular week? Perhaps it was just my turn.

There is something dinosaur-like about these nocturnal predators. It is impossible to look at one alive and not feel that you are looking at something incredibly ancient and significant. For me, the thrill of catching my own swordfish after fifteen years of trying was indescribable, the redemption of years of side-tracks and dead ends. Now I wear a black-coral swordfish with emerald eyes, custom made from the precious stone that grows in the depths of the Yucatan Channel—the waters that, after all those years, sent me the sword I had searched for. After fifteen years of traveling the world in search of my future, I had come full circle, finding my goals where I had started. I had finally earned my sword.

A Day in the Life

MARI LOCHHAAS

0430

IT'S SO HARD to tear my body from that warm bunk, muscles aching, hands burning from a hundred tiny cuts, to roll out into the
chill, damp morning. The steady drip from the camper roof forecasts
the weather for today: FOG.

Not your common garden-variety fog, but blanketing, muffling,
permeating Oregon coastal fog. The type that falls from the rigging in
great dollops, stinging my eyes. It seeps through raingear, wool sweaters and long underwear. The casual observer might call it light rain
or even "Oregon mist," but rain comes down sideways here, and the
complete lack of visibility qualifies it as fog. My enthusiasm, such as
it wasn't, wanes.

I slide down the ramp and sleepwalk down the dock. The ghostly
boats float dreamily in the fog, awaiting their masters' awakening. I
step aboard my dory by habit, assuming it's in the same spot. If someone else tied up here I'd probably fish their boat until noon before I
realized why everything was out of place.

The engine coughs and rumbles, then purrs. I thaw out the day's
bait and put on my damp raingear. It's better this way, damp. I'll be
soggy in an hour, anyway. I may as well start out that way.

I wipe the fog from the inside of the cabin windows. The open-
backed overhead cover, common to dories, can't keep the fog out. I'll
need to be sharp with the loran this morning. I wait for its blinking
yellow lights to settle on coordinates. My loran is outdated: its LED

shows only two five-digit numbers, which correspond to my position on a grid that is superimposed on charts of the coastline. I must depend on my water-logged, fish-blood-splattered notebook for the coordinates of buoys, jetties and other fixed objects.

Beside the list of coordinates for navigating the channel are compass courses to steer for the next buoy. This technique of navigating with compass, loran and notebook usually works, providing I compensate correctly for current and wind. This is a broad provision so early in the morning.

Other pages of the notebook list the coordinates for the other ports from which I fish. Wildly strewn in between are isolated coordinates with "pinnacle," "crab pot" or ⊂⋈ next to them, indicating their value.

The numbers on my loran are now a constant display and correspond to the ones in my notebook. I strain my eyes in the dim compass light to make out the hen scratch scribbling in the notebook. Although I have the courses memorized, a quick review can't hurt. I think, for the two thousandth time, I should get a new loran.

Casting off, I feel my way down the channel, depending on my outdated equipment to make the dog-leg turn at the jetty, hidden in the fog. The ebbing tide humps up a bit at the bar, but it's not even rolling, so I'm off to the fishing grounds.

0930

I wake up. Somehow, someone set the trolling poles, ran to the grounds, set the gear and landed twenty-five chinook and seventeen coho salmon. As I am the only one on the boat, and it is a very small boat, I will have to assume it was me. I wish someone had told me I was going fishing; I would have brought a warmer shirt. It's wet and cold out here, but at least the wind isn't blowing. Yet.

I decide to run the gear, to see what I set while sleep-fishing. I engage the gurdy and its hydraulic spool begins pulling up the thin stainless steel cable, with its fifty-pound lead, from thirty fathoms below. I have six of these wires, theoretically separated from one another by differing lead weights, floats and attachment to the trolling poles. Occasional tangles due to the current, fish or bad timing attest to the reality of the system.

I watch the first line snap coming up the wire, like a stainless steel clothspin caught between the brass stops. A pair of these stops on the wire every three fathoms keeps the snap in its place and gives me an easy way to measure my gear as I let it out.

I peer back from the snap along the imperceptible monofilament leader to the bright spinning flasher. Behind the flasher darts the hoochie, a fake replica of a squid, this one painted with red-rimmed eyes and blue and yellow stripes that hide the hook in the white tentacles. I watch its action and make a mental note to increase my speed. Trolling at two knots, slight speed changes can alter a salmon's opinion of my gear. I remove the snap and coil and leader in the gear box.

The next spread, as each snap-flasher-hoochie unit is called, has a fish. A shaker, a salmon under legal size, futilely pulls at the hook. I pull the leader down, draw my gaff up on the barbless hook to slip it from the fish's jaw, and the shaker darts away.

There's a chinook on the next spread, maybe a shaker, maybe a keeper. I hoist it aboard and lay it gingerly against the measuring line. It's a quarter-inch too short. The hefty fine that accompanies illegal fish decides its fate. I gently return it to its home. It leaps clear of the water, then furiously charges the next flasher. I laugh at such arrogance. That one will be fun to catch when it grows up.

The following three spreads have no fish. The wire suddenly pulls back, and I realize something strong has been sleeping on the next spread. I stop the gurdy as the snap comes up, place the gaff within easy reach. Slowly, I pull in the leader until I see a twenty-pound chinook, only lightly hooked. I quickly check for any nearby boats, then concentrate on the fight.

This fish will bring sixty dollars at the dock. I must strike exactly right with the gaff; its sharp steel point must hook to hold. I balance its familiar weight on the two-foot-long wooden handle. My favorite gaff, don't fail me now! I gently play the fish up to the boat; it veers and sheers away, I play it back again. It runs twice more, then, in a moment of fatigue, it slows a little too close to the boat. I plant the gaff, full force, in the gill plate and haul up with both hands as the fish thrashes to break free. I drag it over the transom and it's aboard! For a moment I atavistically rejoice in the triumph of the primitive battle, then I mercifully dispatch my opponent with a sharp blow to the head.

Still thrilled with the success of landing such a fish, I go quickly back to running the gear. I pull up the next spread and quickly land a nice ten-pound coho. As it hits the deck, it spits the hook, slithers away from the gaff blow, flops its way forward, over the other fish, over the coaming and into the cockpit, splashing blood and slime everywhere. Disgusted with the extra trouble this fish is causing, I climb out of the gaff hatch to retrieve it.

A boat suddenly looms ahead, seemingly inches away. But it's an illusion. We are really several yards apart, probably a full minute from complete disaster. I pull the old "dory doubleback" spin on my gear in a 180-degree turn. It's my friend, Big Boat Bill. His schooner is three times bigger than my boat and not nearly as maneuverable. He apologizes for the close call. Apparently, he hadn't picked me up on radar. Over the radio, he admonishes me to get a radar of my own.

I know, I know. Last year I bought a new engine. I'm just getting enough ahead now to buy new electronics. They will do everything for me: lorans that store a hundred waypoints, tell my course and speed, my ETA (estimated time of arrival), my sister's birthdate and the number of calories in my last meal; radars that plot the true course and speed as well as sexual persuasion of the captain for every boat within sixty-four miles. Marvelous technology that I can hardly wait to own.

But when was my last meal? No dinner last night, too tired, no breakfast yet. Let's see what's dry and easily available. I still have to keep a constant vigil for fellow fishers. No, I'd better run through the gear, I see a few fish shaking the lines.

1340

At last, the hot bite has tapered off, the fish are all cleaned and the fog has miraculously lifted. I can see now that forty boats have been working this thirty-fathom curve, yet I had seen only seven in the fog. Of course, I had a distressingly close look at the rigging of each of those boats. With the improved visibility, the boats work closer together, plying a glassy sea beneath an impossibly blue sky. A rare day on this coast.

I dodge a crab pot, long stuck in the sand and lethal to my gear.

That pot could strip my lines of flashers, leaders and leads, costing me hundreds of dollars and a couple of hours re-rigging (a write-off I could do without), yet I have fished around it all day. Lucky. I write down the loran coordinates to increase my luck in the future.

I finally wolf down a dubious-looking cheese sandwich and some slightly fermented juice (I really should get some groceries soon) while chatting on the radio. There is always a fisherman willing to talk in times of boredom or panic. They have always been such a help, advising on mechanical difficulties, or offering hints on what to fish with, or how the weather is, or who is really catching, most of it lies. And they *never* offer "where."

Everyone must learn "where" alone. It's part of initiation. If I survive long enough to accumulate a few fishing holes, then locales will be exchanged, in limited quantities, with liberal embellishments, misleading hints and probably in code. It's all part of the game.

I finish lying on the radio and return to running gear in the glorious sunshine. I've wandered into a patch of hake, a ubiquitous junk fish. I wander out of them, stripping the squishy fish from my gear. As there is no reasonable market for them, I leave them floating in my wake. I feel badly about the waste of time, bait and fish, but not as badly as the hake feel when seagulls swarm down to shriek last rites.

1930

The salmon start biting in earnest again. I've been trolling toward home, but must back tack to return to the best fishing. I warily watch the fog bank crouching offshore, awaiting to return with the night. I don't want to get caught out after dark in the fog. The hours it takes to grope my way back into the channel without a radar are a bad memory of times when greed kept me out too late.

The fog bank holds steady. The fish continue to climb aboard until the sun vanishes into the encompassing shroud on the horizon. I pull my gear on board and push the throttle—WIDE OPEN!

I feel great now, flying across the still water, burning past larger trollers in a flash of fossil fuel fury, fish hold full and planing over the bar. Around the corner by the small boat docks, I slow to haul my trolling poles. An older woman tends her crab ring in the twilight. She smiles and raises her hands in question. I flash seventy-five fingers and call out, "A great day!" Then I spin the wheel and race to the fish company.

While waiting for another boat to unload, I wonder about the woman. Did she once work a job, rewarded with pay and benefits? Did she work at home, rewarded with fine children and love? Or did she work, like so many, for no reward at all? I wonder if she was one of the forerunners, the few women who broke the ground for me. They walked a more precipitous edge and made my break with tradition a little easier.

It's my turn. I whirl to the dock, jump off, tie up, swing open the hatch. A couple of loitering fishermen groan. The buyer rolls his eyes, his helper comes down to unload. I accept the proffered beer and the compliment, in a soft foreign accent from the helper, "You've done the best today, so far." I thank him and glide over to the slip. Exhausted, I tie up the boat, clean the fish hold, turn off the electronics. I stumble up the ramp, pick up my fish ticket and another beer and crawl into my camper.

2230

Contemplating the effort required to cook the snapper I filleted this afternoon, I opt for more sleep. As my mind quits churning with the thousands of projects to be done, I question my motives for choosing this line of work. A thousand-dollar day does add incentive, but most days aren't this productive. I'm not working for the rent, and I'm certainly not here because of the fantastic lifestyle of working and sleeping as total existence. Maybe I'm working to fulfill the dreams of my aunts who read my letters, vicariously living the adventures they missed. Perhaps it's for the men and women who financed my operation or generously taught me their trade. Or maybe it's for my friend's young daughter, who, when told by the boys, "A girl can't be the fisherman in the 'Fishing' game," adamantly stated, "Well, Mari's a girl, and she fishes."

As I drift off to sleep, I hope I take a warmer shirt, tomorrow.

ICE FISHING

JOAN ACKERMANN

YOU EVER SEE HUMMINGBIRDS MATE?" Taylor Streit asks me, swerving around a tight turn on Flaming Arrow Pass. "The male will fly wa-ay up and then dive straight down one hundred miles an hour—this twisting diving motion. Swooooosh!" As his old Saab careens around another hairpin turn, Taylor is swooshing inside the car in the opposite direction, twisting over the stick shift, sinking behind the steering wheel like a dive-bombing hummingbird.

We are on our way up to ice fish at Eagle's Nest, New Mexico, a ten thousand-foot-high valley. It's my third outing in this grand wilderness with Taylor, a professional fishing guide, friend of a friend, and I am almost accustomed to riding the crosscurrents of his tumbling conversation—down canyons, up mountains, over miles of sagebrush on deeply rutted dirt roads. I've rescued him once, hauled him out of a river he'd fallen into, drunk and still talking. I've gotten stuck in the mud with him in his jeep after fly fishing in the Cimarron River, watched him tie flies in his shop in Taos and eaten venison at his home with his Mexican wife and little boy. I've been in New Mexico three weeks, having left Massachusetts and an eleven-year marriage behind. There is a pain in me as big as eastern standard time.

"Look over there." He sits bolt upright, pointing out the rear right window. "I've seen so many elk right up on that hilltop. Elk leave a lot of sign." He reaches for his binoculars behind my seat and gazes through them from beneath the broad brim of his fly-studded beaver hat. "Winter time they wander for miles and miles at night." He whips around, remembering an arroyo where he shot a coyote. The next second he is plunged deep in an explanation of trout genetics; his right hand swims along the bottom of the dashboard, quivering like a trout dropping a flash of red roe. "Once we catch a spawning trout, we'll use the eggs for bait to catch salmon. So that's the deal, see. That's what we'll try to do." He grins, staring at me with crystal blue eyes, a penetrating gaze that could nudge the backside of a slumbering trout at the bottom of a lake. I nod, clutching the door handle as the imaginary red roe continue to sift down.

The sky is blue, ceramic blue, royal blue, all shades of blue blueing away at once, lit by a high-noon sun. Four hours south, nine thousand feet lower, this blue sky does tricks with the red in the dirt and rock of New Mexico's deserts, adding red specific gravity to the landscape, but here, in the north, it's a brilliant backdrop to a wintry scene, tall pine trees glistening with snow. We wind our way up the pass.

I'm writing a piece about Taylor for a national magazine. He claims he's "a prisoner of a magazine girl," but he doesn't seem to mind. So far, he has taught me not only how to cast a fly rod so that the line whips smoothly through the air and lands flat on the water exactly where it needs to be, but also how to shoot a double-barreled shotgun, how to read water, why our national bird is rank ("a nowhere's bird"), approximately two hundred and sixty-three miscellaneous bits of information about wildlife—from a lecture on the water ouzle, the only bird who strolls along the bottom of a river, to the correct way to remove a bobcat's fur ("pull if off like a sock")—how a surveyor triangulates and how to use the hose from a vacuum cleaner as a stethoscope to locate exactly the creaking grind in my 1968 Volvo.

"Is that the lake where we're going ice fishing?" I ask him, watching some distant figures off to our right. We've climbed through the pass, up out of the trees, and are tootling along across an open valley.

"Aren't too many lakes out here," says Taylor, who has been clocking the speed of a raven flying directly in front of us. "You see a lake, it's probably the one you're going to. Hmm," he says, looking at the speedometer. "Flying thirty miles an hour." He pulls himself forward over the steering wheel close to the windshield and peers up to study the raven, following the bird more than the road.

Half an hour later, we are out traipsing across the ice toward a distant grove of cottonwood trees that doesn't seem to be getting any closer. The lake is a huge expanse of white that blends into the rest of the wide snow-covered valley, rimmed on all sides by mountains. "This is the coldest place in the States," says Taylor, pulling a sled with our tackle, food and extra clothes. I am wearing, among other wooly items, three pairs of socks and two down parkas. "People in Eagle's Nest are real weird," he says. "They get depressed and drink a lot. The cold makes them crazy." We tromp on. I wonder if the cold makes the fish weird and crazy, too.

"Look for old holes, ones with blood near them," he says as we finally near the trees. "Signs that fish have been caught. I reckon that's a hole over there."

We find an old hole with telling stains of blood nearby. After smashing the thin layer of ice covering the hole with a rock, Taylor offers me some bait. "Gonna be fishing with a smorgasbord today— frozen corn and salmon eggs. Why do they eat this stuff? Cause they're nuts. Stocked trout will eat anything. Wild trout would never touch this stuff. I have much less feeling for stocked fish than I do for wild fish. Now, if you see the bobber go boink, boink—*strike*; pull up hard and yell for me."

I sit down on an abandoned piece of Styrofoam and proceed to watch delicate sheaths of ice close in on my fist-sized hole which I scoop out with a little aquarium net. The fishing line drops from my mittened hands, threading me to another world where genetically disturbed trout drift in their wintry hold, propelled to spawn by aberrant urges from unrelated gene pools. The line feels like an antenna, a live wire vibrating with dim half-frozen thoughts. I'm hanging on by a thread.

"Hey!" Taylor calls out to me from twenty yards away where he sits hunched over a hole. "See the snow fleas? They live just below the surface of the snow. Don't know what they live on." He pulls up his line and puts on some fresh bait. Those are the last words I hear him say for a long time.

Though I don't fish often, I enjoy it. When I was a kid I used to catch eels on the pier in front of my grandparents' house on Cape

Cod, and I'd fish in the Charles River in Cambridge where I grew up. Once my friend Keil Choi and I caught eleven sorry-looking slimy catfish on a Saturday afternoon using bamboo poles and worms and a red plastic bucket. We fished off the end of the dock at the Cambridge boathouse by the Eliot Bridge. My wedding reception was held at the Cambridge boathouse; the nicest wedding picture shows the whole family out on the dock, cousins, uncles, best friends, smiling—unseen catfish lurking below. It was the grueling finish of that eleven-year marriage that had sent me packing out to New Mexico, to realign myself, to see different colors in the earth, a new palette, to soothe a scorching pain.

I often think of fishing when I'm writing. You put out a little bait and wait. Sometimes you get a nibble, sometimes nothing. You stare at the still blank piece of paper, like the smooth unruffled surface of water, waiting for some sign of life, some inspiration. When you begin, you often don't have a clue what lurks in the depths; it might be a lone sardine or a rich run of blues. You go through little rituals—brewing coffee, tidying the desk, resetting the thermostat, unwrapping the gum. You sit and wait, tossing out one idea after another, hoping one of them will attract a stream of others. If you're patient and lucky, words may start to surface. Sometimes they're keepers; often they're not.

Hours go by. The drips from my nose freeze up. As my state of mind ices over, "ice fishing" becomes redundant—noun and verb freezing over together in suspended animation. The sun wheels across the sky and the snow fleas calm down and eventually stop jumping. What do they live on? What's in the snow that nourishes them? Maybe the same thing that is nourishing my soul at the moment, in the vast frozen stillness. I feel an enormous peace. I am content to sit here for hours and hours, sitting on water, out on the middle of a lake, ostensibly doing nothing, doing something, holding a line. I'm sitting on the floor of the sky, the ceiling of the lake, ten thousand feet high, in the coldest part of the States, suspended in cold, ice fishing—fishing for ice. It's a blissful meditation; cryosurgery of the psyche.

After lowering great quantities of bright yellow corn and hot pink salmon eggs, beaded in different designs on my hook, I try an experiment. I break off a little bit of a corn chip, Frito-Lay, and manage to hook it. I lower this genetically disturbed form of corn down through the hole that keeps trying to freeze over. There is an immediate response. Taylor is standing silhouetted against the rich gawdy reds and purples of the sunset, doing a kind of jaunty cowboy jig with his hands in his pockets, when I yell. "Whoah!"

"Come on through, baby. Come on through," he coaxes, at my side in an instant as I pull up the line. "Man, be a crying shame to catch a fish and not be able to pull him through the hole. Come *on*, baby."

The fish suddenly slips up through the hole, thrashing and thwacking its tail, doubly shocked by its own birth into a waterless world and by its own gasping death. Taylor removes the hook, measures the fish to be fifteen inches and lays it down in the snow; its warm blood slows through the ice.

"Back East, a fish like that is one in a hundred. She's healthy. She'll have pink meat and taste real good."

Later, as we drive home in the dark, Taylor tells me that trout despise sunlight, that the hour a nymph spends swimming up to the surface is the most vulnerable of its life, that he once thought a piece of the sky was falling when a great golden eagle suddenly swooped in front of his car and snatched hold of a prairie dog and that he once drove right through a rainbow.

"The rainbow was moving along and we were actually passing through it. I mean, we drove *through* it. I still can't believe we actually ran into the end of the rainbow."

In the back seat of the car, the rainbow trout lies on its side wrapped in a plastic bag, its rigid tail curled, its pink meat clinging to the bone, frozen beyond the end of its own fifteen-inch rainbow. Taylor's voice continues, blooming in the dark with more stories, more outrage about the local pollution, how he feels personally insulted by it, more specifics on the snow fly, more details about the Canada goose he shot and gutted that morning on the Rio Grande.

"The thing is, I feel so romantic about the bird, I can't even tell you," he says. "Some people might think it's strange I say that since I shot him, but I do."

For a while the prisoner of a magazine girl is silent. In the dark, I think of the goose, its long smooth neck, its soft downy feathers drenched in blood, washed clean in the rushing river. I think of my marriage, once a great lovely thing, alive and flying high; I wish its death had been as clean and swift, its spirit released in one violent smokey blast. Both images, the dead bird and my marriage, gain silence in the dark, receding deeper and deeper into it.

We start our descent down the windy mountain road, only one headlight working. On both sides of the road the mountains rise high to a starless sky, their outline barely lit by a sliver of a moon. The romance from Taylor's voice lingers, hovering in place like the tiny beating wings of a hummingbird, warming the cold winter air as we drive back into town.

A Buncha Guys, a Coupla Fish and ME: The Opening of Trout Season, Roscoe, New York

VIVA

WHEN I GOT THE ITCH to fish this spring, I decided to try trout. After some research—including a visit to the World Fishing and Outdoor Exposition (in Rockland County), where I watched a Texan catch bass in a forty-foot aquarium, and to Orvis New York, a sporting goods store, where the kindly salespeople outfitted me with a pair of neoprene waist-high waders and boots ($220) and also volunteered Wes, one of their salesmen, as my guide ("He doesn't have a wife and he also wants to be a writer")—I headed for the Catskills. My destination was the Antrim Lodge in Roscoe, New York, where the season's opening dinner was to be held.

Accustomed to bass fishing, which involves spinning tackle, live minnows and boats, I discovered that fly fishing, as practiced on the Beaverkill (where, devotees insist, it was invented), is as much of a religion as the one at the Siddha Meditation Ashram in neighboring South Fallsburg, where I occasionally spend time. And, in tune with the times, both religions are presided over by females: Gurumayi at the ashram and Lenna Papadimatos at the Antrim.

"Leave your minnows home," Papadimatos told me when I phoned for reservations, and then she launched into an ode to the match-making magic of the Beaverkill. She told me about the bride who had a trout sequined onto her bodice and whose cake was topped by a fish and about the couple who met thigh-deep in the stream, whose rings were trout circles. In her dual role of trout queen and marriage broker, Papadimatos warmly welcomed me into the bosom of the fly-fishing fraternity.

Saturday, March 31, 1991, 3:30 p.m., Roscoe. The eve of the opening of trout season. From behind the wheel of my rented Chevy, I peer through fog and drizzle at the Antrim Lodge, a pile of gray stone and brick covered with yellowish moss and black mold. As a kid in the pre-Lenna era, I used to dine here with my father on the way to Syracuse, and tonight Wes and I have arrived for the lodge's fabled Annual Red Smith Two-Headed Trout and Other Amazing Stories Dinner. Sportswriter Smith named this event in honor of the trout that took so long making up its mind which stream to take at Junction Pool (where the Beaverkill meets the Willowemoc) that the fish grew two heads.

"Typical upstate," I tell Wes. "Gothic Gloom." "Gee, that's good," says Wes from the passenger seat. "Gothic Gloom. I'll have to remember that." Though he's suggested teaching me how to fly cast, he changes his mind now that we're actually out in the murk. "Let's drive around and look at the water where we're gonna fish tomorrow," he says guiltily.

3:40 p.m. Fabled Cairn's Pool in the Beaverkill. Like Junction Pool, this is a deep, wide section of the Beaverkill, which otherwise snakes through the rocks and woods, mountains rising on one side. The dripping trees are black, their budding leaves chartreuse. An empty two-lane blacktop ribbons between the stream and, on the grassy valley side, the occasional ancient cemetery with ten-foot-high wrought-iron gates.

"God, this is so gloomy!" I say to Wes. "Trees," says Wes, "water. At least we're out of concrete and noise pollution." Cairn's Pool is strictly catch-and-release, meaning you have to throw the fish back, a new concept to me, brought up as I was to clean my own fish and stick them in the freezer for pre-Vatican II meatless Fridays.

There's a man up to his hips in the icy stream (you can fish Cairn's Pool year round). I carefully watch his fly-casting technique. Casting with spinning tackle is like tossing a yo-yo out in front of you. The weight of the bait and lead sinker, combined with the force of the arm-wrist motion, causes the automatic reel to unwind. Fly casting involves neither a weight nor an automatic reel. A loosely held length of slack somehow miraculously slithers through the guides, up the rod and out onto the water solely through a deft motion of the forearm. This technique was apparently invented by an English-woman, Dame Juliana, in the fourteenth century.

I hand Wes a notebook and pen and say, "OK, I'm gonna dictate: rear view of mysterious hooded figure in two-tone brown with waders blending into landscape beiges and café au laits in swirling ocher and earth-green water, gracefully flicking his fly rod with beige line snaking out in wicked S-curves. . . . " "Gee," says Wes, scribbling madly, "that's good."

5:30 p.m. My car spins in the mud near a photo opportunity—a stone ruin. Wes, holding the camera, panics and begins to babble. In forty-five minutes we're supposed to be at dinner, so I gun into some dead grass at the edge of a ravine, slam on the brakes and then somehow skid up onto the road. Back at the wicker-furnished Reynolds House Inn, where we're staying, I put on red heels and a tailored French suit, because, when I phoned for sartorial information, not wanting to stick out like a sore thumb, Lenna, in a soft Holy Mother voice, asked me to "wear a dress or a skirt, not pants," just like they do at the ashram. "Wow!" says Wes.

6:25 p.m. Bar-restaurant at the Antrim Lodge. The decor: mirrors and dark mahogany, stuffed fish, fishing mementos, old newspaper clippings. A few older women with scarves, stacked heels and short, functional hair. I stick out like a sore thumb. "Viva! *You're* here? You're going fishing? You actually brought *waders!*" exclaims a middle-aged, distinguished-looking man with white hair, who turns out to be Nick, a sportswriter for *Newsday*. "Now I've got a hook!" I tell him he can't write about me. I'm going to write my story about me. But Nick insists I sit down next to him at the sportswriters' fabled round table instead of the tiny table, No. 20, to which Wes and I have been assigned. Since No. 20, in a dark corner behind a screen, is bereft of food and I'm starving, what with all that oxygen—while Nick's table is loaded with crab salads, crudités and "Trout Town" bumper stickers—I let him kidnap us. They put Wes between *Camping Magazine* and *Field & Stream*. On my left, a balding sportswriter from the Bergen *Record* is earnestly pontificating to a young writer on the reasons why he never accepts a free meal. "I have my ethics," he says.

"Brought his wife," Nick whispers, nodding toward the gold-pinned woman next to Bergen *Record*. "That's something you just don't do."

"...When I go to a place to fish and I only fish four days," Bergen *Record* is telling his disciple, "I want an *intense angling experience*. That's why I made my wife my photographer. 'I'll tell you when you can fish,' I say to her. 'You can fish when you've got *every shot!*' " Nick pokes me, whispering, "Brought her because they're for togetherness."

"...As a result," Bergen *Record* continues, "I've been able to fish intensively."

"That's what they call weekends at the ashram," I tell Nick. "Intensives."

"...I could have put her up as an associate—she's that good," Bergen *Record* says of his wife. "But I haven't. I'm fifty-seven. I figure I got nineteen, maybe twenty Mays left in my life. I'm not giving any of 'em up..."

At Nick's right, Ken from the *New York Post*, a younger writer with a black beard, twinkly eyes, beer belly and khakis, slugs down a drink, rolls his eyes heavenward and asks if I want "a Stoli."

" '...No family parties!' I told my wife. 'No funerals, no weddings...' "

"No vodka," I tell Ken.

"You're not talking," Nick says, leaning over to read my notes. "Aha! You're *actually listening!* Being a reporter is difficult for a woman. Keeping your mouth shut. You got a sexually linked hereditary impediment." Then he tells me the four stages of an insect's life.

"Did I do the right thing?" Bergen *Record* is asking his disciple. Then, without waiting for an answer, "I think I did." At the mike, Father James from the First Presbyterian Church is giving a sermon about Jesus Christ, the apostles, camaraderie, fishing and the one hundredth anniversary of the Antrim Lodge. He ends, "Your breath is in us for creation, so we are restless without you."

Ken has put down his Stoli and, for the first time, is scribbling notes, presumably on the sermon, when the two-headed trouts arrive. Someone points out that the heads are at each end instead of two at the top, the way they're supposed to be. And then we notice that Nick, with the sermon transcript in his hands, has aced out all of us.

"How'd you do that? I ask.

"Easy. You know why? Because I'm a reporter!" He looks at the tape recorder that's just blinked out on *Field & Stream.* "Bah! Electronic reporting!" Nick snorts. "How about breakfast at eight at the Roscoe Diner so I can interview you some more?" Nick asks me. "I'm going fishing at six," I reply.

Lenna sidles up behind me and complains that I'm not "meeting people, talking to them." "Take your notebook," Nick sneers, before I get up and march over to the nearest table, where a genuine fisherman named Chuck tells me that he himself is the "most boorishly sexist person" he knows and "my girlfriend's taken up fishing since she read *Wade a Little Deeper, Dear.*"

I stretch my cramped legs out on the aisle and ask, "Who wrote it?"

"*Not a lady, a woman,*" Chuck says. "Not an astronaut's wife, more a Liv Ullmann—of fishing." He cranes his neck to read what I'm writing. "No. Change that to Sigourney Weaver."

9:00 p.m. At the podium, Lenna has been introducing all the sportswriters, bemoaning the fact that Nelson Bryant from *The New York Times* couldn't make it (I guess I have his seat) and promising to introduce "a little later, the woman writer," before she launches into her own sermon on Jesus Christ, the apostles and fish.

"I used to be able to get away and come up here," Chuck is complaining over my pleas to shut up, "and now *she* wants to come up. It's a way to attack me. As a man. I say, 'Where do I hide?' " Lenna's talking about St. Peter, doubtful fish stories and the nature of doubt in general. From Chuck, "Lenna's very religious... I mean do I hafta hide in the *bathroom?*"

"Shhhhh," I hiss.

"Chuck," from the microphone, "stop talking!" "You know, my girlfriend's sister is a Ford Foundation artist," he continues. "She uses piscatorial motifs." "Letters?" I whisper. Realizing that Lenna is staring at what, in this place, must be considered an obscene stretch of leg, I inch my skirt down. "No. Fish. *Piscatorial,*" he says.

To shut him up, I hand Chuck my notebook and a pen and he

writes, "I started out in my early twenties as an exceptionally sexist guy. In retrospect, however, my present relationship has had a noticeable effect in subduing this."

I hear my name called over the microphone: ". . . who walked in this afternoon and remembered this place from her childhood, called earlier and said, 'What shall I wear?' I said, 'Black pants and a white blouse with a collar.' 'Collar?' she said. 'Does it have to have a collar?' I said, 'And I have an apron for you.' 'Apron?' she said. Well, I thought she was the new waitress. But she's a writer. What paper is it, Viva? *Women* something? . . . *Women's Wear?*" More speeches; dancing by the Papadimatos children to the strains of "Never on Sunday."

10:30 p.m. Keener's Pool Bar at the Antrim Lodge. Ken has just handed me a *New York Post* card, offering, "call me if you need any help," when Lenna takes me aside and complains that "I'm the rudest person" she's ever met. Then, in a deadly undertone, *"Interviewing someone while I was talking!"* "You asked me to," I remind her, *"and I told him to shut up three times!"*

"That's not what he says!" "Then he's lying," I shout, the entire population of the restaurant and bar staring at me, except for Ken, who is suddenly engrossed in the wine list, not even raising his eyes when I plead, "Help me out. She's attacking me!"

I ferret out Chuck and his friends at the other end of the bar, but they just sneer. Meanwhile, Lenna has raised her voice. "Plus you were supposed to sit at table No. 20! And you sat with the invited guests, the *writers!* You knew where you were supposed to sit!" I rush back to Ken. "Nick begged me to, right?" I implore, but Ken buries his nose deeper in his Stoli.

"You weren't invited. I'm sending your magazine a bill!" Lenna thunders over her shoulder as she marches away, her bottom and shoulders twitching, "Imagine, *interviewing* someone while I was talking!"

"Why do you believe Chuck and not me?" I yell pathetically after her. She turns and fixes me with a fishy stare. "Because he comes here every weekend and you don't!" Wes, embarrassed, hustles me out the door, saying that even though the evening is young I've obviously been ejected. He just hopes I've garnered enough material to have made it all worthwhile.

April 1, 8:00 a.m. Socrates (I kid you not), the Holy Mother's husband, is serving coffee laced with ouzo from the back of a station wagon. I ask for mine straight (ouzo) and am being politely turned down when his wife appears, snarling, "You haven't left yet?" and, wagging her finger in my face as I try to explain one more time, exclaims, "The Lord sees what you did." As she turns her back on me and sashays down the road, I head for the water, where the newly embarrassed Wes has already fled and where seventeen nonjournalist fishermen in waders and a couple of wives shout, "One lady caught a trout" whenever a newcomer arrives. And to think I'd always believed you had to be quiet to not scare the fish away!

Nick has appeared on the rocky shore to tell us he's going up to Cairn's Pool. "We'll miss you," I lie. But a couple of local reporters, along with the *Post*'s Ken, in loafers and khakis, remain along the shore and roadside banks in case anything of note happens. When a large fish is brought in by a waderless local, sheepishly using a spinning reel and worm (because his five-year-old son wants to catch a fish), it turns out to be only a catfish. "They'll bite on anything," I tell the crowd. A collective sigh of relief can be heard from the as-yet-unsuccessful fly-fishing purists. Wes, only ankle-deep in water, though he's wearing neoprene waders, tells me his boss said he was crazy to come with me.

Salvation appears in the form of Eric, the game warden. In a navy-blue uniform encrusted with lots of gold braid, badges, et cetera, he grabs my rod, saying, "Here, lemme show y' how t'cast. Y' gotta *whip* it! Like this!" and demonstrates, whipping the line over and behind his head several times like a cowboy preparing to lasso a calf.

"Watch it. People behind you," I say as the line snakes between two men and a little boy. "Oh I ain't gonna *touch* 'em," he assures me, whipping like mad and catching his hook on the upright rod of one of the fishermen standing behind him, about four inches from the man's left eye. "They shouldn'ta moved! They were supposed t' stay put!" the game warden wails.

The victim, remarkably unconcerned about the near-loss of his left eye, somehow manages a smile that is both sheepish and affable. "My feet are cold," Wes announces. "You should ski. Like me," I say. "Mine are warm as toast. I could stand in this water all day, thanks to the $220 neoprene waders and boots you convinced me to buy." I whip the line like crazy, three or four times, and then cast it out over and over. This is more like it. I'm finally having fun.

"You should roll, not whip. I'm teaching you how to roll-cast because there's so many people around," Wes says, grabbing my rod and executing a subtle roll, which now seems quite wimpish. "I like whipping." "But you whip too fast."

12:30 p.m. Commotion. A young guy in blue jeans and boots has actually caught a trout. It's barely over legal limit; he's holding it up like an Oscar winner with his trophy, but unlike the Oscar, the poor fish is gasping for air. Summoned by Ken, who's been observing from the edge of the water, the *Post's* photographer is squatting on one knee, trying to focus while the little trout twists and squirms. "Why don't you kill him if you're going to eat him?" I suggest. "*Shuddup, lady,*" screams the photographer, "*get the hell outta here!*" Embarrassed again, my "guide" has scrambled up the bank and is walking fast toward Cairn's Pool. I follow him. "Let's get into the water," I say, watching four or five fishermen, hip- and chest-deep in the swirling, wilder section, catching nothing. "You don't wanna get in that icy water," says Wes. "You might slip. Better to just observe."

Up on the road while I'm "observing," another writer tells me that when a friend claimed he'd caught thirty-seven trout one morning in (catch-and-release) Cairn's Pool, he replied, "You mean you caught the same trout thirty-seven times." As another fisherman with fly rod and waders comes up behind us on the road, I'm telling the writer that the American Indians claim that catch-and-release is playing with God's food. "But actually it's like a Nazi concentration camp," I offer. "I don't see the analogy," grumbles the newly arrived fisherman.

Winking, the writer hands me his card. Maybe I want to go fishing with him for shad on the Hudson. Or out in Montana where they never heard of fly fishing. Where they call it that "effete eastern stuff." Ken appears to say he wants to catch just one fish before he goes home to write his story, so he's going to the Eldred Preserve. Why don't we meet him there?

On the way, I stop, makeupless, in waders and stocking cap, at the Antrim to pay my dinner bill. A waitress tells me, "There was a model here last night who was really out of it. Hopping from table to

table." While Wes is actually *thanking* Lenna and I'm meditating on
the apparent cowardice of all men, I realize the waitress was talking
about me.

1:30 p.m. Way past the Neversink Reservoir, Wes, who, armed
with the map of Sullivan County, has been driving ahead of me at
around thirty-five miles per hour, pulls over to say we've been going
in the wrong direction for the past forty minutes. Furiously yelling
that he drives too slow anyway, I take the lead but lose him entirely
and end up, off course, somewhere beyond Monticello.

3:00 p.m. The Eldred Preserve turns out to be three or four pitiful
little ponds, possibly the source of the phrase, "like shooting fish in a
barrel," with entire families lined up on the banks shoulder to shoulder.

Since I don't see Ken anywhere, I head for the bar. Ken is drinking a Stoli. "You're the lady who screamed at me," says his photographer. "No. You're the man who screamed at me." I turn to Ken.
"What about your fish?" I ask. "I already caught it. What about
yours?"

4:00 p.m. Getting colder. I rent a lowly, dreaded spinning rod,
buy a bobber and a can of worms and end up borrowing a minnow
from a friendly car salesman from Peekskill. "Thank God," I tell
him, "you're not an effete eastern fly fisherman." "Those guys over
on the Beaverkill," he says, "the snobbier they get, the more coarse
and vulgar I get. But I'm big. They don't dare get snotty with me like
they get with you. They know I'd lay 'em out flat."

A woman fishing in a white jumpsuit and white boots, with white
platinum hair, says, in a thick Irish brogue, "I never seen a woman
fly fishin'. Only the men fly fish." "Do you kill your fish and eat
them?" I ask.

"Sure I do. Jesus and the apostles ate fish. But the thing is, they
haven't stocked the pond."

"Hey," Peekskill calls out, "wanna pull this trout in?" I take the
rod. "Get a feel of the *weight* of it," he says. "That's right. Atta girl,
good girl! Feel that *weight!*"

I feel barely anything. A bass one-third this size would have me
holding on for dear life as it dove for the bottom. The bottom of the
pond is about six inches from the top; the overfed trout is acting like a
drugged log. Peekskill's friend gets the net (hardly necessary, since the

fish seems so eager to flop into the frying pan), and a worker from the preserve says, "See! And that woman in white complained there weren't any fish!"

7:00 p.m. The Eldred Preserve Restaurant. The cleaned, iced, rainbow trout (sold to me at $3.90 per pound) is sitting in a plastic bag under my chair while Wes and I partake of the free dinner offered by the Eldred's owner after I recount my tale of persecution at the Beaverkill. I'm eating rack of lamb; Wes, blue trout, while we watch through the window the only wild things we've seen so far, a doe and her fawn scenically grazing.

"You should learn not to hold a grudge," Wes says. "And you'll never be a writer until you learn how to hold one," I tell him. "That and fast driving."

April 2, 7:00 p.m. The Chelsea Hotel, my apartment. I ask Gaby, my eight-year-old, who has her own spinning rod and who begged me to bring home a trout, how she likes the one that cost about $883.78 to catch. "It tastes fishy."

MAGADAN LUCK

NANCY LORD

MAGADAN OBLAST, the Soviet Far East, a far-flung corner of the Russian Republic, beyond even Siberia.

We met our Russian counterparts, scientists with the Institute of Biological Problems of the North. One studied the plankton in lakes, another the population cycles of lemmings, still others the successions and distributions of plants.

"And what is your specialty?" they asked.

Our interpreter helped me with "She works for senators," but that brought only puzzled looks. I pantomimed catching fish with a rod and reel, laid my hands—fingers splayed—across one another to look like web.

"Ah! *Ribachka!*" Their eyes lit up. We would go fishing!

The idea of the "expedition" of Alaskans to the Soviet Far East was that we would join with counterparts to work on biological or environmental problems. As an environmentalist and a recent assistant to the Alaska legislature on natural resource issues, I'd anticipated a cooperative effort to plant seedlings or haul tires out of a trashed river. My interest in the trip was based mostly, however, on a long-time fascination with this mysterious northern land to our west, and I wanted to be there, to see for myself the country that's been called Alaska's divided twin.

When I packed my duffel bag for Magadan, I threw in a light-weight spinning rod that had come in the mail one day, a bonus for buying a new outboard. Though I know something about fish, I don't often meet them on the end of a line. In Alaska, I fish commercially for salmon, gillnetting them in beach sets; my idea of fishing is standing knee-deep in sockeyes, snapping web from gill, the muscles in my hands aching. In my circles, to "fly fish" means to load salmon into an airplane and haul them to a processor.

The helicopter landed on a sandbar. The Alaskan and Russian botanists, a black dog the size of a bear and I disembarked into clouds of mosquitoes. We were in the Magadan Reserve, one of the Soviet Union's system of natural areas set aside for preservation and scientific study. A broad, slow-moving river flowed through a landscape of stubby black spruce and birch forests leading into low, purple hills. Several small buildings—the reserve's headquarters, home to its guardian rangers—were half-hidden in the trees, just up from the river bank.

There were more than enough hands to help with dinner, so I took my rod down to the river, tied on a Mepps lure and made some casts. The river was too shallow adjacent to the sandbar, so I walked upstream to where the bank fell off more sharply. The mosquitoes weren't any worse than in interior Alaska, which is not to say that they weren't among the worst in the world.

Vladimir, one of our hosts from the institute, appeared on the bank, sucking on a cigarette. He spoke to me in Russian, none of which I understood, wrinkled his nose, waved derisively with his hand, pointed at my rod, frowned. Translation: This wasn't a good fishing place, and my equipment was totally unsuitable.

For dinner, served at an outdoor table balanced on logs, we had fishhead soup. Gamely, our uninitiated Americans sipped broth from around the staring salmon eyes, the white globs of milt and the legions of kamikaze mosquitoes that dove into their bowls.

After the hours-long dinner, after the speeches and toasts and the exhausting efforts at politeness and communication, I was ready for my sleeping bag. Our interpreter called me over. "You're going fishing," he said. Vladimir was nodding. So was a man who looked like he'd just stepped out of a jungle; he was wearing a mosquito-net hat, the net tied up away from his face, a dirt-colored heavy-duty field suit with a huge knife on the belt, and several days' beard. This was Boris, assistant ranger. Boris pointed downriver. Just over there, we would go, just for a little while, we would definitely catch some fish.

I didn't seem to have a choice. I recruited Debby, one of our botanists, and we zoomed off in a powerboat with Boris and Vladimir.

This far north, early in July, there was plenty of light at ten-thirty. The sky was stretched with cirrus clouds, high and feathery and lit from below with pale pink edges. The river washed past snags of fallen trees and banks overgrown with grasses. Debby peered into the foliage, recognizing a lupine, a spirea. We rounded one bend and another and then pulled up beside a side slough.

Fish waggled in the bottom of the pool. I hadn't known what we were to fish for, but I recognized these by their sail-sized dorsals. We traded our names for them—*kharioos*, grayling—as we readied our poles. Vladimir had a spinning rod with a big, shiny spoon. Boris had the world's largest fly rod, nearly as thick as my wrist at its base, long enough to reach across the slough. Boris looked at my rod and, frowning, said something to Vladimir. His tone was disparaging.

I cast into the pool. On my second cast, a fish swept forward and took the lure.

Boris leaned his own pole into the bushes and ran to help me. Shouting excitedly, he grabbed my line and began to pull it in, fast, hand over hand. Debby and I looked at each other. "Must be the Russian way," I said. Boris yanked the fish up onto the bank, unhooked it and slid a stringer through its gills. It was a nice fish, perhaps fifteen inches long, its scales like rows of silver buttons. We all enthused over it, and Boris and Vladimir took up their poles again with a new intensity. I handed mine to Debby.

Debby caught a fish, and then I caught one. Debby yelled, "*Nyet! nyet!*" and wouldn't let Boris grab the line. "*Americanski* way," we told him and showed what it was like to let the fish take off, to dive and fight and flash and be reeled back in. Boris looked worried and then amazed when I landed the played-out fish on my own. He stretched his rod across the slough and dropped his fly near the opposite bank. Vladimir, farther along, cast and cast again; his reel zinged as he cranked the line in.

Debby caught another.

Boris suddenly became very interested in my rod. He ran his hand over it, testing the flex, pinching the line. He held the lure in the air and let it twist, glinting, back and forth. He mumbled in Russian. "Try it," I said, pushing the rod at him, but he wouldn't take it.

"Vladimir," I said, "try this." I gave him one of my Mepps. He put it in his tackle box. I gave Boris a Mepps, too, and he dropped it into a jar with his homemade flies.

I cast again, caught and played and landed another grayling.

The men exchanged looks. Neither had hooked anything yet.

We heard the sound of another boat. It was Sergei, the head ranger, and two others of our party, fresh from the sauna. They admired our catch as we all swatted mosquitoes. Boris began to take his pole apart. He had an idea. He was going to get his net.

While he zipped back to the camp, the rest of us took the other boat around a couple of more curves to the river's juncture with a side creek. In the creek mouth, we could see where salmon-sized fish were finning, breaking the water into silvery rifts that reflected the remaining light. I flung my lure at them a few times, but it was too dark to hope for more than an accidental snagging. Sergei boiled water on a campstove and served jam "tea"—a spoonful of jam stirred into a mug of hot water.

Boris returned with a pile of tangled gill net. I helped him work through the net, laying it out on the boat's bow—the line with cork floats to one side, the line with metal rings to the other, the web picked free of sticks in the center. "I do this in Alaska," I said. "Five species"—I held up five fingers—"in Alaska."

"*Keta*," Boris said, and I understood. The chum or dog salmon, the one with striped sides—its scientific name is *keta*. I spread my fingers again and made vertical stripes in the air. Boris grinned. We were talking about the same fish.

When the net was laid out neatly, we tied one end to shore where the creek merged with the river's slower water. We pushed the boat backward into the current with an oar, and the net spilled off the bow to lie in a line. We waited, and Boris described what a big splash we would see when a fish hit the net. The fish, though, weren't moving, or they weren't crossing the current, and so we left the net and motored back to camp.

In the morning, we had five *keta* salmon to add to our mess of grayling. Vladimir and I cleaned them. He used my dictionary to tell me that he respected a woman who cleaned fish.

A thousand miles to the northeast of Magadan Reserve, our three powerboats headed upriver, startling moose, reindeer, swans, geese, loons, hares—a richer collection of animals than I'd ever seen in one place. I'd left the botanists and joined another group of Alaskans to fly to the Soviet arctic, to a scientific station on the coastal plain. The scientists here specialized in parasites. None of us knew anything about parasites, but we'd been happy to hike up a mountain, set vole traps on the tundra and eat reindeer stew. Now, our hosts were taking us fishing.

We wound back and forth along the ribbon of river. The mountain we'd climbed previously was sometimes in front of us, sometimes to our right, sometimes behind us. Now and then the lead boat missed the channel and ground up a cloud of river bottom with its prop. I watched the banks; where the river cut into them, it exposed a wall of ice beneath the sod. I was hoping to spot a tusk or a frozen, fleshy leg of a mammoth. In the geological museum in Magadan, we'd seen a cast of a whole baby mammoth that was found in permafrost near here.

Someone pointed. A leggy, flag-tailed, blond and copper-colored fox was racing along the shore. For a second, it seemed as though the animal and we were part of the same stopped action, and that it was the backdrop land that was moving past us. And then the fox was up over the bank and gone.

There were buildings ahead, wooden skiffs pulled up on the beach. We slowed and turned in. A couple of men came out of one of the cabins and watched us from behind a length of gill net that was hung, like a fence, in front of the camp. Wooden barrels were piled to one side.

I reached for my fishing pole, but Valeriy, the chief Soviet parasitologist, stopped me. Not yet. This was, apparently, just a visit stop. Wilhelm, one of our drivers, knew the men here. They were preparing for the run of arctic char that would come later in the summer.

The men were dark, chain-smoking and shy. Wilhelm talked to them while the rest of us stood around awkwardly. I looked into a barrel. It was stuck with lumpy, gray salt and smelled like fish. I looked at the gill net, fingering the web, lifting the lead line. I assumed the net was stretched out for mending, which it needed, but I couldn't find where it had been mended, ever, nor any sign of needle and twine.

The men—Americans, too—had disappeared into one of the cabins. I found them passing around and admiring hunting rifles. A pile of unloaded bullets lay on the nearest bed, sunk into the folds of a faded blue sleeping bag. An electric lightbulb dangled from the center of the ceiling, and the most prominent object in the room was a large television set. I had to look longer to find the net-mending needle, burnished wood, on a nail by the door.

It was time to go. We piled back into the boats and continued upriver, running aground with greater frequency, until we came to a wide curve in the river, a long gravelly beach where we anchored.

The morning's clouds had broken up into scraps of gray fleece, uncovering an ice-blue sky. The sun was almost directly overhead, and there was no shade anywhere. Valeriy pointed at the portion of the river that swept around the curve, indicating that was where we should fish, but the water there looked too fast to me. I took my rod and cut across the top of the beach, through a sandy area where dense, thin-leaved plants were so thickly covered with pink blossoms they looked like bouquets stuck in the sand. I brushed past willow bushes, setting loose an air show of white fluff. The bank on the far side fell off sharply into a deep pool.

Kharioos. I could see half a dozen grayling, all good-sized, all lying on the bottom against the shore. They were finning as though fanning themselves, using as little energy as possible. Clearly, they were not in a mood for feeding.

I cast across the pool and watched my Mepps flash its way back, looking like nothing that might occur naturally in the river. It nearly ran into one fish, which turned to look at it and then, slowly, eased back into position.

I fished for an hour like that, annoying one fish and then another, but never enough to coax them into a hit.

To tell the truth, I didn't mind about the fish. I felt the sun on my face and the arctic breeze, and I listened to the water. I cast and cast again, and it was the motion that mattered—mindless, repetitive, rhythmic. I thought about Norman Maclean, the fisherman-writer whose father had used a metronome to teach him to fish, to melt into the rhythms of the universe.

My mosquito lotion wore off all at once, and, until I stopped to slather more on, I understood the panic of Alaska's caribou and Russia's reindeer, animals that sometimes get driven by mosquitoes to exhausted deaths.

Back down the river, I could see the others, spaced apart, casting into faster water, Valeriy with this thick wool hat piled on his head like a turban. I mentally pinched myself. I was in the Soviet arctic, fishing with Russians for Russian fish. How could I ever have imagined, growing up through all those years of anticommunism and Cold War fear, that this was possible? Here we were, Russians and Americans together, sharing the same universal rhythms, in what must be one of the wildest and most sparely beautiful, not to mention peaceful, places on our shrinking earth.

I worked my way toward the others, testing the faster water. When I reached Valeriy, he told me, in his fractured English, that he liked that I liked to fish and that he was impressed with American women. We—the three here at Ust-Chaun—were the first he'd ever met. I understood him to say that we did everything that Soviet women did and more, and I was embarrassed. I didn't think Soviet women had time for such idleness as fishing; they were all too busy, working double-duty at their paid jobs and their domestic ones—the long hours of shopping for short supplies, preparing meals from scratch, homemaking without the labor-saving equipment Americans take for granted. Even here, among scientists posted to a remote research station, women were cooking, caring for children, attending to chores.

At that moment, from a clearing near where the boats were anchored, Luda called us to tea. She had spread a picnic cloth on the ground and was slicing cucumbers. I carved a loaf of bread on our boat bow. The others trailed in. No one had caught any fish, no one complained, everyone plucked parboiled mosquitoes from their cups of tea. I practiced my Russian. *Komar.* Mosquito. Across the river a swan, its wings walloping the air with a sound like towels being snapped in the wind, launched itself, circled over us and headed east.

We went back to fish some more. Luda stayed by the boats; she did not care to fish, she said.

The sun had fallen considerably, and my fishing hole was now partially shaded by the bank. I heard the fish before I even came around the corner. They were rising through the shade, snatching at mosquitoes, leaving widening rings that merged one into another. They weren't jumping, just snouting through the surface, then falling back again. I cast into the pool, repeatedly. Now and then, a fish would make a run at my Mepps before veering off. I thought of Boris, back at Magadan Reserve, how much he'd love to be here with his giant fly rod. When we left the reserve, I'd told him that when he came to Alaska, I would be *his* fishing guide. It had been the wrong thing to say, of course. We both knew his chances of ever coming to Alaska were close to zero. His chances of ever dropping a line in his own arctic were probably similar.

And I thought again what I had thought a thousand times since arriving in the Magadan region—what right do Americans have, by the accident of their birth on one soil instead of another, to such enormous privilege?

I thought this like a mantra—what right, what right—and I listened to the river. Along the shore, it made a whispery noise, like rough cotton rubbing against itself. Farther out, it rustled around rocks with a silkier sound. After a while, I could hear single pieces of gravel washing past each other, but I still had no answer to my question.

By then, I had sufficiently annoyed the pool of fish that one retaliated by striking my lure. We struggled with one another, back and forth along the bank, until I landed it, gills heaving, in the sand. I fished some more, and I had another. I hooked another and lost it. I caught a third, one so small I would have released it had I not hooked it so well.

I saw Wilhelm crossing a channel farther upstream, and then the others, everyone circling back to the boats. It was all I could do to break away, to reel in and not to cast again, to pick up my fish and leave my piece of river.

Back at the boats, we showed off our fish. With three, I was the highliner again. Wilhelm, fly fishing, had caught only one. He flashed a huge, gold-toothed smile at me.

"You are happy," Luda said.

Yes, I was, and I also knew that was not exactly what she'd meant to say. The Russian language has a single word for both happiness and luck. If you're lucky, you must also be happy. If you're happy, it's not that you have some constitutional guarantee, some inalienable right to be so, but only that you have enjoyed good luck.

"*Ochen*," I said. Very.

MENTORS

MALLORY BURTON

MY FATHER CARRIED MY SUITCASE up the stone steps. I followed with my aluminum rod tubes. He watched as I set them carefully in a corner of the screened-in porch. If he thought it was strange that I'd taken up fishing again after all these years, he didn't say so.

I stepped into the familiar cabin and looked around. The first thing I noticed was the down parka I'd sent my father for Christmas. It was hanging in the closet with all the tags still on it.

"Something wrong with the parka?" I asked.

Dad set down my suitcase and kicked the heavy pine door shut. "Waste of money," he said. "Don't need a coat."

I forgot all the promises I'd made myself about not starting anything.

"This is bloody Ontario. Forty degrees below zero in December. What do you mean, you don't need a coat?"

"When it gets real cold I wear three shirts."

Three shirts. And no hat, as I recall. A fishing guide without a cap was a genuine oddity. Every Christmas a grateful client would inevitably send him a cap which he would toss onto the top shelf of the closet. For all I knew, the hat collection was still there, gathering dust.

I'd forgotten how tough he was, much more rugged than the tourists he took out fishing for muskies and northerns. He'd scoff at their many-pocketed fishing vests and fingerless fishing mitts. God only knows what he'd think when he got a look at my fly rods.

I was beginning to have second thoughts about bringing them at all. This was lake country, big lake country. They fished down deep with thirty-pound test and live bait. The tackle stores sold steel leaders and lures like pan-sized trout. You couldn't walk into a shop and find the times of the hatches chalked up on a notice board. With a fly rod, you were on your own.

Dad struck a match, turned on the gas for the propane light and lit the mantle. "You know where everything is," he said. "I'll see you in the morning. We'll go fishing if you want." He nodded in the direction of my aluminum tubes.

"Sounds good," I said.

When I was a very small girl, I used to go fishing with my father. Sometimes we took the boat. Often, we walked from our place at the seven-mile railroad bridge to the nine-mile bridge, a long walk for a child. My arms always ached from carrying the minnow bucket, but I wouldn't have dared complain and risk being left behind on the next trip. My father took his fishing very seriously and tended to be a bit gruff with anyone who wasn't tough enough or didn't fish properly. Occasionally I'd put the bucket down to pick wild strawberries or to rescue a mud turtle that had fallen over onto its back while attempting to cross the tracks. As I walked, I filled my pockets with dew-bright pebbles, which later faded to a disappointing gray.

At the nine-mile bridge, I was content to sit in one spot, dangling a line over the side while my father paced up and down the bridge. When I grew tired of fishing, I'd lie face down on the ties, watching for fish in the shadow-striped water below. The fish were long, dark shapes in the water, sending sprays of shiners to the surface ahead of them.

"You're not catching anything," my father would say when he came to check on me. "Get a fresh minnow."

The hook went in the minnow's mouth, out through the gills and back through the tail, missing the internal organs. That way, the minnow stayed alive for some time on the hook. Occasionally I think of those open-mouthed, gasping minnows when I am tying on a fly.

When I am releasing a fish, I think of the buckets of fish entrails we used to haul to the dump. My father would scoop the tourists' walleyes out of the live well and clean them expertly and quickly. The filets were always piled neatly on the corner of the table before the discarded fish hearts had stopped beating. He used to show them to me, holding the pulsing hearts up on the edge of his knife before tossing the guts into the garbage pails. I stopped fishing when I was fifteen.

I learned what little I know about fly fishing from books. The literature is full of stories about fishing mentors, those pipe-smoking, tweedy types who provide the initiate with gear, skill and fishing etiquette. I used to think that my mentors were those unknown anglers I first observed on the rivers of British Columbia or the guides who took me out on my first few trips. The truth is, my mentors were gasping minnows, pails of fish waste and pumping fish hearts balanced on the edge of a knife blade.

I slept soundly. The first noise I heard was the sputtering of a boat motor. I rushed down to the dock in my housecoat, so I wouldn't be left behind.

"Daylight in the swamp," I murmured as I stumbled onto the float.

"Been daylight for a couple of hours," Dad replied. "Too bad you missed breakfast. The motor was acting up, or you would've missed fishing, too."

"I'll be ready in a minute," I said. "Don't leave without me."

I pulled on my clothes, ran a comb through my hair and grabbed my gear.

"Since when are you so keen on going fishing?" Dad asked as we pushed away from the dock.

"Since I found out how civilized it can be."

"What's that supposed to mean?"

I fitted the sections of my fly rod together and attached the reel. "Fly fishing," I said. "It's different."

My father slapped his leg. "Well I'll be damned," he said. "Old Man Campbell used to do it."

"What?"

"Old Man Campbell, the guy I bought this place from," he said.

"He used to fly fish. Tied all his own flies with fur and feathers from the game he shot. Crazy old coot used to hold the flies in his mouth while he tied them."

"You're kidding. Was he a good fisherman?"

"People thought he was awful strange to fish like that around here, but he did all right. He used to catch these big silvery-looking fish that nobody else ever seemed to catch. We used to smoke 'em."

I'd seen a picture of Old Man Campbell at the public library in town. He wore a tweed cap and smoked a pipe. Suddenly I felt very optimistic. We rounded the point, and Dad cut the motor.

"We'll paddle down the channel," he said. "The fish are pretty spooky in here. Mind you don't drop anything in the boat."

I rigged my rod and tied on a streamer. Dad looked critically at the setup.

"Be a real shame if a big northern smashed up that pretty little rod," he said.

"It's strong enough," I countered. "Graphite. Best rod made."

We quit talking then. The boat moved into the narrow passage. On both sides of the channel, slabs of glacier-scarred granite sloped gently down to the water. Stands of birch lined the shore, the peeling white bark reflected on the water's surface. Dad let the boat drift, and I concentrated on pitching the streamer against the bank, stripping it back in toward the boat and recasting. It was difficult hauling the heavy sinking line out of the water, and my casting was a little shaky.

My father wasn't fishing. He was hunkered down in the back of the boat with his arms folded.

"Don't worry," I said. "I'll watch my backcast. If it makes you feel any better, the hook's barbless."

"Barbless!" my father snorted. "Bass gets ahold of it, he'll shake it for sure."

A bit later, a bass did get hold of the fly. The fish dived under the boat and came flying out of the water on the opposite side. The bass shook its head viciously and spat out the streamer, which hit the side of the boat hard enough to break the hook point. I had two more bass on briefly, and a couple of takes from useen fish that seemed to simply bite through the leader.

"I'm not much for fishing wet flies," I admitted. "I like fishing small mayflies when they're hatching off the water. Fish flies, we used to call them. Remember how they'd be all over the window screens in the morning?"

"Still are," my father said.

I looked around the boat and spotted a large mayfly on a boat cushion, white wings folded together above its curved, tan body. I picked it up to get a better look, and the forked tails twitched.

"Old Man Campbell was forever doing that," my father said. "Picking bugs up off the water and staring at them."

Just before noon, Dad finally pulled out his spinning rod. "We gotta eat," he said.

A big walleye took the diver on the first cast. I turned my head as my father snapped the fish's neck.

I spent the rest of the day sunbathing and pulling weeds in the garden, trying to restore the flower beds. Toward evening I set up my fly-tying materials and started working on a mayfly imitation that would match the one I'd seen that morning. Just after the sun went down, my father came up to the cabin and rapped sharply on the window.

"The bugs you were talking about," he said. "There's a bunch on the water down by the dock. Some fish, too."

I grabbed my rod and a couple of the new flies. It was a hatch all right, with mayflies coming off the water in good numbers. The pod of fish, splashy risers, was feeding on the surface. I tied on an imitation and cast it into the middle of the rising fish. Despite its light color, I could barely see the fly and lost track of it among the naturals.

"That's you," my father said suddenly. "Set him."

I hate it when guides do that. They must be born with a special kind of radar. What did he know about fly fishing anyway?

I lifted the rod tip and struck the fish. It didn't run like a northern or tug like a walleye. It didn't dive or jump like a bass. It took a bit of line and thrashed around lamely, more like a whitefish than anything else. I glanced back at the pod of feeding fish, the splashy rises, the silvery backs, the big forked tails. Surely there weren't any bloody whitefish in the lake. I let the line go a little slack, hoping to shake it off.

"What's the matter with you!" my father yelled. "Keep tension on him."

He grabbed the landing net and scooped up the fish. It lay flopping on the dock, its small mouth opening and closing. Before I could make any excuses, my father let out an ear-splitting whoop of astonishment.

"It's one of Old Man Campbell's fish!" he hollered. "The big silver smoking fish! I haven't seen one in years!"

The departure of their cousin didn't faze the remainder of the whitefish. They continued to feed noisily on the surface, creating riffles as far as the eye could see in the otherwise glass-calm bay. I could hardly claim that they were an endangered species, and as my father said, we had to eat. Still, if he'd put the fish in the live well, I probably would have sneaked down in the middle of the night and tossed the sorry-looking thing back. But my father didn't wait until morning. He hauled the smoker out right then and there, mosquitoes notwithstanding, and fired it up. Then he got on the radio phone, and by midnight everyone on Seine Lake had heard the story of how his daughter from British Columbia had caught the big silver smoking fish on her flimsy little fly rod with a bug she made out of string and turkey feathers.

"She won't touch a minnow," I heard him say, "but she'll pick bloody bugs off the water all day long. Crazy fly fishers."

"By the way," he said to me between phone calls. "There's a bunch of Old Man Campbell's stuff out in the boathouse somewhere. The rods are only made of wood, but they're yours if you want them."

Reginald Campbell's lines had disintegrated, and the reels had seized up, but his collection of bamboo fly rods, carefully stored in metal tubes, was in perfect condition. They are much too valuable to fish with on a regular basis, but once a year I take one along when I visit my father up the lake to fish for Old Man Campbell's big silver smoking fish.

Casting in the Fog: Reflections on a Fishing Sister

MARY ELLIS

IT IS SIX-THIRTY IN THE MORNING. A foggy and gray Sunday in July in northern Wisconsin. My sister and I step outside our mother's house into an unusually cool mist. We're going fishing, and this is the kind of weather we've been hoping for—when the air is so heavy with water that it sets off an even sharper smell of swamp cedar and tamarack; when the fish seem more inclined to take the hook. We are both grateful for the overcast sky. It releases our eyes from the glare of the sun, allowing us to look comfortably at everything: green moss, pink ladyslippers, the loudmouth Canada jays, or whiskey jacks as they are more commonly called, perched in the tamarack branches above us.

We trudge through the swamp to the lake. My sister, Jane, walks ahead of me. I smile: She is still dressed in her blue flannel nightgown but has on the necessary green rubber boots and a baseball cap saturated with Muskol. She carries a Browning graphite rod with a Shimano quick-release reel and a carton full of worms. I carry my first-of-the-morning cup of coffee.

Despite the squishing of bog under our boots, we try to be as quiet as possible because of a pair of loons that live on the lake. We reach what could be called a dock: an old, slowly rotting barn door sunk into the vegetative bedding of the swamp. I park myself off to the side on a half-submerged log the swamp is also slowly reclaiming and watch as my sister walks further down the bog shore.

Jane moves far enough away so that she can cast comfortably without hooking me. It's a reality and an old family joke. I've either managed to move at just the wrong time, sat in just the wrong place or had the misfortune of being with Jane on a day when her arm was rusty. When we were children, it was my back that got it the most; now as an adult, it is usually an arm, and once it was a finger, a dazzling feat that sent our brother, Paul, who was paddler and navigator on a family fishing trip down the Chippewa River, into a laughing fit that nearly tipped the canoe. I had been pointing out a great blue heron when Jane, casting back, deftly managed to snag just that finger. Now she stands a good distance away from me, but still I keep a careful eye on her casting arm.

The fog drifts over the top of the water, so thick in places that I cannot see the opposite shore. The shoreline we own on this kettle lake has been in our family for almost thirty-five years, and we have never called it anything but "the lake" or "the lake by the house." I don't even know if it has an official name. It is this lake, almost a stone's throw from the farmhouse we lived in when we were very young, that my sister has probably fished and loved the most. It looks, especially now in the early morning, like photographs of Alaska's boreal lakes and forests. Except for an occasional party of crows and, if we are lucky, the loons, it is completely quiet. Sometimes a car or truck rumbling past on the gravel road by the house disrupts the peace, but most of the time, the lake seems to be part of our own private world. When we were little girls, innocent of our effect upon land and its effect upon us, we thought the lake belonged to us and we belonged to the lake. We could have fallen off the bog and drowned, and then we really would have belonged to the lake—our mother warned us about this possibility constantly. We only superficially believed her in our arrogant innocence. We believed we were a part of the lake and land—like an arm or leg—and therefore it would not hurt us. Besides, we reasoned, we had life jackets on, and we could swim.

We applied this same reasoning toward time. Like most children, and especially as rural children, we did not measure time in minutes, hours or days. If we felt it was "time" to go fishing at the lake, we went regardless of whether it was morning, afternoon or evening. We jumped out of bed as soon as the sun hit our faces, not because it was six a.m. And we fell asleep when it got dark and we became tired. As much as we took our surroundings for granted, we were also in daily awe of them. We wondered why the sun was so bright, how caterpillars turned into butterflies, why the lake's surface looked like a mirror on windless days and what it looked like on the bottom. We were in awe of this lake even when we did not know about the tremendous force and power of glaciers (learned about in fourth or fifth grade) that carved out kettle lakes such as this one. And when we did learn about those natural forces, it only increased our love for the lake.

As I watch my sister, I realize that fishing brings her this feeling of time that cannot be measured by a contrived human clock.

Jane reaches into a carton of worms and pulls out a fair-sized night crawler.

"Sorry, wormie," she says, threading the squirming night crawler on her hook. When she is done, she wipes her hand on her nightgown and adjusts the yellow bobber.

"We're goin' for those big ones today!" she whispers and grins. I laugh into my cup. As deep as this lake is, it holds mostly pan fish: perch, bluegills, crappies and sunfish.

She draws the rod back and throws it forward, skillfully releasing the line so a tiny hum sings through the air. The line, bobber and worm-laden hook disappear momentarily into the fog until we hear the splash of contact. Then she slowly reels, pauses, slowly reels and pauses. She stands with her weight mostly on one leg and watches, almost stares, with Buddhist-like devotion at the very faint yellow outline of the bobber.

Except for being an adult, my sister still strongly resembles the child she used to be. She was a teddy bear kind of kid, incredibly good-natured and cuddly, trusting and patient. She crawled out of bed this morning the same way she did when she was four—with that doey brown-eyed happiness that said *fishin'*. Her reddish-brown hair is very short and neatly caps her head. From a distance in a baseball cap, jeans and a sweatshirt, she might appear to be a teenage boy. But when you get closer, the tall and slender figure and sharply defined face become distinctly and elegantly female. It surprises many people to see her, a woman fishing alone. And that, to our family and friends that know her well, is the quintessential Jane.

Looking at her now, I am reminded of how the act of fishing and her experience of fishing are colored by her femaleness.

Absent is the Great White Hunter approach, the camaraderie of beer buddies in the boat, the male bonding of father to son, or the great sporting "wife" to a Hemingway-like figure. Nor is she a snob insisting on fishing with only the most expensive lures or the best rod and reel that money can buy or in an outfit straight from L. L. Bean or Eddie Bauer that would declare her the genteel and well-educated lady fisherman, a word combination that always causes me to smile cynically because of the contradiction in gender and implication of class.

There she is standing fifteen feet away from me, dressed in an old blue flannel nightgown, with sleeping sand in her eyes, and fishing with worms. Although she has and uses more sophisticated lures such as french spinners, rapalas or brightly colored flies for fish such as trout, walleye, muskie and northern, she is just as happy with what other fisherpeople would consider less. Jane fishes, as she says, by "instinct," and if that means a long yellow cane pole such as the kind we used as kids, than so be it.

There are only three things my sister will not tolerate when fishing. She will not fish with drunks or with people drinking in the boat or on shore. (When I say "drinking," I do not mean a beer or two. This rule extends to some family members and an ex-boyfriend of mine who used fishing as a euphemism for getting drunk. I never fished with him either.) She can't stand people tossing cans, paper or other junk into the water or on the ground. And, as good-natured as she is, she hates it when she is patronized or put down for (a) being a woman, (b) being a woman who fishes and loves it and (c) being a very successful angler even though catching is not always her primary goal. The majority of put-downs and comments have come from men, but she has encountered a few women with similar attitudes.

One such incident involved an anchorman from a TV station in north central Wisconsin. Jane was visiting the Eagle River area to do some walleye fishing with our brother Paul on the Big Twin Lake there. This anchorman was not in my sister's immediate party, but was in another boat in the watery vicinity. Nobody was catching much of anything but talk. Jane and Paul were winding up what appeared to be a dismal day for fishing when she landed a thirty-two-

and-a-half-inch, nine-pound walleye that would have weighed twelve pounds if it hadn't spawned out. Paul whooped. It wasn't the record for walleye in Wisconsin, but for that day, or any day, it was a great catch.

It was getting dark, so they headed in and docked the boat. Not long afterwards, the TV anchorman and his party made it to shore. My sister received envious but good-hearted congratulations on her fish from most of the men. However, the anchorman who pointedly ignored her when the day began, continued to do so with barely concealed anger. He, like the other guys, hadn't caught anything either, but it noticeably galled him that the only woman in the group not only caught *something*, but caught a *good-sized something*. Although she thought he was being a jackass when the day began, my sister was still honestly surprised by his reaction.

The walleye was taken to a taxidermist as a gift for Jane and now hangs on the wall by her front door, its mouth gaping with formidable teeth, and fins erect on its arched body. Jane said that when the fish was netted and lying on the bottom of the boat, she felt sad that it was a female walleye but happy that it had at least spawned. Despite the fact that Jane has caught and eaten many fish, she has told me that she often experiences a moment when she realizes that she is taking another life for pride and fun, a moment when she feels the significance of death because as a woman she understands the significance of life. I think this would remain true for my sister if she fished not for sport but to feed herself and a family. And therein lies the irony of the anchorman's reaction. Women have been providing food for their families for thousands of years, and in northern Wisconsin in particular, Ojibway Indian women have fished for that reason. So whether it is for sport or need, women have always fished and always will.

The bobber bobs and then goes under. Jane jerks the rod up and begins reeling. "I'll bet it's a bluegill," she whispers, and sure enough, it is a small but energetic bluegill. They're fun to catch because they are such little fighters. Jane reaches out to grab the line and carefully slides her hand along the bluegill's back to smooth down the dorsal fin so she won't get stuck. She gently pries the hook out of its mouth and, bending down, slides the bluegill back into the water. I see a

flash of butter yellow from its side, and then it is gone, diving for
safety underneath the floating bog shelf. Jane threads the hook with
another night crawler and casts. I slap a mosquito on my cheek, and
the sound seems to echo across the lake. I ask Jane if the mosquitoes
are getting at her legs beneath her nightgown. She shakes her head
and continues to stare at the bobber. I wish I had thought to bring the
camera.

We have several pictures of Jane fishing when she was three or four.
Our family lived on a string-bean economy, what with seven children
and basically one parent, but after borrowing a camera from her in-
laws for years, our mother finally squeezed the money together to
invest in a Kodak.

In a couple of these photographs, Jane is wearing a woman's one-
piece orange swimsuit (minus those torpedo-like padded bra cups),
the crotch of which is hanging around her ankles, the scooped neck-
line framing her navel. Over this engaging outfit, she has on an orange life jacket (mandatory in our family if we were by the lake or the
smaller pond close to the house), and in her hand, a fishing pole. She
is standing ankle-deep in the pond, which is fed by a channel from the
lake. In one picture her face holds that wide beam of baby teeth demanded by a mother wielding a camera ("C'mon now, Janie...
smi-i-i-le"), and in another, she is staring at the pond surface with the
seriousness that a possible ripple or break in the water requires.

Jane would sit on the bank of this pond and happily catch bull-
heads or whatever was biting for hours. If the fish were slow in re-
sponding, she would wedge the end of her fishing pole into the mud
and prop it against one of the iron stakes supporting the bank. She
would then get a long-handled net from the barn and spend the rest
of the morning or afternoon wading in the water and netting polly-
wogs, frogs and minnows, stopping every so often to check her line.
She was an easy child to watch—a fishing pole, worms and the pond
enabled our mother, with a glance out the kitchen window, to keep
track of her youngest daughter. It was considered cute and novel that
a little girl loved to fish so much, and Jane drew patronizing smiles
from visitors, relatives and the like. All the girls in our family were
tomboys, that is, capable of doing "boy" things—shooting a gun, fishing, playing ball, climbing trees, fist fighting—as well as "girl"

things—playing with dolls, playing house, learning to bake, wearing dresses when the occasion demanded it. But the unspoken assumption, as it was with Jane's fishing, was, *they'll grow out of it.*

Obviously she did not.

There is only one incident that might have caused sufficient trauma to stop Jane from fishing. We lived three miles outside of Glidden, Wisconsin, where our great-Aunt Martha had a store. When we stayed with her, we often fished off the yellow bridge above the Chippewa River, which meandered through town. Our aunt kept a set of cane poles in the back of the store, and we dug worms out of her garden. If it was a nice day and we were tired of watching Aunt Martha wait on customers in the store, we would trudge down the hill to the river with our cane poles and worms. Most of the time I got bored and wandered back up the hill to the store, but my sister would stay down there, usually the only girl among the boys fishing off the bridge and river shore. Occasionally one of the patrons of the bar next to the bridge (a pink building called the Y-Go-By Bar) would step out and boom, "ARE YOU CATCHING ANYTHING?!" The old man would wait for the appropriate "yeah" or "nah" before stepping back into the bar to continue his drinking.

One hot summer day when Jane was eight and I was nine, my sister caught something that would rock that little town for quite a while. She was fishing off the shore instead of the bridge when she hooked a snag. She pulled on what she thought was a floating log until a piece of white cloth surfaced. Then it was ensnared by a strong current in the middle of the river, moving it faster while my sister pulled harder. More white cloth surfaced. Jane was about to give up and snap her line when what she thought was a floating log with debris turned over. The boys on the bridge yelled. It was a dead man.

I was sitting on a stool in the store, rapidly wilting from heat and boredom and watching for "shoplifters" while Aunt Martha took turns waiting on customers and chatting with our other aunt, her visiting sister, who was a nun. Her religious name was Sister Mary Alexander, but we called her Aunt Madie for short. I listened to the low hum of their conversation with the increasing desperation that extreme heat and boredom produce in a nine-year-old child who is stuck in a seemingly endless chore. I was close to tears when Jane burst through the screen door.

"There's . . ." puff, puff, "there's . . ." puff, puff, "A *DEAD MAN IN THE RIVER!*" my sister shouted. My mouth fell open, my boredom instantly gone. Jane was sweaty and pale and seemed to be trembling, although I couldn't tell if it was from the shock of seeing a dead man or from running up the hill so fast. There was a long, long silence while the two women stared down at her.

"What did you *say?*" Aunt Martha began. My sister was taking a deep breath, preparing to blurt out the information again, when our Aunt Madie intervened, stepping forward and grabbing Jane by the shoulders. She bent down and looked my sister in the face.

"You," she said angrily, "are lying!" and shook my sister. "You're lying! Shame on you!"

"Noooo!" was all my sister could get out to the daunting figure in a black and white habit.

"Sister," Aunt Martha offered hesitantly, "I think she's telling the truth. Aren't you, Janie?"

I could not get off that stool or speak a word to help my sister. It was as though the heat had melted the seat of my shorts and a good portion of my butt to the wood and dried up my tongue. By now, my sister was badly frightened, and all I could do was watch Aunt Madie continue to shake the daylights out of Jane while Aunt Martha hovered around them in a nervous but ineffective spiral. Then Edgar Schroeder from Schroeder's Hardware Store across the street (and who I thought looked remarkably like Uncle Joe from the TV show "Petticoat Junction") came in the store and said excitedly, "Martha! They just found Mr. Donahue in the river. Somebody hooked'im while they were fishin'!"

Aunt Madie quit shaking Jane, stood up and turned around to address Edgar. I thought maybe she was going to shake him, too, but she and Martha only followed him outside to see if any more news was running up the hill. I finally found the energy to slide off the stool and walk over to my bewildered and forgotten sister, who proceeded to tell me the details of how she hooked him ("I thought it was a *log*").

Mr. and Mrs. Donahue, she in her early sixties and he in his seventies, lived on the outskirts of town along the river's edge. Mrs. Donahue, bedridden with cancer and in extreme pain, couldn't take it anymore and slit her wrists and throat. Mr. Donahue came home from work at lunch, found her and took an understandable dive into hysterical grief. He left his wife, went to the Y-Go-By Bar, got very drunk in a short time, went home, tied rocks to his feet and, finally, jumped into the river the day before my sister hooked him. It had been a very hot summer, and the Chippewa River is not as deep through town as it is in the bottomlands outside of town; the combination of shallow and warm water caused Mr. Donahue's body to bloat quickly and rise toward the surface, making it easier for a little girl with a cane pole to snag him.

It was the talk of town for weeks. Aunt Madie didn't apologize to Jane for doubting her. I listened to my sister's nightmares (I slept on the top bunk, and she on the bottom), and we didn't fish the river in town for quite a while after that. In the sensationalism of such deaths, people forgot that it was Jane that hooked him although my sister has never forgotten. Now when we drive through Glidden and across the yellow bridge, it still reminds her of Mr. Donahue and that childish, superstitious feeling that the fish in that part of the river might turn into dead men when you put your line in.

A loon appears through the fog. Jane quietly reels her line in and waits. Even from a distance, it is remarkable how big a loon is compared to most water birds. We watch it turn its head from side to side, gauging our position, maybe even our intent. The loon stays silent while it swims in our direction. "I wonder where its mate is," I whisper. Before Jane can answer, the loon suddenly gives a short, sharp cry. Minutes later my question is answered: The mate appears out of the gray sky and makes its long and magical landing, skipping across the surface and then, breast up, skiing into the water. We watch for a while hoping they will come closer, but they stay toward the middle of the lake.

It must be seven-thirty by now. Jane bends down to pull another night crawler from the carton. I watch her cast into the water in front of me, listen to the squish of her boots as she shifts position. She has caught several fish but kept none, disengaging the hook from their gills or mouths carefully before returning them to the water. Her fishing style is gentle, much like teasing a good friend but ultimately being respectful of her feelings.

Jane absent-mindedly hikes up her nightgown to scratch her

knee. Her water-dwelling playmates, the bluegills and crappies, are not taking the worms as fiercely as they did an hour ago, and now the bobber registers nibbles, not fully engulfed bites. Jane reels once and lets the bobber sit in a new place. She sighs deeply. I can't tell whether the sigh signals contentment or sadness, but I think it's a mixture of both. The fog is slowly lifting, and with it goes some of the morning's mystery that touched us when we first got out of bed and headed for the lake. We are no longer little girls who sneaked out of the house in our nightgowns while our mother was asleep. And soon, we must return to our adult lives.

But the morning's stillness has given us the comfort just to sit, just to *be*, instead of going, going, going most of the time. It allows us to be sisters in the way we were years ago, when the blood connection between us was so strong we never had to think about it. Jane for years was my closest playmate. Her fishing was a variation of something *I did*, what *we did* together and what we learned and became in our private rural world. It was not a sport, it was not a whimsy. It was putting a line in the water to see another part of ourselves, scales and all. And unlike hunting, you can catch a fish and not kill it, if you choose to.

I laugh to myself on this last thought. It is no doubt preferable to some men to have women fish rather than hunt. A woman with a fishing pole is less threatening than a woman with a gun.

"Are you getting tired?" Jane asks. I shake my head even though it's true—I am a little tired. The white blanket of fog over the water has thinned in places, and I can see the opposite shore rimmed with tamaracks. Jane grins at me and adjusts her cap before reaching down for another night crawler. The loons give off their peculiar laughing cry, and we listen as their voices trail off. Jane threads the worm on the hook. Then her right arm gracefully arches behind her, poised like a messenger bearing gifts of food. She swings it forward, and I watch as my sister casts into the fog.

JOAN ACKERMANN is a freelance journalist who writes for the *Atlantic, Time, Sports Illustrated* and many other magazines. She is also a playwright, and her play *Zara Spook and Other Lures* is currently headed for an Off-Broadway production. She lives in the Berkshires in western Massachusetts.

MARGARET ATWOOD is one of Canada's foremost writers and the author of many books of poetry and fiction including *The Handmaid's Tale, Cat's Eye* and her latest collection of short stories, *Wilderness Tips*.

JUDITH BARRINGTON is a poet and the author of *Trying to be an Honest Woman* (1985) and *History and Geography* (1989), both published by The Eighth Mountain Press. She is the founder of The Flight of the Mind, an annual summer writing workshop.

DAME JULIANA BERNERS, a hunting writer and compiler, is said to have "flourished in the year 1430." Legend places her as both nun and noblewoman and the first woman to be published in the English language.

JANNA BIALEK lives in Baltimore, but is originally from Cincinnati. A freelance writer, she has published essays and articles with Jewish and feminist themes. Her fishing experiences in Ontario's Georgian Bay and Whitefish Falls area culminated in a battle with a twenty-three-pound great northern pike, which she consumed with great relish and can still taste today, twenty years later.

BETSY BROWN is a lesbian separatist who lives in Eugene, Oregon. She is a former member of the collective that publishes *Womyn's Press*, one of the oldest feminist newspapers in the United States.

MALLORY BURTON lives on the coast of northern British Columbia, where she teaches English as a Second Language and fishes for salmon and steelhead. She spends her summers writing and fly fishing in Montana and Idaho. Her serious and humorous fiction appears in *Fly Fishing, The Flyfisher* and *Flyfishing News, Views, and Reviews*. She is also the author of an award-winning Native Studies curriculum.

ALBIA DUGGER is the editor of *Sport Fishing* magazine, contributing editor of *Sea Frontiers* magazine, and has won awards for her articles on billfish conservation. She received a masters in fisheries science from the University of Miami and is a licensed captain.

MARY ELLIS was born and raised in northern Wisconsin and educated at the University of Minnesota. She is a freelance writer and is particularly interested in feminist, African-American and Native American writing.

ELIZABETH ENRIGHT began her career in the field of children's literature, first as an illustrator and later as an author. Her stories appeared in *The New Yorker, Harper's* and other magazines. She is the author of three collections of short stories: *Borrowed Summer* (1946), *The Moment Before the Rain* (1955) and *The Riddle of the Fly* (1959).

SUGAR FERRIS is the founder and President of Bass'n Gal, a women's bass fishing organization, and is the publisher and editor of *Bass'n Gal*, a bimonthly magazine. She lives in Arlington, Texas.

TESS GALLAGHER'S work has been honored with fellowships from the National Endowment for the Arts and The Guggenheim Foundation. Her books include *A Concert of Tenses, The Lover of Horses, Amplitude, Moon Crossing Bridge* and the forthcoming *Portable Kisses*. She lives in Port Angeles, Washington, where she was born.

LEWIS-ANN GARNER lives in rural Northumberland, England, with her husband Michael. Together they plan forays into remote and isolated parts of Scotland. Since the age of six she has spent all available free time in search of wild brown trout, leaping salmon and elusive sea trout. Her two passions are writing and the great outdoors.

SHIRLEY GILLEY grew up in the country in Oklahoma where fishing is a favorite pastime. When she's not fishing, Shirley enjoys writing short stories and composing songs on her guitar. During the week she works as a nurse.

LORIAN HEMINGWAY, half Cherokee Indian, was raised in the Deep South. Her many fishing pieces have appeared in *The New York Times, Sports Afield, America, Ocean Fantasy, Pacific Northwest* and *Horizon* magazines. Her passionate interest in the natural world plays a strong role in her first novel *Walking Into the River*, forthcoming from Simon and Schuster.

LINDA HOGAN, a Native American and a member of the Chickasaw Nation, is the author of several books of fiction and poetry including her most recent, *Mean Spirit*. Her work deals with questions of spirit, peace, environment, healing and daily living. She is involved with the Birds of Prey Rehabilitation Foundation and lives in Idledale, Colorado.

KERI HULME is of Nga Tahu, Orkney Scots, and Lancashire ancestry. Her novel *The Bone People* won the New Zealand Prize for Literature, the Pegasus Prize and Britain's prestigious Booker Prize and was published in the United States in 1985. Hulme describes herself: "I am: a rather reticent and timid person who gets fierce about deliberate ignorance, cruelty and intolerance, unnecessary waste, and any threat to any of my family....One day I hope to develop gills." She lives in Okarito on the West Coast of New Zealand, in a house she built herself, where she makes her living as a writer, painter and whitebaiter.

MARY S. KUSS has been active in a variety of volunteer service, including conservation work with several Trout Unlimited chapters and environmental education work with Boy Scouts, Girl Scouts and many local conservation organizations. She has taught fly fishing to individuals and groups for The Sporting Gentleman Orvis Store in Media, Pennsylvania, since 1980. She devotes much of her time to fly fishing, wood carving, gardening and other creative pursuits.

GRETCHEN LEGLER is a graduate student and instructor in the creative writing program at the University of Minnesota. She has also been a newspaper reporter and a freelance magazine writer. She is currently working on a series of essays having to do with her experiences as a woman in the outdoors.

MARI LOCHHAAS fishes commercially in Alaska. In addition to providing a livelihood, fish are an inspiration for art. Her fish prints are displayed in Alaska, Oregon and New York. She lives in Port Orford, Oregon.

NANCY LORD lives and fishes commercially for salmon in Alaska. She traveled to the Soviet Far East in 1989. She is the author of two short story collections, most recently the book *Survival*, published by Coffee House Press.

AUDRE LORDE is an African-American lesbian poet and writer. She is the author of many books including *Zami: A New Spelling of My Name*, *The Cancer Journals*, *Sister Outsider* and *A Burst of Light*.

MARYA MOSES, a Tulalip Indian, was born in 1911. She has fished commercially in the Pacific Northwest for more than forty years.

MARGOT PAGE is the editor of *The American Fly Fisher*, the quarterly journal of the American Museum of Fly Fishing, located in Manchester, Vermont, and a freelance writer whose articles on fly fishing and other life matters have appeared in *The New York Times*, *Trout*, *Fly Rod & Reel*, *New*

Woman and *American Health*. She and her husband, Tom Rosenbauer, live with their young daughter, Brooke, not far from the Battenkill, in East Arlington, Vermont.

JEAN RYSSTAD lives in Prince Rupert, B.C., with her (commercial) fisherman husband, Tom, and their two children. She has published both fiction and non-fiction in various magazines, including *Westcoast Fisherman* and *Western Mariner*. Her first short story collection, *Travelling In* (Oolichan, 1990), focuses primarily on the fishing lifestyle. She also writes drama for CBC Radio.

LE ANNE SCHREIBER was born in Evanston, Illinois. She worked at *Time* magazine, writing on foreign affairs, then covered the 1976 Olympics, and began a career in sports journalism, first becoming editor-in-chief of *WomenSports*, then editor of *The New York Times* sports section. In 1980 she left sports coverage to serve as the deputy editor of *The New York Times Book Review*, and four years later left New York City altogether to fish, tend to her garden and write. She lives in Ancram, New York.

SANDY SCOTT was trained at the Kansas City Art Institute and worked as an animation background artist for the motion picture industry before turning her attention to etching and printmaking in the 1970s and to sculpture in the 1980s. She is a licensed pilot of twenty-five years and maintains studios in Fort Collins, Colorado, and on an island on Lake of the Wood in Ontario, Canada.

JENNIFER SMITH is a licensed Montana fishing outfitter and professional fly casting instructor. She has written for *Fly Rod & Reel, Fly Tackle Dealer, Scientific Anglers Guidebook* and other fly fishing publications. Jennifer has fished in Alaska, Florida, Canada, Argentina, and was recently invited to Sweden to teach fly fishing. She is an instructor at the Dan Bailey Fly Fishing School in Livingston, Montana, and regularly holds casting clinics during the Federation of Fly Fishers annual conclave.

SABRINA SOJOURNER was named the 1990 Pioneer Black Journalist in Editorial by the Atlanta Association of Black Journalists. She is the first openly gay person to be honored by the group in its fourteen-year history. She is a Designated Spiritual Leader for the First Existentialist Congregation of Atlanta. In addition to fishing, Sabrina enjoys sailing, birdwatching, playing with clay and hanging out with good friends.

LIN SUTHERLAND is a freelance writer of twenty years, specializing in humor, travel and people. She has been published in numerous magazines, and has a weekly humor column in the *West Austin News*. She lives in Texas.

AILM TRAVLER lives in northern New Mexico where she writes, teaches and farms. She is the author of several essays on fools and clowns and a book on Native American sacred systems. She has also published poetry and recently completed a novel.

VIVA has been an actress, a model, a movie producer, a photographer, and has published two novels and written for numerous magazines and newspapers. She is currently a contributing editor to *New York Woman* magazine and a freelance writer and a painter. She has two daughters, Gaby and Alexandra, eight brothers and sisters, and twenty-two nieces and nephews. She lives in New York City.

KATHARINE WEBER, a writer and book critic, is at work on her first novel, *Objects in Mirror Are Closer Than They Appear*. She lives in Connecticut with her family and spends summers in Ireland, where her two daughters enjoy fishing for mackerel from their dinghy.

CARLETTA WILSON's poems and fiction have appeared in a number of publications, most recently in *Poets. Painters. Composers.*, *Prism International* and *Exhibition*. A cassette of her poems, *In Here By Turns*, was released in 1988.

JOAN SALVATO WULFF has written a fly casting column for *Fly Rod & Reel* since 1981 and has written for many other outdoor publications. She is the author of *Joan Wulff's Fly Casting Techniques* and *Joan Wulff's Fly Fishing: Expert Advice from a Woman's Perspective* (Stackpole). She lives in Lew Beach, New York.

About the Editor

Holly Morris is an editor and an avid angler who fishes the rivers of Montana, Utah, Oregon and Washington. She lives in Seattle.

Selected Titles from Seal Press

LEADING OUT: *Women Climbers Reaching for the Top* edited by Rachel da Silva. $16.95, 1-878067-20-6 Packed with riveting accounts of high peak ascents and fascinating narratives by some of the world's top climbers, this exciting collection is an inspiring testament to the powers of discipline and desire.

THE CURVE OF TIME by M. Wylie Blanchet. $12.95, 1-878067-27-3 This is the fascinating true adventure story of a woman who packed her five children onto a twenty-five-foot boat and explored the coastal waters of the Pacific Northwest in the early 1920s.

WATER'S EDGE: *Women Who Push the Limits in Rowing, Kayaking and Canoeing* by Linda Lewis. $14.95, 1-878067-18-4 An inspiring book that takes us inside the world of competitive rowing, kayaking and wilderness canoeing through ten profiles of women who have made their mark in these sports—from the first pioneers to today's Olympic champions.

DOWN THE WILD RIVER NORTH by Constance Helmericks. $12.95, 1-8786067-28-1 The remarkable Arctic wilderness adventure of a woman and her two teenage daughters who voyaged down the Peace, Slave, and MacKenzie river systems in a twenty-foot canoe.

RIVERS RUNNING FREE: *Canoeing Stories by Adventurous Women* edited by Judith Niemi and Barbara Wieser. $14.95, 1-878067-22-2 This spirited collection spans a century of women's canoeing adventures and is sure to please the avid canoeist as well as anyone who has been attracted to the romance and excitement of outdoor adventure.

HARD-HATTED WOMEN: *Stories of Struggle and Success in the Trades* edited by Molly Martin. $12.95, 0-931188-66-0 Women employed in non-traditional work—ironworkers, carpenters, firefighters and more—vividly describe their daily experiences on the job.

SHE'S A REBEL: *The History of Women in Rock & Roll* by Gillian G. Gaar. $16.95, 1-878067-08-7 This fascinating story of the women who have shaped rock and pop music for four decades is filled with interviews, facts, photos and lively personal anecdotes from both performers and women behind-the-scenes in the music industry.

SEAL PRESS, founded in 1976 to provide a forum for women writers and feminist issues, has many other books of fiction, non-fiction and poetry. You may order directly from us at 3131 Western Avenue, Suite 410, Seattle, Washington 98121 (add 15% of total book order for shipping and handling). Write to us for a free catalog or if you would like to be on our mailing list.